Loose Lips Sink Ships

Frederick W. Sarkis

authorHOUSE®

AuthorHouse™
1663 Liberty Drive
Bloomington, IN 47403
www.authorhouse.com
Phone: 1 (800) 839-8640

© 2019 Frederick W. Sarkis. All rights reserved.

No part of this book may be reproduced, stored in a retrieval system, or transmitted by any means without the written permission of the author.

Published by AuthorHouse 07/31/2019

ISBN: 978-1-7283-2115-8 (sc)
ISBN: 978-1-7283-2114-1 (hc)
ISBN: 978-1-7283-2113-4 (e)

Library of Congress Control Number: 2019910691

Print information available on the last page.

Any people depicted in stock imagery provided by Getty Images are models, and such images are being used for illustrative purposes only.
Certain stock imagery © Getty Images.

This book is printed on acid-free paper.

Because of the dynamic nature of the Internet, any web addresses or links contained in this book may have changed since publication and may no longer be valid. The views expressed in this work are solely those of the author and do not necessarily reflect the views of the publisher, and the publisher hereby disclaims any responsibility for them.

Introduction – Who I Am

I'm a 93 year old World War II Naval Veteran. I was born in Rochester, NY, the second child of a Syrian-Lebanese immigrant father and an American born Lebanese mother in a family that grew to nine children. Seventeen years ago, I authored my biography which I titled *"Prisoner of the Truck"*.

A prisoner is what I felt like, when at age eight; my "Pa" would have my "Ma" wake me up in the summer time at 5 AM to go with my Pa on his fruit and vegetable horse and wagon.

My Pa would drive the horse and wagon to the Public Market in the center of Rochester where regional farmers would rent covered outdoor stalls where they would park their horse driven trucks for unloading and display of their products for huckster's to buy. (That's what they were called, "hucksters").

Hucksters' would then take their horse and wagons down the narrow streets in Rochester NY to sell to housewives who would come out to the wagon to buy their products.

Then Ford began production of the Model T Ford Truck which replaced the horses.

From age eight to twelve, in the summer I was on that Ford truck for six days a week. My only job was to carry the baskets into the ladies home as an extra service which other hucksters did not have. On summer Saturday's my Pa's last stop was at a bar around 8 PM. I could not go into the bar.

Until around 10 PM when we left, I had to keep an eye on the open truck to insure that no one stole anything from it.

I loved the winter for one reason. I could go to school and get off that prison-truck. However, I dreaded winter Saturdays. My father had a carpenter enclose the truck. A kerosene lamp inside the back of the small truck would keep the fruits and vegetables from freezing.

Our housewife customers would put on their warm clothes and enter the truck for purchasing their fruits and vegetables or they would simply order them inside their homes. My job, just like the summer, was to carry the baskets into the home and return the baskets to the truck where my father was waiting. Remember, this started when I was eight years old. I often wondered why he even needed me.

Again, in the winter, I dreaded the last stop at the bar. My father locked me up in the back of the truck. From 8 PM to 11 PM, full of self-pity, I huddled next to the kerosene lamp to keep warm. I had a glass quart of water to drink out of and an empty quart to pee in. (Even at 93, tears come to my eyes, as I type this).

However, four years later at age twelve, three five minute lessons with my immigrant father as noted in autobiography Prisoner of the Truck, changed my attitude. As he suggested, I turned the truck into a study center and the results are both in my auto-biography "Prisoner of the Truck", and it's free digest on the www.YesPa.org website.

In over ten years, hundreds of schools in the US and English speaking schools throughout the world have freely downloaded *Yes Pa* for use on their Smart Boards. *Yes Pa* is a six-week character education program that uniquely links the parent, teacher and child.

Simply stated, taken from the free Yes Pa book freely and easily available on my website, I write of the three five minute lessons (at age 12) that changed my attitude and my life forever… which lead to remarkable success in school, in life and in business.

At age 16, I graduated from a Catholic business school, skilled in typing, bookkeeping, short hand and business law. This led to a job as a speed typist in a transportation company preparing the transportation bills for the truck drivers. I earned five times minimum wage and before entering the US Navy in WWII, at age 18, as the eldest son, I bought my mother of ten children a home on Park Avenue in Rochester, NY. (My Pa, with the help of my younger brother Joe, continued to sell fruits & vegetables to customers at their homes).

At age 18, I served two years in the Navy. At age 20, I got a job with a plumbing and heating company as a billing clerk. In the morning, I would attend a school for Veterans to earn my high school diploma. In the afternoon, I would work as a billing clerk for a major plumbing and heating company. From 20 to 22, as a WWII Veteran with free tuition, I attended night school at the University of Rochester earning an Associate's Degree in Business.

At age 22, shortly after my father's death, I became involved in a business startup, selling a 5 cent cup of coffee out of a vending machine. This involved a frozen coffee concentrate, fresh cream and sugar in the form of simple syrup. A stick would come out of the machine to stir the contents.

From 22 to 30, with my brother Joe's outstanding sales skills, I became the coffee king of Rochester, NY which led to a complete line of vending machines for corporations large and small and contracts for managing cafeterias for major corporations. This led to merger with a national company where I became the Vice President of Food and Vending Operations for the Northeastern US. This involved the management of 6,000 employees with four key company executives that led to a ranking of #1 in the company I merged with. An example, at Xerox, in its prime, we managed all of their cafeterias and vending machines.

At 30, my younger sister Ann introduced me to Helen O'Hara, who became my dear wife, mother of my five children, and major supporter in both good and bad times.

From 40 to 60, my business ventures involved the founding of major ski area with two General Motors engineers who were pioneers in the development of snow making machines and the start of a new Cliffside-Lakeside village of 350 homes with a Robert Trent Jones Golf Course and a 128 Slip Marina.

At age 70, interest rates of 20% led to the loss of the ski area and a significant amount of my wealth. In addition, after 18 years, with interest rates and the energy crises, I lost my investment in Bristol Harbour Village. However, I again became involved in Bristol Harbour and then sold my interest.

These financial difficulties led to the start of an automated blood pressure machine business in pharmacies, now owned and operated by my sons. Royalty payments since then have enabled me to focus on my not for profit mission.

And over these many years, with great gratitude, I have received many awards in service to others during my business career as well as in my active and ongoing character education for middle-school students as well as prisoners in jail. The down- to- earth message to prisoners in jail is this. Do as Fred did on his father's prison truck from age 12 to 14 - turn your prison into a study center.

As it relates to my concern for the future of our children in America, what follows is my book on the Loose Lips of Donald Trump, our current President of the United States.

As my mission relates to my <u>ongoing work with Prisoners in Jail</u>, here is a quote from a September 31, 2014 letter to me from Christopher Doser, 2014 Prison Program Coordinator, the Newman Club, University of Rochester, NY led by Father Brian Cool. *"For the past eight years, students and leaders in the society have been involved with your "Yes Pa" program. Together with the Monroe County Correctional Facility, we have conducted the program each semester and have had as many as three groups at a time holding discussion sessions for the inmates. Your story and program have touched the lives of both inmate and athletic, and often result in valuable discussion for the life lessons".*

(Note – As I write this in May of 2019, this now totals 13 consecutive years of counseling with prisoners).

As it relates to the free availability of the Yes Pa program via the www.YesPa.org website, here is just one of hundreds of written testimonials received from teachers over the past years.

"I would highly recommend reading Yes Pa in the High School population. The character building aspect of your book is wonderful. Students of all ages often vacillate between their belief system, peer conscience and what's working for them in the moment. Yes Pa can reinforce values or at least offer another choice to them. You offer the voice of a Grandfather or Uncle our students may have had but, never had the chance to learn their life story with ups and downs. As a bonus, your life parallels periods in time that we are studying in other classes. Your firsthand accounts of the Great Depression and World War II are invaluable.

Fred, hopefully your extreme generosity and time will be appreciated by the US Government, Our First Lady and Arne Duncan to freely use your Yes Pa materials. I wish you the best of luck with this endeavor and hope you are successful."

Yes Pa: An Educator's Appreciation

From: William Cahill, 6th Grade Teacher, Volney Elementary School, and Volney, NY, May 15, 2013.

"The second decade of the 21st century so far has seen us evolve into a society about me. We seem a bit obsessed with celebrity as Kim Kardashion's every move receives more attention than our troops who have sacrificed their freedoms to protect ours. College advisors are stunned at the number of parents showing up on campus to complain about their child's (18-24 year olds) schedule and grades. Employers are worried about the sense of entitlement that many young people entering the work force seem to have and the concept of personal responsibility seems to have long gone the way of the buggy whip. In the world of education, expertise is judged by your net worth not your diploma, and the government thinks of our students as pieces of data rather than children. Many teachers are asking themselves how we can return to a more common sense approach to education and a more selfless society as JFK envisioned fifty years ago? Unfortunately I have the answers to very few of these concerns, but for the last decade I have used a classroom resource that is as powerful as anything I have come across in my twenty years as an educator.

Thanks to a teammate, eleven years ago I was introduced to Yes Pa, the abridgement to the autobiography The Prisoner of The Truck by Fred Sarkis. One year later we contacted Fred to see if he would come to our school, and he's been coming to impact the lives of our students ever since. During this time period many states like New York have mandated that schools adopt character education programs (as if teachers had not been teaching and modeling character since the days of the one room school house, but I digress) to help students become good citizens as well as students. I have yet to see a character education program that is as real world, practical, powerful and as impactful as the Yes Pa experience is.

If you were to attend any STEM conference, you would hear employers tell educators that they are not looking for workers who had "good test scores." What you would hear is their desire for workers who are; enthusiastic, resourceful, problem solvers, personably accountable, honest, and people who are good team players with high moral standards. Yes Pa and the lessons it teaches are a blue print for to teach the character traits that employers are desperately looking for. The three lessons that young Fred learned in the summer of 1938 are as relevant today as they will be fifty years from now, they are timeless.

I read Yes Pa every fall with my sixth graders and use it as a road map for academic and behavioral expectations for the rest of the school year. My students annually list learning the life lessons of Mr. Fred Sarkis as one of the highlights of the school year; I could not give it a higher recommendation as an educator, or as a parent.

On a personal note, after ten years of working with him, I am honored to call Fred Sarkis my friend. I love this man, I love his message, and I love the fact that at age 93 he selflessly proves that Tom Brokaw was correct when he named Fred's generation the greatest. He could be spending his golden years working nonstop on his formidable tennis game but that would be so un-Fred like. (Note: Fred in the 85-90 age group, achieved a ranking of #1 in the US). Fred continues to live by the virtues of the Yes Pa story, he has goals, he works hard at achieving them, and he continually gives back to his fellow man and tirelessly makes lemonade out of lemons. He is the epitome of what we want our students to be; kind human beings who make the world a better place."

And honored by one of the nation's leaders in Character Education - November 25, 2013

To whom it may concern:

For more than 40 years, my work as a developmental psychologist and educator has focused on helping teachers and parents develop good character in youth. For the past 20 years, I have directed the Center for the 4th and 5th Rs (Respect and Responsibility) at the State University of New York at Cortland. It's been our privilege to know and work with Fred Sarkis, a wonderful human being who, with the help of some talented teachers, has created a wonderful character education program, Yes Pa, for middle school students.

We hold Fred's work and his personal character in such high esteem that we devoted most of an issue of our Center's newsletter, The Fourth and Fifth Rs, to telling the story of Yes Pa. That issue includes an article by psychologist Dr. Rob Ellis summarizing his evaluation study showing that 6th-graders who experienced the Yes Pa program were six times more likely than control group students to show gains in self-efficacy (the belief that they can, by the choices they make, affect their success in school and life). We regard that as solid empirical evidence of effectiveness.

There are lots of good character education materials, but what makes Yes Pa unique is the person behind it. Fred embodies the qualities of character we all want kids to develop: positive attitude, perseverance in the face of adversity, a sense of humor and humility, and the desire to give back to others. His life story, beginning in the Depression, makes these character lessons come alive and take root in the hearts and minds of students. They say things like, "Wow that dude had a lot of problems, and he beat them all." "If Fred can do it, so can I." Said one father - "My kid never talked to me like he has since he started reading "Yes Pa."

As reflected in the science-based research on the www.YesPa.org website, of great significance, the professional videos of Fred's talk to students were ranked higher than Fred's live talks to students – which make international coverage of Fred's mission via the Internet far easier.

Yes Pa can also help to combat the bullying that has plagued so many of our schools. In telling his story, Fred recounts the teasing, exclusion, and other cruelty he experienced at the hands of schoolmates and how he overcame it—and even used it to motivate him to study and excel in school. Yes Pa can help to empower kids who experience peer cruelty and encourage all students to take a stand against any kind of bullying in their school.

It's not surprising that to date nearly two thousand schools in the U.S., Canada, and Mexico have downloaded the Yes Pa materials. We hope many more will take advantage of this rich (and free) character education resource created by a most remarkable man and his colleagues.

Sincerely,

Tom Lickona

Thomas Lickona, Ph.D. Director, Center for the 4th and 5th Rs (www.cortland.edu/character) Professor of Education, Emeritus, SUNY Cortland, the Center for the 4th and 5th Rs (Respect and Responsibility, located in SUNY (State University of NY) Cortland's School of Education was founded in 1994 by education professor and psychologist Dr. Thomas Lickona. Its mission is to promote the development of performance character and moral character – excellence and ethics – in schools, families and communities. Its staff includes Dr. Lickona, director and Marthe Seales, office manager. It has trained more than 25,000 educators and parents from 40 states and 26 Countries.

Note: There is one primary reason for reflecting the above endorsements of my mission to help kids be the best they can be. It involves character education. And in Loose Lips Sink Ships, I am referring to the character of Donald Trump, the current President of the United States.

- I sincerely thank FactCheck.org as well as Thom Hartmann, the author for allowing the reprinting of the article regarding Attorney General William Barr that follows.

Regarding the Title of my Book

During WWII, I clearly recall the cartoon on the front cover of my book as well as the following cartoon as reflected on Wikipedia, the free encyclopedia.

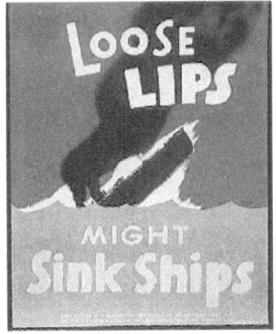

"American World War II poster by Seymour R. Goff, who signed it with his common pen name 'Ess-ar-gee' **Loose lips sink ships** is an American English idiom meaning "beware of unguarded talk". The phrase originated on propaganda posters during World War II. The phrase was created by the War Advertising Council and used on posters by the United States Office of War Information."

The poster was part of a general campaign of American propaganda during World War II to alert service men and workers in industry who working on key government parts for war equipment to avoid careless talk about their roles in such productions.

And this book is about the "unguarded talk" of Donald Trump, the President of the United States.

Introduction

ROBERT F. KENNEDY
NEW YORK

United States Senate
WASHINGTON, D.C.

March 22, 1967

Dear Fred,

I am grateful to you for the fine time we had skiing together last week at Bristol Mountain. It was good of you to spend your time with me.

I enjoyed meeting you and hope that we can ski together again sometime soon.

My very best personal regards.

Many Thanks to you

Sincerely,

Bob

Robert F. Kennedy

Mr. Fred Sarkis
199 Ambassador Street
Rochester, New York

As a World War II Veteran, the following named Chapters were taken from my "Prisoner of the Truck Book" published on June 23, 2003. These Chapters serve as an introduction to my background as I move on with the Loose Lips of our United States President, Donald J. Trump.

Chapter 17 – Prisoner of the Truck - Prisoners of Political Madness

The USS Guam was anchored in Buckner Bay, Okinawa, less than 310 miles south of Japan, when the first Atomic Bomb was dropped on Hiroshima on August 6, 1945. Three days later, the A-bomb was dropped on Nagasaki.

On August 6, 1945, all of the sailors rushed topside when the news of Hiroshima was announced over the public address system. It seemed clear to everyone that the war would soon be over and we would all return home. I stood among my cheering shipmates with mixed emotions. The ship's newsletter included data on the population of Hiroshima and the estimated number of dead and wounded. Hiroshima was about the same size as Rochester, the home of my warden father, my mother, my eight brothers and sisters, our home, schools, hospitals, churches, parks, Eastman Kodak, Bausch & Lomb, Gleason Works, Rochester Gas & Electric, Rochester Telephone Company, Democrat & Chronicle, etc.

The Japanese and Germans had shocked the world with their sophisticated war machine. Hitler had been working feverishly to perfect an A-bomb. During WWII, it was common talk among citizens of Rochester that our city would be one of the enemy's prime targets for air raids. Rochester was the home of Gleason Works, the maker of sophisticated gears, essential to the war effort.

The destruction of Gleason would cripple the country's gear manufacturing capability, essential for the running of our ships, tanks, airplanes etc. 1293 Park Avenue, the home of my parents, brothers and sisters was only 2 miles from Gleason Works. That night on August 6, 1945, I found solitude in the aft of the Guam anchored in Okinawa. I meditated on the destructive power of the Atomic Bomb. These were my thoughts. I could not help but think that if Japan or Germany had perfected the Atomic Bomb ahead of the United States, Rochester could have been Hiroshima. My entire family, relatives, schoolmates, teachers and friends would have suffered or died. I would eventually return, if at all, to a devastated city to visit the ruins. I wondered where I would erect a memorial to my dead family.

At 19 years of age, there was no doubt in my mind that my country was on the offensive due to the provocative attacks of the enemy. America and its Allies were engaged in World War II in the defense of liberty. Yet, on this night of August 6, I felt compassion for the Japanese military men whose families were in Hiroshima. What mental anguish did these men suffer when they heard that their city and their families were wiped off the face of the earth with a single bomb? Did these Japanese military men come to the realization that their government's fanatic and insane leadership caused such misery and pain?

I tried to put myself in the shoes of a 19-year old Kamikaze pilot and other young Japanese military soldiers who were taught to believe that they were serving their country with honor when they sacrificed their lives in suicide dives to destroy or cripple an American Naval Vessel. I thought of the Japanese soldiers. They bitterly defended the island of Iwo Jima right to the end, in spite of a war they knew they were losing, without thought of surrender. If I had been born Japanese, would I have had the same suicidal willingness to die for my country based on a strong spiritual conviction instilled in me by my country and my parents? Would I have considered it an honor to commit combat suicide for a cause that offered no victory?

I thought that if I had served in the US Army and came into hand to hand combat with the "enemy", I would have fought vigorously to save my life even if I had to plunge a bayonet into the heart of another 19 year old enemy soldier. I wondered whether that would have been an act of self-survival rather than an act of bravery in service to my country. I wondered how sick I would be when I saw an "enemy" soldier, 19 years old, gasping for his last breath as I watched him die. I wondered how I would feel about his parents who spent all those years raising him to manhood.

I was happy that the Atom Bomb would end the war and hasten my return to my family and to my future with them. However, as the former Prisoner of the Truck, I felt a deep compassion for all military and civilian casualties in World War II. Whether friend or foe, my heart went out to all mothers and fathers who lost loved ones, or for the military personnel who returned to a destroyed town to find that their mothers or fathers were killed in the war.

I thought of the Japanese civilians as brainwashed victims of war, victims of an insane political system that sought war in the pursuit of economic or territorial gain. I thought of my father's customers, most of them German immigrants, who were examples of goodness, skills and generosity in the Rochester community. I wondered how many of their relatives in Germany, caught in a web of insanity, had no choice but to bow to the power of Hitler, his Army and Gestapo for fear of death or imprisonment. I just thought and wondered. In a long period of peace, from one generation to the next, it is easy to forget the horrors of past world wars.

I researched the Internet for the impact of wars for the past hundred years and to give thought, not to winners or losers, but to humanity as a whole. (Matthew White, HistoricalAtlas of the Twentieth Century, 1999)

Examples of the number of people who died in all the wars, slaughters, oppressions and man-made famines:

Oppressions 79,000,000
Military Deaths in War - 38,000,000
Civilian Deaths in War - 21,000,000
Man-made Famine - 44,000,000
TOTAL - 182,000,000

These numbers are staggering. We can only pray that reason among world leaders and their people will prevail over insanity in the new Millennium.

Otherwise the devastation of the next 100 years will surpass the horror of the last 100 years. How many of those who suffered or who witnessed suffering, were prisoners, "shut up against their will or not free to move"?

Even the Bible makes reference to the insanity of leaders. ".... when David returned from the slaughter of the Philistine, the women came out of all the cities of Israel, singing and dancing, to meet King Saul, with timbrels, with songs of joy, and with instruments of music. And the women sang to one another as they made merry. 'Saul has slain his thousands, And David his ten thousands.' And Saul was very angry, and this saying displeased him; he said 'They have ascribed to David ten thousands, and to me they have ascribed but thousands...' And Saul eyed David from that day on." 1 Samuel 18:6-9

On board the USS Guam, I served with two ships in Task Force 58 that represent the two worst casualties in US Naval History. These following figures represent a very small percentage of 182,000,000 who died in the past 100 years. Yet, they are examples of the human suffering caused by war.

This is a record of that disaster, taken from the Internet Web Page of the USS Franklin (I mentioned the USS Franklin in my September 7, 1945 letter to my family):

"Headline: *Mar. 19, 1945 - USS Franklin (CV 13), which had maneuvered closer to the Japanese homeland than any other U.S. carrier, was attacked by a single Japanese plane which dropped two armor-piercing bombs, devastating the hangar deck and setting off ammunition. Franklin was enveloped by fire. Casualties totaled 724 killed and 265 wounded. Franklin remained afloat and proceeded under her own power to Pearl Harbor for repairs.*"

"*The Franklin, which was loaded with fully gassed and armed planes and hundreds of tons of explosives was herself a 30,000 ton floating bomb. After the initial blasts of the two bombs, the Franklin's open aviation lines ignited. The planes warming up on her flight deck turned into raging infernos; their bombs and rockets adding to the conflagration. 40,000 gallons of aviation fuel poured out of Franklin's hangar deck in a flaming niagra. Every last soul on the hangar deck was vaporized in the flash of an instant. Raymond Milner, Smith's best friend on the carrier, had passed into the pages of history along with several hundred other sailors."*

Shortly after March 19, 1945, throughout the United States, there were 724 gold stars and 265 silver stars that were hung in the front windows of the homes of parents and wives — all caused by one Japanese pilot — all in a matter of minutes.

USS INDIANAPOLIS

The USS Guam served with the USS Indianapolis in preinvasion raids on Okinawa. The Indianapolis was damaged in this invasion and returned for repairs. After repairs, while on another assignment, having just completed a special mission, the USS Indianapolis was torpedoed by a Japanese submarine on July 30, 1945, only six days before the 1st bomb was dropped on Hiroshima. The ship's compartments were not sealed and it sank in 12 minutes. The USS Indianapolis website records the event of 883 dead out of 1,199 on board. There were 331 sailors who survived after spending 4 to 5 days floating in life jackets in shark infested waters. There was a major error in communication regarding its departure & arrival. It was fortunate for the 331 survivors that they were spotted by an aircraft that was not engaged in a search.

Another 883 gold stars in the windows of parents throughout the United States — all caused by one Japanese submarine eight days before America dropped the first A bomb on Hiroshima.
Note: *For ships at war, the Franklin and the Indianapolis suffered the worst casualties in US Naval Military History.*

Hiroshima and Nagasaki

Japanese estimates placed the total number of dead from the two Atomic bombs of Hiroshima and Nagasaki at 240,000. The pre-raid population of both cities totaled 450,000 people. The deaths, not counting the injuries, represent 53% of the population of these two cities.

To comprehend the destructive power of the A-bomb, the US sustained 292,000 battle deaths throughout six years of WWII. Whereas, within three days of each other, in a matter of seconds, 240,000 Japanese people died from two Atom Bombs.

Cost of the War

(Free Concise Encyclopedia — An Encarta Article titled World War II)

"World War II's basic statistics qualify it as by far the most costly war in history in terms of human and material resources expended. In terms of money spent, it has been estimated at more than $1 trillion, more than all other wars combined. The human cost, not including more than 5 million Jews killed in the Holocaust, is estimated at 55 million dead—25 million of those military and 30 million civilian. The human cost of the war fell heaviest on the USSR, where more than 20 million were killed. The Allied military and civilian losses were 44 million; those of the Axis, 11 million. In terms of global politics, the most significant casualty was the world balance of power. Britain, France, Germany, and Japan ceased to be great powers in the traditional military sense, leaving only two, the United States and the USSR."

There were others wars after WWII. I salute the US military forces of *all wars* in the past 100 years, both living and dead, who fought for democracy and peace. I pray that the next century will be one of peace for all nations; that hunger, famine and disease, including the growing threat of world AIDS be wiped out; that the rulers of all nations become rulers of peace instead of power and madness; that the people of every nation, for the good of humanity as a whole, never again allow themselves to become prisoners "kept shut up against their will or not free to move"; that future generations of men, women and children of all nations be spared the fear and the destructive power of War.

Prejudice

Hitler's persecution of the Jews was a Living example of insane prejudice. In the United States, the discriminatory treatment of African-Americans since Lincoln's Emancipation Proclamation of 1863 is a sad example of justice moving too slowly. The World

Book Dictionary for the definition of prejudice — *"an opinion formed without taking time and care to judge fairly; applies to an opinion or judgment, usually unfavorable, formed beforehand with no basis except personal feelings."*

It is time to end prejudice against one's race, creed, color, physical appearance or sexual orientation. It is time for all of us to come together as good neighbors. It is time to "Love your neighbor, as you love yourself". It is time for the Golden Rule to flourish, *"Do unto others as you would have them do unto you"*.

Chapter 20 - Prisoner of the Truck

A New Family Beginning and Miracles

1950-51 - On March 14, 1950 my father was laid out at home in the living room. Relatives had taken over the kitchen, preparing food and refreshments for all those who came to pay their respects. There was nothing our family had to do except to stand in line to receive the condolences of relatives and friends. For two days, there were afternoon and evening hours. First the visitors paid their respect to my Father with a silent bow of the head or a knelt prayer. They then expressed their sympathy to the family. First, my Mother, then Betty, Fred, Joe, Anne, Jim, Vicky, Deanna, Kenny and Lee who was then four years old. It was a very emotional scene for those expressing sympathy. In the kitchen, the women who prepared the food were talking and laughing as if they were catering a party. In the living room, all was quiet and sad. I could tell that Lee and Kenny were hurt and confused by this contrast. Several times in those two days, I would kneel down to Lee's level and give him a kiss and a hug to comfort him. Kenny was 8. I did not have to kneel for Kenny but in between the great number of visitors, I managed to hug him as well.

Both sides of Park Avenue for a half mile, on either side, were crowded with parked cars. We were all surprised by the number of our Father's customers who paid their last respect. We learned that he was well loved by all of his German, Irish and Scottish customers, many of whom remembered me as a little boy. They wanted me to know how much my Father loved me. They said that he carried my Father's day letters in his pocket so that he could show his customers. A countless number of them said, "He was so proud of you." Others had saved the newspaper clipping of one of my Father's Day letters that he had taken to the Democrat and Chronicle for publication.

After the Mass at St. Nicholas church, all ten of us, my mother, brothers and sisters sat closely together into one funeral van. It was a cold March 16. Monsignor Hallak, the pastor of our church and frequent visitor to our home, conducted the ceremonies at home, in Church and at the cemetery.

After the cemetery services, shivering with cold, the ten of us huddled closely together in the funeral limousine, gathering warmth from each other. We were very silent. No one was speaking. My Father's death seemed to bind us together more closely than ever before. It was as if it would be a new beginning for all of us. In my mind, I felt that my Mother's life would be easier. I loved my Father but I never liked the frequent hurt that his unpredictable moods and temper caused her, especially since she valued peace in the household. I especially remembered the times before I began my first full time job, at age 16, when they would speak in Arabic. His tone of voice seemed to be filled with anger. I assumed it had something to do with her needs for money for groceries and household expenses. Yet, In spite of his faults, she always defended him and encouraged us to forgive him because of the pressures he had to live with.

The day of his burial, I not only resolved to keep the promise made to my Father but I was determined to go further. I would do everything possible to insure that my Mother lived in a house of predictable peace.

The Big Business Events between 1950-51

In April of 1950, Kwik Kafe was two years old. Mr. Hunting sent potential buyers of Kwik Kafe to see the barbershop headquarters and to meet me, his manager, to answer questions. I could see that my future as a manager was limited. I knew that the business, as it was, did not justify a purchase at $60,000, ($637,000) in 2009 dollars), the amount Mr. Hunting sought to recover. The return on investment did not justify this value. In addition to Canteen of America, there were local, highly competitive companies beginning to offer the complete package of vending including the powdered coffee unit referred to in a previous chapter.

In May of 1950, just past my 24th birthday, I asked for a meeting with Mr. Hunting. I told him that I knew he wanted to sell the business and that he had received offers for less than $30,000 ($318,000 in 2009 dollars). If sold, I told him that made my continuity as his manager seemed uncertain. I said that I would like to be considered among the parties interested in buying the business. I advised him that anyone who bought the business would have to either run it or hire someone for a higher salary than I was receiving, a salary that could very well wipe out the cash flow that I was generating.

He asked if I had an offer. I said, "Mr. Hunting, if I gave you $30,000 for your business, you would have a $30,000 loss. You could take this loss and deduct it from Hunting Company profits and save $15,000 on taxes. You can than wipe your entire hands of this bad experience with a $15,000 loss instead of $60,000. Please consider that I have been responsible for running the business for one full year and had accumulated $10,000 ($106,00) in 2019 dollars) in cash. If I had not remained involved, it is very possible that this business would have folded and you would have taken a $60,000 loss. ($637,000) in 2019 dollars."

Suspiciously, he said, "Where on earth do you suppose you can get $30,000. I said, I have generated cash of 10,000 that would go to you; you would take a two year note from me for $10,000 backed by collateral on the equipment and I will raise $10,000 by getting a mortgage on my Mother's house." Mr. Hunting said that this was a very poor offer and was unacceptable. I then gave Mr. Hunting a choice of selling the business to me or finding a replacement for me within 90 days. Again, it was the strawberry story – a choice between one or the other. I explained that I still had six months to take advantage of the GI Bill of Rights and I wanted to enter Notre Dame University in September of that year. Mr. Hunting continued to politely refuse the offer. I thanked him and said I would do my utmost to train a new manager in the next 90 days – and I meant it.

In the latter part of May of 1950, Mr. Hunting sent his son to "look over the business" and to take an inventory. I spent a week with Mr. Hunting's son reviewing the management systems that I developed for the control of cash and product in every machine. I reviewed all of my sales records and promotional efforts. When he took inventory for audit purposes of the products in the former barbershop, he put a half filled box of pencils on a table and preceded to slowly count them one by one. I knew then that he was not cut out for this business.

In early June of 1950, one month after my talk with Mr. Hunting, I received a phone call from Mr. D'Amanda. I said, "Mr. D'Amanda, I will not talk to you. If you want to speak to me you must speak to my lawyer, Jack Conway." He said, "Fred, as you discussed with Mr. Hunting, you just tell Mr. Conway we will take the $10,000 from Kwik Kafe's account, we will take your $10,000 note if you show up with $10,000 in cash within the next two weeks. He can handle the paper work for our approval."

I hung up and stood on my head on the desk, supporting my body with my feet on the wall. Mr. Knox said, "Are your going crazy?" Still upside down, I said, "No Lester, I just had a miracle. I'm going to own this business. It is a miracle. Thank you, Carmelites."

Since my dad's death, I promised to give a dozen eggs a day to the Carmelite Nuns on East Avenue, not far from where I lived. This was a cloistered order of nuns who prayed for world peace and for the intentions or petitions of those who came to them. They were not allowed to talk or to see outsiders, except to acknowledge gifts that were hand delivered to them within the small entrance. There was a bell and a revolving platform. A donor would ring the bell and speak through a screened device. The object would be placed on the revolving platform. The sister would respond by asking, "What do you seek from our prayers?" The donor's answer could pertain to health problems of the individual or a loved one, or success in business, education or simply for a special intention.

I rang the bell. I heard a voice say, "Yes?" I said, "Sister, I made a promise to deliver a dozen eggs a day to the sisters." She advised me to put the eggs on the platform. She revolved it and said, "What do you seek from prayers?" My answer was, "Sister I am the manager of a business that I want to own. I need prayers to help make it happen."

The routine was the same every morning. I'd say, "Here are the eggs Sister." She would say, "Same intention"? I'd say, "Yes Sister, same intention " and be gone.

When I was 12 years old and we lost our home on 470 Driving Park Avenue for failing to make the mortgage payments, the memory of my Mother's tears and sadness, were still fresh in my mind. I remember thinking, "Maybe when I grow up, I can get my Mother a new home and there would be no mortgage on it".

It was only 6 years later, before I turned 18, that I bought 1293 Park Avenue for my mom and family and paid off the mortgage. How could I possibly ask Mother to risk a $10,000 new mortgage on our Park Avenue home? Her response was one of joy and enthusiasm. She simply said, "Fred, I believe in you. I know you will make it a success. Do it." I was only able to get $8,800. I cashed my $500 in war bonds. Betty had enough saved for the remainder. I rushed to Jack Conway with the $10,000 ($106,000 in 2019 value) in cash the deal was quickly closed.

Right after the closing in June of 1950, at age 24, I went back to the Carmelites with my dozen eggs. "Same intention?" the Sister asked? I said, "No Sister, I want the good sisters to pray that my company will be given a chance to test our coffee machines at Kodak." Each morning, I would drop off the eggs. "Same intention?" "Yes, Sister, same intention."

In March of 1950, my brother Joe turned over my Father's business to my cousin Paul Sarkis. Leo Kruze, the Personnel Manager of Fasco, hired him for $1.50 per hour. After I bought the business from Mr. Hunting in June, Joe left Fasco Industries to join Kwik Kafe. Joe relieved me of the hours I spent servicing machines so that I could spend full time to sell, a plan that did not have the approval of Mr. Hunting prior to my purchase of the assets.

In July of 1950, I made my periodic phone call to Gordon McKay, the Personnel Director at Kodak Park, a division of the Eastman Kodak Company. I saw Mr. McKay at least four times a year. He was always gracious enough to give me an appointment. At each appointment, I would fill him in on our progress and present letters of satisfaction from companies that we were serving. I always asked him for another appointment. Again, as in the strawberry story, I would say, "Can we meet again in six months, say June or July?" In our July meeting, I told him of the new ownership of Kwik Kafe. Again, I politely asked if we would be allowed to have a side-by-side test either in August or September. Mr. McKay had checked our references from companies we were servicing and received good feedback. He respected my enthusiasm for our product. In addition, every time we signed up a new customer in competition with Canteen, I would tactfully write to Mr. McKay to advise him of our growth. However, at this July meeting, Mr. McKay repeated, "Fred, things have not changed. We are happy with our service. Canteen is doing a good job. There are no complaints from our employees. Stay in touch and we welcome any news of your progress." I kept dropping off the eggs to the Carmelites on East Avenue every morning. "Same intention?" "Yes, Sister, same intention."

In October of 1950, Paul Sarkis, gave up my Father's business and joined our company as a coffee service man. My full time effort in sales and a bigger risk-budget for direct mail advertising began to pay off. We successfully converted all of the 25 coffee vending poor sellers into good sellers. In addition, we purchased 20 new units through a payment plan with a local bank. It was no different that purchasing an automobile. For each machine purchased, I had a separate payment book of 48 monthly payments. I would clip coupons each month for each machine and send a check for the total to the bank. We were generating sufficient cash flow to make the payments.

In trade magazines, I advertised the 20 fruit juice machines that had been gathering dust in the garage. These machines had cost $1,000 each but Mr. Hunting would not let me sell them for less than $700. I sold them for $500 each. In October of 1950, I went to Mr. Hunting with a check for $10,000 to pay off the note. He was shocked and somewhat suspicious. He said, "Where did you get the $10,000." I told him I found a buyer for $500 each for the 20 fruit juice machines that you wouldn't let me sell. He smiled at me, signed the release of collateral prepared by Jack Conway and said, "Fred, I know you will make this business very successful and I wish you the best of luck."

I continued to drop off the dozen eggs. "Same intention?" "Yes Sister, same intention". On November 1, 1950, All Saints Day in the Catholic Church, at 9:45 AM, I received a phone call from Gordon McKay. He said, *"Fred, I want to talk to you about a side-by-side test, when would it be convenient for you to come to my office?"* Consistent with the strawberry story, I tried to keep my cool. I politely asked, *"This morning or this afternoon?"* He must have known the strawberry story. He said, *"No, I can't do it today. How about tomorrow or day after tomorrow?"* I chose tomorrow. I again stood on my head on my desk with my body supported by my feet against the wall. Mr. Knox said, *"Now what?"* Again, upside down, I said *"Another miracle. We get a side-by-side test at Kodak Park."*

At my appointment with Mr. McKay, he told me that Canteen had, without Kodak permission, changed all of their heavy weight paper cups to a light-weight paper cup. The result created havoc. Coffee cups were leaking at work stations, executive desks, in containers that held multiple cups, on the production lines, etc. Drippings of coffee on the floor were a hazard for a slipping accident. This change represented a savings of one-half cent per cup. At 5 cents a cup, this represented savings of 10% on the sales price. This was a major blunder by a national company on the NY Stock Exchange. It would have been far wiser to increase the volume of sales by a better quality than to save dollars with a reduction of quality.

We were spending a penny for our heavy weight, plastic-coated paper cups to eliminate a cardboard taste to protect the flavor of our coffee. Canteen quickly converted back to a heavy weight cup but they were not plastic coated.

We had our first trial in building 6 at Kodak Park. Unlike most companies with staggered breaks, certain departments in film production had to take 15 minute breaks at the same time in the morning and afternoon. My brother Joe was in charge of service. He and the Canteen service man were allowed to watch the 15 minute break but were not allowed to speak to the employees. The first few days were not measurable since curiosity would attract people to our machine. But at the end of a two week period, employees would wait in a long line to use the Kwik Kafe machine. The only use of the powdered machine came from people who were too impatient to wait. Kodak ordered several other trials in other buildings. The results were the same. On average, Kwik Kafe was outselling Canteen seven to one.

I dropped off the daily dozen of eggs to the Carmelites. *"Same prayer?"* "No, Sister. We won the trial. Pray for all of Kodak."

The word spread throughout the various divisions of Kodak. The results were the same. Kodak management decided to centralize their decision making process. We were asked us to bid on all 268 coffee vending machines for all 36,000 employees at Kodak Park, Kodak Office and Camera Works. We bid at 5 cents a cup and a realistic 10% commission on sales. We won the bid. Our superior quality resulted in a 28% increase in vended coffee sales at Kodak. It was a win, win situation for all. Kodak employees enjoyed a better cup of coffee. Because of the increased volume, the monthly commission checks to Kodak were higher.

I dropped of the daily dozen of eggs to the Carmelites. *"Same Prayer?"* "No sister, just prayers in thanksgiving for intentions favorably received."

The Kodak experienced led us to believe that we should separate ourselves from our full line competitors. We did not need to offer all products through vending machines. In the fields of medicine and law, there were many specialists. We picked up on this theme and aggressively promoted ourselves as quality-control specialists in the consistent delivery of the best cup of coffee available from a vending machine. We guaranteed every coffee drinker his money back if he or she was not satisfied. In addition, we wanted every service man, every machine and every vehicle to look neat and clean. We installed a full length mirror in our new Portland Avenue headquarters. Each man had to pass that mirror every morning before he departed on his route. A sign above the mirror read, *"This is how I look to my Customer."* Consistent with the policy, procedure and training manual, the service men had to sign when hired, there were questions on either side of the mirror which read: Are my shoes shined? Is my shirt and uniform clean? Am I wearing my tie and cap? Is my hair cut? Are my finger nails clean? Am I clean shaven? Do I daily check the amount of liquid coffee, cream and sugar dispensed, to insure consistent quality? Do I check for the proper temperature of the water? Do I empty the over flow bucket daily and sanitize it properly to prevent odors? Do I keep my station wagon and advertising cup on top clean? Do I record the meter, tests and refunds properly to assure an honest monthly report to the customer on every machine?

We beat our competition in many ways. One significant cost saving was related to the cost of operating a fleet of trucks. We required each coffee service man to purchase his own station wagon to be used for business and for pleasure. Kwik Kafe rented the vehicles from the service man for a sum equal to the monthly payments, plus a reasonable estimate for gas, oil, maintenance and a small profit. In addition, if expenses exceeded the rental income, they were tax deductible. Each service man was required to strap a large metal Kwik Kafe Coffee Cup with our phone number on top of his vehicle, serving as advertisements for Kwik Kafe day and night. This also eliminated the need for a large parking area for trucks.

Another important cost saver was my family's involvement. We added fresh doughnut machines to our coffee service in several locations. The bakery delivered the donuts to 1293 Park Avenue. In the basement of our home, my young brothers and sisters would get up one hour earlier in the morning before school to pack the doughnuts in sealed bags. Joe would take them in his service vehicle to the office for distribution to the other Kwik Kafe service men. Our family was united with one goal - - to grow the business and to pay off the $10,000 mortgage on our house. No one could match our total service program, high volume, good quality, honest count, low labor and operating costs and a reasonable selling price.

My sister Ann was another key person in the growth of the business on Portland Avenue. Ralph Clausen was the manager of the Rochester division of Canteen Company of America. We were to meet at lunch to discuss the threat of license fees on food and beverage machines. He arrived at our headquarters. I was ten minutes late in returning to our headquarters. At lunch that day, Ralph Clausen said, "You have no parking lot. All your men own and maintain their own vehicles, therefore, they are well cared for. You have family members working for you in all departments. I watched your sister Ann while I was waiting for you. A delivery of cups arrived in this freezing weather. Ann put on her overcoat, opened the door and told the delivery men where to stack the huge delivery of paper cups. She was counting money from each vending machine and keeping a record of sales for that particular machine. She was answering the phone. She locked the money in a safe. She excused herself for a few minutes to go down to the cellar to throw some coal in the furnace. She kept the entire working area clean. My God, Fred, be reasonable, how the hell can I compete with you guys?" (Ralph Clausen joined our company a few years later to assist with our rapid growth into other products and services.)

On October 3, 1951, on the occasion of my Mother's 48th birthday, the family presented my Mother with a beautiful plaque showing a scenic view of a home that read, "God Bless Our Un-Mortgaged Home." She lost her home in the depression. She would never lose it again. It was a day of joy and peace. Ann and Deanna brought out their guitars. Kenny and Lee were now harmonizing songs together as were Ann, Betty, Vicky and Deanna. Joe and I entertained with a comical "Dem bones, Dem Bones, Dem Dry Bones" and joined the others in favorite family songs, including of course my Mother's favorite. It seemed as always, when we sang these words, we would direct our united attention to Mother and would watch the tears of happiness flowing from her peaceful face.

"You are my sunshine, my only sunshine,

You make me happy when skies are gray,

You'll never know dear how much we love you,

Please don't take our sunshine away".

In our singing, we included religious songs in praise of the Lord who gave us this wonderful family gift of joy, love and togetherness. This was a very special time in the life of Frances Sarkis and her children. She was at peace. I was only 25 and full of creative ideas for our growing business. In partnership with the Holy Spirit and an assist from the Carmelites, I felt that nothing was impossible to achieve. It was only five years ago that I ran an ad that read: "20 year old WWII veteran seeks part time office work, shorthand, bookkeeping, typing, what have you?"

Chapter 21 - Prisoner of the Truck

Age 24 to 34

Building a Business – Becoming Rich

In 1952, Kwik Kafe was featured on the front cover of a national trade magazine for the perfection of the first computerized system in the nation to report sales by each coffee machine to a customer. In cooperation with the local IBM service bureau, we developed a "marked card system" for our service men to use. These cards were fed to a super computer at the IBM center. For each machine, it recorded the daily meter readings, the number of tests and refunds given, the amount of cash collected and the shortage or overage. This report accompanied the monthly commission check paid to the customer.

In the vending machine business, a customer relies on the cash sales and commissions, as reported by the Vendor. If the Vendor reports sales less than actual, the client is denied its rightful commission. The combination of our high quality, good service and professional computerized reports, served to give us an image of impeccable integrity in our operations.

From 1952 to 1956, we remained coffee vending specialists. In the national Kwik Kafe franchise system, we achieved the highest penetration of market for six consecutive years. The combination of market penetration, excellence in quality control, sanitation and superior service by our personnel led to six consecutive First Place National Awards at the annual convention of franchisees. I took my Mother to these annual meetings and she assisted me in accepting these national awards. Rudd-Melikian, our manufacturer, in a national trade journal featured a picture of our family around our home picnic table. Ann was playing the guitar and we were all singing. When the picture was taken, Betty, Joe, Ann, Vicky, Jim and myself were working either full or part time in the business.

In the vending industry, we were the first in the nation to introduce a profit sharing plan for all employees that equaled the 15% maximum allowed by IRS. We had no employee turn over. Most of the men, including Joe and I bowled once a week with our service men and technicians and played euchre afterwards. It was a great family spirit.

By 1958, we had 35 employees and over 450 coffee vending machines on location. We were selling over 15,000,000 cups of coffee a year. We were Rochester's King of Coffee Sales. Personnel managers, who were not satisfied with their full line vending providers, asked us to take over all the vending machines in their plant including candy, snack, cold drink, cigarette, milk and ice cream.

In 1958, we moved to a new headquarters on Maple Street, opened up Rochester's first commissary for vending food products and introduced the first automatic cafeterias for those companies that did not have manual cafeteria operations.

From 1958 to 1961, we were the first company in Rochester to develop a complete package program for our clients. My associate, John O'Donnell was a key man in helping us to build a new division that specialized in cafeteria and other food service programs for business, hospitals, schools and colleges. John was a graduate of the Cornell Hotel School with extensive executive experience in what was called manual food service programs. There were other key men in the organization too numerous to mention.

Our business continued to rapidly grow. We operated over fifty vehicles and had over 600 employees. We were early birds in the development of a computerized center that produced professional monthly reports for our food & vending customers. We built a strong chain of command with excellent training, motivation and supervision programs that focused on maintaining high employee morale while meeting the wants and needs of our customers with high quality products, in a cost effective manner. The Golden Rule applied in our organization. "Do unto others as you would have them do unto you."

With the assistance of what was then the Association for Retarded Children, we earned a national award from President Eisenhower for the employment of the handicapped - - the largest employer of handicapped in the Rochester area. The program worked because one or two handicapped adults were assigned to each of our cafeteria operations for side-by-side motivation and training.

Our work with the handicapped included the employment of a blind salesman. From his commissioned earnings, he would pay for a driver and escort. The man was Matt Katafiaz. In early chapters, Matt was the man I worked for when I was a 16 year old billing clerk at the Universal Carloading Company. Sugar diabetes lead to his blindness and ended a brilliant career. He was the Southern District Manager for Universal Carloading Company before he went blind. At Universal, his performance was outstanding and he was being considered for the national Presidency prior to the loss of his vision. I ignored the criticism of competitors who accused me of using sympathy to get sales. Once Matt began his dialogue with the prospect, they forgot that he was blind and respected him for his listening skills, knowledge of product and brilliance as a salesman.

My Mother was an important part of our business entertaining. When we introduced the first automatic cafeteria, we impressed our customers and prospects with Lebanese food prepared by my mother and vended at the drop of coins. In addition, we held annual parties for customers with Lebanese food prepared by Mother. She was an important part of building public relations with our customers.

My work, in our national and state trade associations and in the Rochester community, was extensive. I received major recognition awards from the Junior Chamber of Commerce, the National Automatic Merchandisers Association, the Greater Rochester Chamber of Commerce and the United Way. I also served on the Board of Directors of these Organizations and several others. I served as Chairman of the United Way's Speaker's Bureau and was an invited speaker for food service seminars, American Management Association, Kwik Kafe Conventions, National Automatic Merchandisers Association, Boy Scouts of America, Junior Achievement, Danny Thomas Fund Raising and many other Civic and Church Groups.

The volunteer work that I loved the most was working for Richard P. Miller, the executive director of the United Way Campaign. He allowed me to bring fun and humor into the campaign. There was a full week of reporting toward the end of the campaign. Over 600 volunteers would attend the reporting luncheons. Massive display boards reflected how each Division was doing. As Chairman of the Individual Subscribers Division, I developed a theme for each day of the luncheon that brought laughter and a competitive spirit between various divisions of the United Way. These themes were so popular that I was asked by Carl Stevenson, Treasurer of Kodak, to come up with a plan that would add spice to the pledge that Kodak would annually give to the United Way. At the luncheon, Carl announced that Kodak's pledge was so significant that they had to retain someone who could guarantee it's safe delivery. With the pre-planned background music, I rushed into the heart of the large hall of the Chamber of Commerce dressed as Batman carrying the pledge card in my hand.

As Chairman of the Speaker's Bureau, I traveled and gave talks to companies who were responsible to solicit their fellow employees. Mr. Miller loved the strawberry story of the Prisoner of the Truck. He encouraged me to tell it to these volunteers. I would conclude my short talk with, "Never ask, do you plan to give again this year? Ask if you will increase last year's pledge by 5% or 10%."

I cherished my role as head of house, as anointed by my father. I found my job and my community activity to be exciting and challenging. This left little time for dating. During these years, every Sunday was family day. My family would squeeze into one car and go to St. Nicholas Church on the corner of Leo & Remington Street in Rochester. It was a small church. My father was one of the 1927 founders. Monsignor Hallack was our pastor and very close to our family. He joined us on Park Avenue frequently on Sunday's following the Mass. Mass was said in Greek, Arabic and English. We were Eastern Rite, Roman Catholics. I sang in the choir and served as President of the Youth Council.

In 1955, when I was 29, on our way to Church, my sister Ann wanted me to stop and pick up one of her girlfriends, Helen O'Hara. This was not too uncommon. It seemed as if we always had a friend of a brother or sister who wanted to join us for Church as well as the delicious Sunday "Zlabee" breakfast that my mother made. Zlabee, made from flour and yeast. The mixture had to rise overnight at the right consistency, removed in portions by hand, fried and served with butter and syrup. Accompanied by fresh eggs and fresh fruit, it made for a wonderful Sunday event, usually followed by singing in the living room by family and visitors.

While eating breakfast, my hand hit a full glass of milk and because Miss O'Hara was across from me at the table, I was somewhat embarrassed by my clumsiness. My brother Joe had gone to Monroe High School with Miss O'Hara although they were not in the same class. He knew Miss O'Hara by her looks. I was surprised to learn that Miss O'Hara's father was one of the Hunting Company salesmen that I took dictation from. My cousin Richard, who was studying to be a Doctor, was also at our breakfast, which was not too uncommon because Joe and he were very close cousins and had many double dates together. After our song fest, Miss O'Hara and my sister Ann went up to Ann's bedroom. While they were there, Joe and Richard made remarks about Helen's attractiveness. When Miss O'Hara came down the stairs again, I took a much closer look. I did not know this but Ann had brought Miss O'Hara home, hoping there would be a connection between Miss O'Hara and me. Disappointed in my lack of attention, Ann announced that they were going bowling and off they went.

Suspecting that Ann had brought Miss O'Hara home to meet me, I asked Ann for her phone number which Ann readily provided. I caught Miss O'Hara at the wrong time. She was on her way to Ft. Lauderdale with friends. Miss O'Hara was a graduate of Brockport State Teachers College and was in her first year as a teacher of Physical Education and Health at Monroe High School. She was popular with her students. My father once said, *"Fred, if you don't marry a Lebanese girl. You should marry a German or an Irish girl but first meet their parents. If you fall in love with the mother, then you should think about marrying the girl."* I thought, "Well, if I date Helen, I'll meet her mother and then take one step at a time."

I found myself taking time to evaluate my commitment to my Father. I was so wrapped up in building the business and so heavily involved in community affairs that I had little time to think about dating or marriage. There was a young German girl on Portland Avenue that I dated. She came from a large family but she showed no interest in a second date. I must have been a boring klutz. I kept remembering the seven course dinner she ordered at a fancy restaurant. For each course, she would eat about a third of her serving and the waiter would take it away. That included the dessert she ordered as well. I kept wondering why anyone would order more than they could eat. In our household, that was a major offense. Then there was Lorraine Hajjar, our choir leader at St. Nicholas Church whom I faced every Sunday in the choir. She was four years older and more like a sister than a potential marriage partner. There was the girl that my cousin Richard introduced me to but that date was a major failure on my part for reasons I cannot mention.

Lee was now 11, Kenny 15, Deanna 18, Vicky 20 and married to Bud Rosa, from New Jersey, who asked me for her hand in marriage. Jim was 22 and in the major seminary, Ann was 24, Joe was 26 and married to Josie, Betty was 31 and unmarried and I was 29 unmarried.

Mr. Melikian, the inventor of the coffee machine said that I should get rid of my marriage checklist for dating a girl and just date for fun. My check list was something like this. I must love her parents; be sure she wants to have all the children that God will send us; not be wasteful about anything and eats what she orders; be fairly attractive; have a lovely figure; be outgoing, warm and friendly, intelligent and have a strong belief in God.

I decided I would try to date Miss O'Hara for fun and get rid of the check list. My fatherly role as head of the house was diminishing and I could still care for the needs of my mother and younger brothers if I were married. I did not plan on getting married like Joe did and bring his wife to our home to live until they found a place. Josie would go to the only bathroom and lock the door. That completely disrupted the routine of the household. One night I tried to use the bathroom. Josie was still in there and I had to go outside in the back yard and wash up in the kitchen sink. I woke up the next morning and she happened to be there again with the door locked. I knocked on the door and said "Josie, when are you going to give the rest of us a chance. You've been in there all night. My God."

Nor did I want to play pranks like I did with Josie. Joe suggested that I get in their bed and cover my head with a sheet while he hid in a closet. I went along with it. I was getting extremely nervous when she got into the bed and cuddled up next to me. I turned around and she screamed, fleeing the room in panic. Joe, in the closet, was rolling over with laughter.

It was spring break and Miss O'Hara was going on vacation to Ft. Lauderdale. I asked if I could call her for a dinner-date when she returned. She was friendly and said "OK." She returned. I made the date. I went to her home. I met her mother and father. Her father and I spoke of the days at the Hunting Company and the people who were no longer there. I fell in love with her mother. (Check list). I brought surprising news to Miss O'Hara. I forgot that it was bowling night and wondered if she would mind watching us bowl and we would then go out to dinner. She was delightful in her reaction - a good sport. She seemed to enjoy watching the boys bowl and the boys enjoyed meeting and watching her and whispering to me about what a hot chick she was. The bowling ended. We went to dinner. Miss O'Hara ate everything she ordered. I drove her home, walked her to the door and said goodnight, I'll be calling you again if you would like. She said, "OK".

We continued to date. We were having fun like Mr. Melikian said. I was very attracted to her and loved every moment I spent with her. She said she liked my reaction when I spilled the glass of milk at my mom's breakfast table. She was sweet, gentle and loving. She had class. My sister Ann knew what she was doing. My best date was the summer of that year when Miss O'Hara was the Waterfront Director at the YMCA Camp Onanda on Canandaigua Lake. I drove down from Rochester for a breakfast date. I asked for Miss O'Hara. No one seemed to know who Miss O'Hara was. Suddenly someone said, "Oh, he means skipper, the one who takes us for overnight stays in the river south of the lake." Wow! I was impressed. The area south of the lake was full of wildlife, mosquitoes and even snakes. They found Skipper and we drove to Canandaigua for a breakfast. Skipper ordered a heaping platter of pancakes, eggs and home fries. I thought she was going to lick her plate. We were having fun like Mr. Melikian said and my check list was working well except I didn't know how many children she wanted to have if this fun dating got serious.

We were engaged on Christmas 1955, six months after our first date. Miss O'Hara and I spent New Years Eve with my mother, Kenny, Lee and Deanna. They all loved Miss O'Hara. Photographs of our New Years Eve Party reveal the joy of that evening. A few months later, as we were heading for the Springhouse on Monroe Avenue for dinner, I started talking about a wedding date. Miss O'Hara became nervous and thought it was premature. I spun around the parking lot and took her home. Seriously wounded, I said something like, "I'm going to be 30 years old. I've been respectfully courting you with the intention of marriage and a family of our own. I don't know what you were thinking when we got engaged but that was what I was thinking."

We had made a previous commitment for dinner with my cousin Amelia and her husband Faye Reynolds, the following night. Before I left the curbstone, I said I had to live with the commitment and would pick her up. She said, "OK". After the dinner at the Reynolds home, as I parked in front of her home, she tenderly and sweetly reached over for my hand and said, "I'd be honored to be your wife." I said, "You'd better think about it a bit more" and swiftly drove away.

On our next date, she shared her feelings with me. There were good reasons for her concerns that helped my understanding. She said she had confronted her reasons and they were not justified and not only that, she would have as many children as God sent us. So I had fun as Mr. Melikian said I should, and my check list was complete. Helen Margaret O'Hara and I got married on June 30, 1956, bought a house on Pinnacle Road in Rochester. Our first born in December of 1957 was named Regina Marie. Our second child, a son, Gregory John was born in May of 1960.

In 1961, Mr. Fishman a co-founder of a company called Automatic Retailers of America (ARA), with $18 million in sales flew into Rochester. Our sales were $3 million. After an evaluation of our books, he and an investment banker made an offer to buy our company. I told them that I was only 35 and had no thought of selling. They said, "At 35, you could become our national president when Mr. Davidson and I retire. Mr. Fishman was 48 and Mr. Davidson was 52. I turned the matter over to Jack Conway, my attorney and Brendan Meagher, the Managing Partner of Price Waterhouse in the Rochester branch. ARA offered $1.4 million. I told them to ask for a non-negotiable $2 million, thinking they would go away. ($2 million equates to $29 million in year 2019). After much haggling between my accountants and attorney, they met the price. Both advisers, aware of our financials, highly recommended that I proceed with the closing.

I became the Vice President of ARA for the Northeastern United States. I was put in charge of acquisitions and the development of the Northeastern part of the United States. We bought a home on 199 Ambassador Drive. It was a magnificent 6,000 sq. foot home in an exclusive neighborhood, plenty of room to raise a family with good schools and a Catholic Church and School nearby.

I could not be a happier man. The skinny, bow-legged, knock-kneed, pigeon-toed, dark skin boy, bullied in school, graduated first in his Commercial School class at the age of 16, found a job paying six times minimum wage and at age 17 before enlisting in WWII in the United States Navy, and after his father's death, bought his mother of ten children a house on Park Avenue in Rochester, NY. And at age 35, became a multi-millionaire with a wonderful mother, wife, brothers, sisters and children, all happy and healthy. Praise God. What a blessing. I recalled what one of the Notre Dame Sisters said, *"Fred, sometimes God gives you a cross to bear and it can be many years later when you discover that the cross can often be the stepping stone to future happiness. It depends on how you work with the Holy Spirit."*

News of the success traveled throughout the Rochester community. I was on Rochester's hit list for contributions. I was a Rochester young man's success story from rags to riches. Helen and I were invited to parties by high level executives and bankers along with other prominent Rochester people. Early after the sale, I made a major contribution to relatives from Lebanon who were all seeking money for various reasons. I resolved the Lebanon requests, with the help of a Bishop in Lebanon. I donated sufficient funds to build a medical clinic near my father's village that to this day, continues to serve this small village community.

I knew I needed to make a major contribution to the Rochester community in which I was raised and in which I was successful. It had to be different. It was in my nature. I had this track record of creativity, of being a pioneer in the first coffee vending machine, the first central commissary for the preparation of packaged foods, the first automatic cafeteria and the first to offer industry a total package including vending machines, employee cafeterias, executive dining rooms, etc. In my volunteer efforts, I developed ideas and programs that helped to raise a greater number of dollars or a significant increase in membership such as the Rochester Chamber of Commerce.

With my new found wealth, I wondered, what contribution do I give back to the Rochester community? I needed time to think.

In the meantime, I focused on my goals as a corporate vice president of ARA. Other Kwik Kafe dealers in New York State and New England became aware of my merger. We knew each other from national meeting of franchised dealers. They had a great respect for our 1st place achievement as Kwik Kafe dealers. From the time of my merger with ARA in 1961 to 1963, through acquisitions and an aggressive marketing and sales thrust in this ten state area, my responsibility for Business & Industrial food service operations grew to close to $100 million in sales, and 4000 employees. This involved 1500 individual customers from large to small. Our success at Kodak sparked the interest of many major corporations, including the major IBM plants in NY State.

Our "Northeast Area" headquarters was expanded on Maple Street in Rochester. I had an excellent group of regional vice presidents who reported to me. To assist the regional vice presidents, I had a staff of area dieticians, chefs, cafeteria and vending design specialists, computer experts and an administrative aide. They provided major assistance to the Regional Vice Presidents for the opening and operations of all profit centers under their control. For example, in Rochester, we assisted Xerox with the design, construction and operations of all of their cafeterias and vending services.

In 1963, I had received the top national award from ARA for my operational achievement and community activities. At these national meetings, at the closing dinners, for entertainment purposes, I was allowed to humorously impersonate the various speakers including the ARA President and other corporate officials. Somehow I was able to accomplish this without offending any of them. If I missed a few top officials, I discovered that it was a disappointment to them.

At 37 years of age, I could not be happier. I was happily married with three children. My mother, brothers and sisters were cared for. Tuition was available for any brother or sister, if they chose to further their education.

My older brothers and sisters were not burdened with the need to support my mother. They were free to move to the vocation of their choice.

I lived in Rochester's most exclusive neighborhood. I was one of Rochester's success stories, "from rags to riches." Parties held at my home for business entertainment, or community fund raising, were publicized in the Democrat & Chronicle. My staff of catering professionals was available to make these parties unique in every respect.

The invitation for one party read, "Join us for an Arabian Night". On a perfect warm summer night, a Turkish rug ran from the curb to the front door with a mini-tent over the entrance. Guests were greeted by a seven-foot giant dressed in colorful Arabic clothing with golden slippers. The three-car garage was converted to a tent decorated with Arabic art. Inside the tent, two Turkish pipes were available for guest smoking. A lady relative experienced in palm reading and dressed in Arabian clothing, read the palms of our guests. A photographer took photos of couples smoking the Turkish pipes. Flaming torches lit the back yard and patio area. Arabic food was plentiful, identified in Arabic with an English translation.

My loveable Mother, with humble pride, stood next to the serving table, introducing herself and answering questions about the preparation and ingredients of the Arabic food. She won the hearts of all of our guests and her memory for the names of clients was remarkable. The Arabic food was prepared in our central commissary. My Mother supervised the preparation. On the generous sized patio, stations of mini-grills were on fire, awaiting the guests who cooked them to their desired choice. After dinner, a belly dancer entertained with a group of Arabic musicians from Utica, NY. My wife and I entertained our guests with Arabic dancing that we practiced together for our wedding, seven years before. Guests were from all walks of life – government officials, clients, relatives, community leaders and friends. It was called the "party of the year" by a Democrat & Chronicle reporter.

I was destined to become the national president of a $2 billion dollar company. My family would move with me to the Philadelphia national headquarters. I would take the lessons I learned as Prisoner of the Truck and lessons learned in service to the Rochester community and be involved in national rather than local worthy causes.

I went to bed after the Arabian Night Party wishing that my father had been there to celebrate the success of his son - - to see what patience, study, hard work, education, integrity, salesmanship, human relations skills and excellence in product and service had achieved - - all seeds planted in the Prison of the Truck.

At the age of 37, I had a new dream for my future with ARA. I would become its Chief Executive Officer. I would move to Philadelphia, grow the business and serve on national committees. I was committed to the Creeds espoused by the Junior Chamber of commerce. Among them were, "Service to humanity is the best work of life." "Earth's greatest treasure lies in human personality." And, "Economic justice can best be won by free men through free enterprise." The sky was the limit. I was convinced that nothing was impossible to achieve, if I put my mind to it.

Little did I realize that I would soon create a new 25-year Prison, one that I would impose upon myself, a prison for which I had to accept full responsibility.

Chapter 22 – Prisoner of the Truck

Age 34 to 54

New Prisons - Self-Made – Becoming Poor

How does one measure success or failure, happiness or sadness? Is it measured by an entrepreneur spirit that makes one rich? Is it in facing defeat and turning it into victory? Is it perseverance and patience in facing adversity? Is it faith that sustains you in your trials and tribulations? Is it knowing that you gave it your very best? Is it in searching for the good that comes from failure and turning failure into success? Is it a sense of inner peace and trust in God that sustains you in good or bad times?

Bristol Mountain Ski Area

In 1963, at age 37, I decided to take the after tax $1.5 million dollars ($12,500,000) in 2019 dollars in the sale of my company and invest $300,000 ($3,500,00 in 2019 dollars in a project called Bristol Mountain Ski Area). The mountain land was located in the Bristol Hills, 30 miles south of Rochester, NY, in the Finger Lakes Region of New York State. With local financing, this new one million dollar facility (equivalent to $10 million in year 2019 dollars) would be my payback to the community. It was not a hospital wing or school addition. It was not a get rich quick scheme. It would be profit motivated because only through profits can a regional recreational facility grow and flourish in its service to the total community. Like the 1500 profit centers that I was responsible for in ARA, I would be highly dependent on the management skills of the individuals involved. I would take great joy in school programs for children at a discounted price, special programs for the handicapped, bringing an exciting new winter recreational facility for family enjoyment. Our team would work toward affordable season passes and flexible skiing hours for day or night, seven days a week.

The news media found the plans to be very exciting. I was invited to speak to several luncheon meetings about the plans. My ski area associates had created a brilliant slide show for presentation of the plans. One luncheon involved the Chatterbox Club of Rochester. This was a group of affluent ladies who were active in service to the community. They were the wives of the leaders of the community. I asked my mother to attend the luncheon. The group reflected great excitement in the plans. My presentation involved humor and the laughter. The response was rewarding. During the question and answer period, one of the ladies asked me how I got started in the coffee business. I traced the events including the $10,000 ($140,000 in 2019 dollars) mortgage on my mother's home that led to a $2 million ($12,500,000 in 2019 dollars) company sale in 1956, eleven years later. A lady stood up and said with a bit of humor in her voice, *"That was a courageous gesture by your mother, Fred. I would never mortgage my home for my 24 year old son, no matter what business he wanted to start."*

At that point, I introduced my mother, who allowed me to mortgage our 1293 Park Avenue home for $10,000 ($140,000) and who, indirectly, made it possible for me to speak to their group about our ski area plans. I asked my mother to stand up. She was a sweet and loving five-foot tall lady. She was greeted with a big round of applause and shyly bowed to the audience. Another lady remarked that her son was interested in the Kwik Kafe franchise but after discussions with family attorneys and accountants, the family was discouraged from making the investment. (I was glad that I could not afford either an accountant or a lawyer when I entered the coffee business). When the meeting concluded, I found more attention given to my heroic mother than to me. I was as proud of her as she was of me.

Shortly after this talk, I went to inspect a new cafeteria that we designed and were operating at Xerox Corporation. As I was about to enter the door, a group of Xerox executives were leaving the cafeteria to greet a bus occupied by several men of Japanese heritage. I stood to the side to allow room for the meeting. Joe Wilson, the founder of Xerox, recognized me. I spent several years with Joe Wilson working on United Fund Campaigns. He was familiar with the laughter that I brought to the campaign lunches as well as my performance in the Chamber of Commerce Membership Campaign. Joe stopped short of the bus to quickly greet me and said, "My wife was at the Chatterbox Club a few weeks ago. She heard your talk and liked your plans. She gave a brochure to me. I used that brochure to convince two key IBM executives, who were close to the ski areas of Vermont, to come to work for Xerox. Your plans for the ski area did the trick. It's a great contribution to the community." I said, Thank you, Joe", as he quickly moved toward the bus for welcoming the bus group.

The Bristol Mountain Ski Area was proposed to me by two bright young men, Ron Ratnik and Larry Demarse) ages 30 and 27, professional engineers at General Motors in Rochester. They put together the land package. They did their homework. They knew that snow making was the key to the success of the plan. They needed an investor. Their timing in talking to me was right. They were willing to leave General Motors to work full time to make the ski area a success.

Before I committed to an investment, I took a two week vacation and visited every ski area in the Northeastern United States. Of all of the ski areas that I visited, there were two that stood out in my memory. One was a three day meeting with Cal Coniff, the young manager of Mt. Tom, a ski area in Holyoke, Mass. The average snowfall was 48" compared to 82" for Rochester; the average winter temperature was 3 degrees warmer than Rochester, yet Mt. Tom operated 90 days a year with. Mt. Tom was a small ski area with a vertical rise of only 400 feet compared, for example, to 2,100 vertical feet vertical north of Mt. Tom in Vermont. Mt. Tom was opened from top to bottom – all on man-made snow. Skiing conditions were from good to excellent. The entire mountain was lit for night skiing. I watched the long lines at night and during the weekend. Cal was open enough to show me his financial results for the previous years. The cash flow was not encouraging for a return on investment but the operations for the three previous years were in the black. Cal was encouraging with the plan. He felt that Bristol Mountain with a higher vertical, snowmaking, night lights and close proximity to a much larger city had great potential. His night group programs for schools and colleges were a great success. He believed that ours would be too.

The other memorable, but opposite, experience was with Walter Schoenknect, the owner-developer of a major ski area called Mt. Snow in Vermont. Walt was about 55. I was then 37. Walt was well known in the industry as a pioneer in ski area development. Mt. Snow operated only in the daytime and did not have snowmaking. The only way I could get to see Walter was at 6 PM in a hot tub at the Snow Flake Lodge where I stayed. He said he could only budget 30 minutes and could not have dinner with me. Typical of Walter's creativity, was the lodge that provided a cable ride over the roads right to the base of the ski area.

After I explained our plans for Bristol Mountain and my visit to Mt. Tom, while we were up our chins, submerged in the hot tub, Walt asked, *"What business are you in now?"* I told him. *"Why do you want to build a ski area. They are not good investments?"* I said that I was not seeking big profits; that I believed we could develop a positive cash flow to take care of annual upgrades and improvements. I spoke of our proximity to Rochester and our plans for day and night skiing - - getting twice the mileage out of the same investment. I said this would be my way of giving a portion of my wealth back to the community that gave me the opportunity for success. Walt said, *"Frankly, I think you should stay in the business you are in. You are going to underestimate your investment requirements and discover that you will be constantly pouring more money than the $300,000 limit that you have established. If you want my opinion, I think you're crazy, but it sounds like you have already made up your mind. So, good luck, I have to go."* The last I ever saw of Walt was the back of his red body as he emerged from the hot tub. However, as events turned out in future years, I never forgot his comments.

Otto Schneibs, a professional ski area designer was retained to layout the slopes and trails. Otto promised a trail and slope design that would *"pamper the beginners and intermediates"*. We all believed that this was the market to pursue. This was also the recommendation of the ski area managers that I visited.

Bristol Mountain Ski Area, when completed in 1994, was referred to in publications as the most modern ski area in America with the most advance technology in snow making, lighting and food service systems. My two associates earned high praise in the ski industry for completion of this complex project in time for December 1994 opening.

In its first year, the design did not succeed in serving the intended market of beginners and intermediate skiers. The snow making capacity was too small for a long season or a quick recovery from major thaws. The ski area had a significant loss in its first year. I faulted the famed designer, Otto Schniebs. We did not meet the income projections. The narrow trails and slopes created a crowded feeling. Skiing conditions were too variable due to need for a greater snow making capacity. Families were disappointed. The first year failure was not unlike the opening of a restaurant or business cafeteria. First impressions are most important. If a restaurant or cafeteria food service gets off to a poor or a good start, the news spreads rapidly. So it was with the Bristol Mountain Ski Area. Regardless of the good planning, the first year's experience for beginners and intermediate skiers was bad and that impacted on skier use and confidence for the balance of the year and the few years that followed.

The design failure lead to the development of Ski Valley and Hunt Hollow, two nearby private clubs and another public ski area called Swain. These Rochester developments used the technology of snow making pioneered by Bristol. Swain and Hunt Hollow were carefully planned for the novice and intermediate market. The impact of this new competition had a negative impact on Bristol's share of the market. Our bank was disappointed with the results. In the second year of operation, I had no alternative but to invest another $300,000 to cover losses, expand the snow making system and to widen the trails and slopes.

Ron Ratnik left Bristol to successfully market his expertise in snow making systems to other ski areas outside of the Bristol Mountain market. Larry Demarse was determined to turn the huge first year losses into a gain. With the expansion of snow making facilities and the widening of trails and slopes, the season of 1965-66 was an improvement over the first year but not enough to generate sufficient capital for improvements. In 1967, a $100,000 new slope for beginners, significantly improved the image of the ski area for "pampering beginners" but reasonable profits were still not attained. Fierce price competition from the Swain ski area also had an impact on profitability.

Robert Kennedy

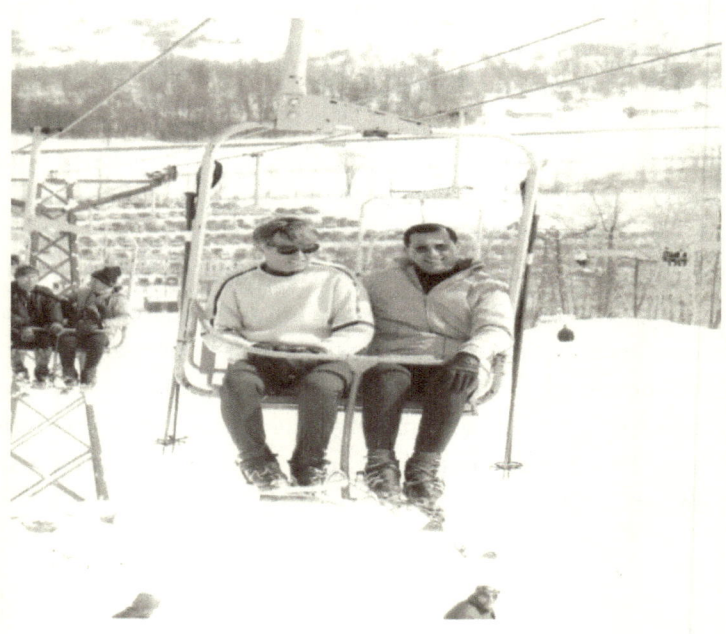

In 1964, while he was running for the Senate, Robert Kennedy could not appear for the ribbon cutting ceremony as he planned. However, he promised to return. In early March of 1967, I received a call from one of his assistants. He said that Senator Kennedy would keep his promise to return on March 18, 1967. It was a cold sunny day, excellent for skiing. Larry Demarse arranged for me to ski with the Senator. We took eight rides up the chairlift together. Each ride took approximately 10 minutes to get to the top of the mountain, a total of 80 minutes of one on one conversation. Senator Kennedy skied with wild abandonment. Had it not been for his falls, I would have been unable to keep up with him. One dramatic fall was caught on film and years later sent to his wife at her request.

I was 41 and the Senator was 42. At first Senator Kennedy talked about my family, mother, brothers, sisters, wife and children. He became aware that I became head of the household when I was 24 and the success that I achieved. We found similarities in the large families we came from. We were closely knit. We played football. We had many family gatherings. We were Catholic and devoted to our religion. Then his conversation shifted to questions. When did my father die? What was my first business venture? What got me into the ski business? What did I want to do with the rest of my life? Are you interested in government service?

I did not hesitate. I answered his last two questions, "I would like to take the tightly controlled management experience that I gained in the food and vending business and put it to work in government service. I would like to be the man in charge of seeing that the food for hungry nations actually gets to the hungry and is not intercepted somewhere by corrupt politics or governments." The Senator replied, "Fred, I will remember this conversation".

I firmly believed that if he became President, I would be called to serve. If called, I would have ditched my investments as well as ARA and moved my family to Washington. Senator Kennedy was shot fifteen months later on June 4, 1968 in California on his way to becoming President of the United States.

The Beginning of Bristol Harbour Village on Canandaigua Lake, NY

In 1963, shortly after the sale of my company in 1963, I had purchased 3 acres of land and 450 feet of cliff waterfront on Canandaigua Lake, 15 minutes from the ski area. The cost was $42,000. I rented a boat on the north shore of the lake and pulled up on the beachfront with my wife and said, "Surprise, this is where we will build our tennis court on the cliff will be vacation home and a stairway will bring us down to the tennis court and waterfront for boating and swimming." The surprise backfired. My wife was not in favor of a vacation home where she would spend all of her time worrying about children on the edge of a cliff or down at the waterfront or entertaining visiting relatives all summer. So this land remained vacant for four years.

In the fall of 1967, I read an article in Ski Area Magazine, the national publication for the ski industry. The article stated that ski areas needed to expand into resort property development in order to enhance their potential for profits, using the ski lodge as a marketing center.

On a winter Sunday in 1967, after attending Mass at St. Januarius Church in Naples, New York, I wanted to get away from the pressures of my work at ARA and the Ski Area. In order to get to the lake property that I had purchased in 1963 for a vacation home, I walked the long right of way at the foot of Seneca Point hill to the beach portion of the property. Canandaigua Lake runs north and south. It is 17 miles long, 1 ½ miles wide and over 200 feet deep. The waters are pure and clear. The city of Canandaigua is on the north shore and Naples, NY is close to the south shore. The hills surrounding the lake are over 1,000 feet high. The winter view was postcard perfect. The unfrozen waters rippled onto the shoreline. In the quiet of this environment, I counted the blessings of my mother, brothers, sisters, wife and children. They were all happy, healthy and doing well. Yet, I was troubled with the great drain of my financial resources, my responsibility to ARA and my commitment to make Bristol Mountain a success.

I thought about the ski area's struggle to make snow only to watch it melt on warm and rainy days and start over again when it got cold. In many ways, the weather patterns of running a ski area where not much different than the management of farms - both were vulnerable to bad weather cycles. I thought of the grape farmers and the frequent local newspaper reports of weather that threatened the quality and quantity of the harvest. I became sensitive to the crises that all farmers faced, in both crop production and financial needs. The quiet meditation in this winter setting seemed to refresh my spirit.

I walked back to my car and headed up the steep hill on Seneca Point Road. As I approached the top of the steep hill, I saw a for sale sign in the woods adjacent to my property. It read 24 acres and 2,000 feet of cliff frontage. I parked my car along Seneca Point Road to walk down the sharp slope. I partially walked and slid downward on slippery snow, through the forest of trees to the edge of the cliff. The views to the north, east and south were among the most beautiful I had ever seen in my travels or on TV or in magazines. A tree, near the edge of the cliff, had formed a bench for me to sit on. In the silence and privacy of this God created environment, where Seneca Indians once resided, my hand felt the St. Januarius Missalette that I had put in my ski jacket at Mass that morning. I checked the index for "How Great Thou Art." Mesmerized by the magnificence of the views, I sang aloud:

"O Lord, my God, when I in awesome wonder,

Consider all the worlds they hands have made,

I see the stars; I hear the rolling thunder,

Thy pow'r throughout the universe displayed.

When through the woods and forest glades I wander,

And hear the birds sing sweetly in the trees;

When I look down from lofty mountain grandeur

And hear the brook and feel the gentle breeze;

Then sings my soul, my Savior God to thee;

How great thou art! How great thou art!

The following day, I thought that this wondrous location, combined with frontage I already owned, could be divided into twenty-six 100 foot lots for the construction of 26 homes with a commonly owned stairway to the beach and 26 boat slips. I had no experience in land development. I naively thought that this could very well be the land development mentioned in Ski Area Magazine that could generate significant cash flow for Bristol Mountain. I would reach for a profit of $10,000 per lot and hand $260,000 over to the ski area. Again, in year 2000 dollars, this would be comparable to $2,600,000.

I phoned Herb Ellinwood, the broker. The California owner was asking $47,000 for the property. I told Mr. Ellinwood that I would like to put in a purchase offer. He phoned me a few days later and said that a "group" of lakeside property owners from Seneca Point heard about my interest in this property and also wished to submit an offer. The "group" was aware that I was in the ski business and they suspected that I was purchasing the cliff for development purposes.

They wanted to block me from buying this property for fear that I might create some kind of development that tied in with the ski area. Mr. Ellinwood said that he was obligated as a broker to submit all offers. In year 1967 dollars, I estimated the combined wealth of Seneca Point, Canandaigua lakeside property owners at $50 million or more. I had no intention of starting a bidding war. I earned many friendships from several of these property owners for my success in business, my community activities and in the development of the ski area. I was an accepted member of the "group" and invited to play in the annual Seneca Point tennis tournament.

With this in mind, I advised Mr. Ellinwood to simply submit an offer for $1,000 over the full asking price. The "group" submitted an offer for a sum less than the full asking price. I was shocked to learn that the owner, in California, accepted my offer.

Little did I realize what a dynamic and difficult impact this purchase and this plan would have on the next twenty years of my life, one that would significantly require me to borrow from the Seven Gifts of the Holy Spirit – Wisdom, Understanding, Counsel, Knowledge, Fortitude, Piety and Love of the Lord. These gifts, kept alive, helped me to survive the

Prison of the Truck. With God's help, they would help me to survive the feeling of being trapped - the self-imposed "Prisoner of a New Venture."

Shortly after closing on the sale of the land, I toured the property with a surveyor to lay out the lots. He shocked me by saying that rocky condition of the cliff could not handle 26 separate septic systems. I retained Paul Russell, a sanitary engineer from Harnish & Lookup. He confirmed the opinion of the surveyors. He said it would require a modern sewer treatment plant to serve 26 lots. I asked him what the cost would be. His shocking answer, "$250,000." I asked how about the capacity of the plant. He said it would serve 250 housing units.

<u>A Bigger Plan for a Village</u>

After several meetings, we concluded that it would be feasible to build five story buildings totaling 250 units on the cliff's edge. However, he said that we would need additional land for the sewer treatment plant. I reasoned that if we could build chairlifts for ski areas, we could build a vertical lift from the edge of the cliff to the beachfront for 250 units as well a given number of boat slips. Larry Demarse, a remarkable engineer and President of Bristol Mountain, knew how to put the engineering and construction team together for such an effort.

At a profit of $5,000 each in 1967 dollars, this would eventually generate $1,250,000 in cash for the ski area as well as repayment of loans that I had to make to keep the ski area going. Our sanitary engineer said that the sewage treatment plant would require 10 acres of land and suggested that I inquire about the land for sale across the street from this Cliffside property. We were not worried about zoning approvals. The Town of South Bristol did not have a zoning ordinance.

I spent the next weekend negotiating with the landowner across the street from the Cliffside property. He owned 110 acres of land, with many great lake views. In the middle of this acreage, he had built a magnificent home with a dramatic lake view to the south that eventually became our operational center. He agreed to trade his land for stock for a plan to put the ski area and land development into one package and to sell shares of stock to the public. In addition to that, Mack McCabe, a local realtor and friend, handled another land purchase of 110 acres called the German parcel. This would be for a future golf course.

Resigning from ARA

In 1968, when I was 42, I was called into Philadelphia for a meeting. In spite of my outside investment pressures, I was actively involved in my responsibility to ARA during the week and actively involved with the ski area on weekends. During the weekdays, I met regularly with my key ARA regional vice presidents and staff. Our ten state area performance was the best in the United States. Based on this, I was asked if I would assume the Presidency of the Business & Industry Division of ARA, a division that was approaching one billion in sales. It was made clear that as President of ARA, I should expect to be traveling at least 60% of the time. I would meet with the vice-presidents of the six areas in the United States for performance reviews at their headquarters. I would be involved in the opening of cafeterias of any of the Fortune 500 cafeterias in the United States. I knew that the next step could be the CEO of all of the ARA Divisions approaching $3 billion in sales. The founders Bill Fishman & Davre Davidson were keenly aware of my ARA national achievement awards for exceptional profit performance, excellent team building skills and award- winning community service.

I now had five children, ranging in age from one to twelve. I shocked Ralph Globus who was retiring as President of the B&I Division when I very reluctantly said, "Ralph, I cannot take the job for two reasons. One, I must be close to my family and two, my investment in a ski area and in resort planning are consuming my capital and both will need more of my time. I am honored by your offer but I find myself in a situation that is a conflict of interest and I believe I should resign. Ralph asked me to stay on for another year to allow the new area president to determine my replacement. This was a difficult decision. I believed that if I became CEO of ARA, I would be able to make community contributions on a national rather than local scale. My heart was always into maximizing whatever community service I could render.

Moving Forward with the Plans for Bristol Harbour Village

In 1968, I still had sufficient funds to retain professionals for the development of the 258 acres and half mile of Cliffside lake frontage we now controlled. Larry Demarse played an active role in meeting with architects and engineers. His experience as an engineer and in the construction of Bristol Mountain was invaluable to the planning process, enabling me to continue to perform my duties with ARA. The ski area was not producing any significant cash flow. There were limited funds for expansion.

Every town in Ontario County had some form of zoning in 1968. As early as 1964, when Bristol Mountain was completed, I attended a Town Board meeting and urged the Town would to develop a zoning ordinance. Unwisely, the Seneca Point Group, in the Town of South Bristol, opposed it. They wanted to build or add on to their lakeside homes anytime they pleased, without any red tape.

In August of 1968, James Johnson, our architect, Larry Demarse and I presented an "initial" plan to the South Bristol Town Board calling for 200 condominiums on the edge of the Cliffside. About 70 persons from South Bristol attended including vocal members of Seneca Point, under the guise of Canandaigua Lake Area Association Inc. They expressed their intense disapproval and concerns about the plans. Intense pressure was put on the town fathers to create a zoning ordnance, one that would block our plans.

There was a great amount of publicity, letters to the editor and appeals to town, county and state authorities and politicians. The scrapbooks of news articles and letters to the editor for the next three years are over two feet tall. They reflect the attempts of the Seneca Point Group to prevent the master planning or the financing of Bristol Harbour Village. A petition of 5,300 signatures was sent to Governor Rockefeller "requesting that he and all other public officials responsible for health and the purity of our water deny permission for construction of Bristol Harbour Village near Seneca Point on Canandaigua Lake."

Urged by the misinformation of Seneca Point group leaders, I personally received over a hundred letters in opposition. Some letters suggested that my children would forever be hated if my plans were successful. Other letters, including one unauthorized letter, on Kodak letterhead, suggested that my plans could affect the business that ARA was doing with Kodak.

Joe Wilson, founder, Chairman and CEO of Xerox

In early September of 1968, in the midst of this intense opposition, I received a phone call from Joe Wilson, founder, Chairman and CEO of Xerox Corporation. It was in 1963 when Mr. Wilson spoke to me about the two IBM executives he recruited because of the ski brochure his wife brought home from the Chatterbox Club. Joe said, "Fred, a group of influential people have asked me to get involved in attempts to block your planned lake development. I believe it is only fair for me to hear your side of the story before I make a decision. Would I be able to meet with you, your architect and engineer to review your plans?" (Mr. Wilson had built a vacation home on a large piece of land overlooking Canandaigua Lake not far from Seneca Point).

We met at the office of Jim Johnson our architect. Paul Russell, our sanitary engineer joined us for this meeting. They both did a masterful job of explaining the plans to Mr. Wilson, an objective listener. He was impressed with the environmental sensitivity in which the plans were developed and the team of professionals involved. He wanted to know more about overall benefits to the community and the business and financial plans for Bristol Mountain and Bristol Harbour. I discussed the contributions Bristol Mountain had made to the Naples, NY community. Naples was wine country in both the growing of grapes and the production of wine. In the winter, Bristol provided many jobs for young and old in Naples and surrounding community. I spoke of the plan to take snowmaking crews in the winter who would become golf maintenance crews in the spring, summer and fall. The same would apply to food service personnel who would move from the ski area food service facility to the clubhouse restaurant for four-season employment. I spoke of the economies involved when one management team focused on both a ski area and a resort, providing year round steady employment. I predicted that Bristol Harbour would be primarily a community of adults seeking a maintenance-free second home. There would be little or no impact on the Naples School District so school taxes on homes at Bristol Harbour would enhance the quality of education for the Naples School District. He was aware of public offerings that were being made during that time with little substance. He felt that our public offering for the sale of shares in our combined ski-lake plan, was sound and had merit since it would minimize high interest costs that could endanger the plan.

I knew of Mr. Wilson's interest in people, who sincerely believed in service to their community. He said and believed that recreation was an essential industry that served the needs of people. I also knew of his reputation for hands on management and walking around his company, remembering the names of his employees as well as those he worked with in the community. If there was someone he did not know, he would introduce himself, seeking the name of the other party. He was a gentle man, a man of compassion and sensitivity for the needs of the total community. He was also a brilliant leader and motivator.

Joe Wilson did not know that I had such a high respect for his brilliance, character, humility, courage and achievements that I would have dropped the plans for Bristol Harbour Village if he asked me to. I was aware that both Kodak and IBM had turned down Howard Carlson, the inventor of Xeroxography. Joe Wilson had the vision to see its potential and the "Fortitude" to risk his entire business and fortune on the idea. And even more, he was a religious man. He did "Counsel" with me. He did search for "Knowledge and Understanding". He did it as a "pious" man. He had the objective "Wisdom" to know that the planning was sensitive to the environment. The seven gifts of the Holy Spirit were simply inherent in Joe Wilson's nature.

I knew that if Joe Wilson asked me to drop the plans for Bristol Harbour, he would have also advised me how to minimize my losses and exit the plan graciously. I had this admiration for Robert Kennedy that I wrote of earlier, but no one, not even Bob Kennedy, earned my respect more than Joe Wilson. I loved that man for his impeccable integrity, his goodness and his concern for his fellow man – one that extended down to the janitors in his company. With the expansion of Xerox throughout the world in his business plan, this man was, nevertheless, taking time to listen to the plan for Bristol Harbour and Bristol Mountain before he signed a petition against it. That is greatness; that is class; unequalled by any man I ever knew. When the meeting was concluded, Mr. Wilson said, "Fred, I do not intend to sign the petition against your project. This does not mean that you can say that I endorse your plan. However, I do wish you and your people good luck and success in this endeavor".

Shortly thereafter, a major leader of the "group", a vice president of the Canandaigua Lake Association, made it her full time personal goal to block the various government approval requirements. She even organized a group of people to solicit protests in public parks in Rochester, 35 miles from Canandaigua. The misinformation passed out implied that Bristol Harbour Village was the lake's biggest polluter, when in fact a shovel had not as yet been turned into the ground. Albany is the capital of New York State and a six hour drive from Canandaigua. She made several trips to Albany and to local political officials in an aggressive attempt to block state approval of the plans for both the sewer treatment plant and the marina.

Throughout this period, I kept thinking. This is the United States of America. I served in WWII to protect the democratic process. I am not planning anything illegal. I am cooperating with every NY State agency that the law requires. In spite of the fact there was no town zoning, these other NY agencies will not permit me to go forward if the plans will harm the environment or the lake. I want to do it right. I value the input of the community. I am sensitive to their concerns. I will make changes that make sense. If the plans disturb our neighbors, they would also disturb the people we would be trying to sell. For all these reasons, I thought, I will commit every last dollar and every ounce of my energy to prevail.

<u>A Shocking Meeting</u>

After the South Bristol Town presentation of plans, I spoke to the Seneca Point Group leader and the vice president of the Canandaigua Lake Association. I asked if I could bring my architect to a meeting with her "group" to address their major concerns. She approved of the meeting and suggested that it be held in her home in Pittsford, NY. I thought this would help me to "Understand" their concerns and help them to "Understand" the controls that we would be put into place to make Bristol Harbour Village a good and peaceful neighbor. This attempt to "Counsel" and search for "Knowledge" could alleviate many of their concerns. At this meeting, I explained that the Condo plan had to be approved by the Attorney General of NY State. There would be rules & regulations governing the quality of usage such as noise control, exterior maintenance of the buildings, balconies free of hanging towels or wet clothing, etc. I tried to reason that no one would buy into the project if there were no legal controls for the orderly usage of each living unit. These controls would minimize any disturbance to condominium occupants as well as the "four" Seneca Point lakeside homes adjacent to the planned development. The Seneca Point Group knew that other homes were far removed from the project and could not see the condominium from their properties.

Our architect explained the "initial plan". We made it clear that we would address their concerns and make adjustments wherever we could. Good questions were asked. One rendering showed a multi-story building rising from the beach, 100 feet, to the top of the cliff. It also showed other buildings on the cliff itself. Inside the beach building, an elevator was planned to take residents to their units or residents from other buildings down to the beach area. A member of the group asked, "That is such a small beach area. Shouldn't that area be left as a beach only? Isn't that best for your long term plans?"

Indeed, in our planning process, we had failed to consider the negative impact this beach building would have on neighbors as well as future residents of BHV. Preserving the one-half mile of cliff without a single building fronting it was the most significant and helpful input gathered from this meeting. Anyone standing on the Bristol Harbour Village beach in the future could enjoy the natural wonder of the 2,600 feet of the cliff water frontage without seeing a condominium building.

After a brief deliberation with my architect, our response was, "Yes, you are right." The architect put an X through the beach building on the drawing and I said, "It's gone. What else?" Questions regarding the size, quality and estimated sales price of the units were asked? It was to be a high quality product that would attract affluent buyers.

Others asked, *"Can you take those five story buildings and nestle them into the trees so that they are somewhat concealed?"* We stated that was in the plan. Another good question was asked, *"Have you been to Bermuda and looked at all of those pink buildings? Can you match the exterior of the buildings as close as you can to the color of the exposed cliff?"* I thought we were making great progress. They were providing input important to future residents as well as our neighbors. The answer was "Yes."

Then the tide turned. Another question was, *"Fred, you are noted for your community good work and a good neighbor. Many of us have been your friends. Can't you pick another spot on the other side of the lake and do your development there?"* This question was supported by several others at the meeting who suggested possible sites. No one voiced objection to this question. My answer was the truth, *"No, for marketing reasons, we want to be within fifteen minutes of Bristol Mountain and this is the only land available on the west side of the lake that provides access to the lake."*

(This question reminded me of my community service in Rochester, NY when important community leaders would support certain housing projects as long as they were not in their back yards. If I write another book, it will be called NIMBY (not in my back yard).

No one seemed to care about the potential convenience of an adjacent golf course, clubhouse and restaurant in their back yard nor the sensitivity given to the careful environmental planning, nor the controls that would be put into place. They simply did not want Bristol Harbour Village to become a reality. They wanted the 2,600 feet of lake frontage to be vacant as if it were their own private frontage. Even though they previously opposed zoning, even though they did not own the land, they treated the land as if it was their private preserve and we were going to despoil it. The 27-acre,

2600 feet of cliff property had been for sale for four years. All they had to do was to chip in to buy it as a private preserve and control of its usage.

It became obvious that the group was not there to listen to reason. They hid under the banner of protecting the lake from our development - yet no one found fault with the suggestion of moving the project to the *"other side of the lake."* They simply wanted us to go away. If we did not go away, they would use pollution of the lake, overly crowded boating conditions and depreciation of property values as their banner. This would unite the entire lake community with fear and misinformation. Politicians and governmental agencies would get involved. This could have a negative impact on governmental approvals. Funds obtained from the entire lake community could be used to litigate to the fullest extent.

Contrary to the fact that the lake belonged to the people of New York State, they were opposed to sharing it. This included their opposition to the state operated marinas on the north and south of the lake as well as our planned development.

Data they promulgated regarding pollution of the lake was based on sheer unwillingness to accept scientific fact. Data that Bristol Harbour would destroy the values of the property *would prove to be inaccurate. Data that the marina would overcrowd the use of the water ignored the* aerial evidence that showed there was ample room for additional boats.

(The living history of Bristol Harbour Village in the year 2000 would serve to prove that the seeds of fear and panic that they spread throughout the lake and in the Rochester community in these earlier years regarding noise, safety, lake pollution and unreasonable boat density were totally unjustified. An award winning golf course and restaurant in their back yard significantly enhanced their enjoyment and contributed to a great increase in their property values. The project made significant tax contributions to the Naples School District with less than a dozen children going to school. Jobs were created and $30 million was added to the tax base with little demand for town and county services. On all counts the opposition was proven wrong.)

In their public attempts to discredit the plan, there was the pretense of protecting the lake *"for all people"* but in this particular meeting in Pittsford, New York, it was clearly shown that the motive was to protect what they perceived to be *"their portion of the lake."*

At this 1968 meeting, a shocking question was asked by someone, without objection by anyone present. *"What will happen to future sales if the Fight Organization wants to buy the first building of 14 units?"* The Fight organization was a group of African Americans and others, who among other causes, wanted to eliminate the prejudice that existed in buying homes in white neighborhoods. I answered that I did not believe the Fight organization would be interested in buying 14 expensive condominium units in a resort environment.

Another question, *"Well, Fred, of course you know the people who will be buying your condominiums?"* I replied, *"People who can afford to buy them"*. *"No Fred"*, came back the reply, *"you know, it's the people who are buying condominiums in Florida?"* I was still naïve. I did not understand. Finally, *"Fred, with your Lebanese heritage, you should know what we are talking about?"* Still, no one at this meeting raised a voice in protest of the question. (Unlike New York State that had few condominium projects during this period, Condominiums were very popular in Florida. It was true that the Jewish community valued this maintenance free lifestyle in Florida and were large buyers of condominium units.) I raised my voice in righteous anger and said, *"Oh, now I know what you are talking about and I do have an answer for that question. We will sell the first building to the Blacks, the second building to the Jews, the third building to the Irish, the fourth building to the Germans, the fifth building to the Italians, the sixth building to the Lebanese Arabs, etc., and we will change the name of Bristol Harbour Village to United Nations Village and we will fly both the American flag and the flag of the other country above each of those buildings."*

Then I continued without pausing, *"Look you all know that I had my start in the coffee vending business. Each of my machines was taught to automatically accept the nickels of all customers regardless of their race, creed or color so as to conform with the law of the land, and the law of the land is no different in regard to real estate sales. There shall be no discrimination in the sale of real estate. Are there any more questions?"* One prominent voice of the Rochester community said, *"Fred, I want to be disassociated with the questions that have just been asked."* There were three or four others who asked to be disassociated with these questions. I asked to be excused from the meeting and the architect and I left.

When the meeting had concluded, I reflected on my childhood and my hatred for any form of discrimination. I was proud that I had the gift of Fortitude to speak out as I did at this meeting. This meeting fueled my determination to make Bristol Harbour Village a reality even if it took me and my family to the door step of personal bankruptcy. There would be one exception. I would not put a mortgage on my mother's home. If losing the battle was God's will for me, I knew that with my experience and determination, I could rejoin ARA or find employment anywhere in these United States. However, I knew that my sarcastic responses to the "group" would only serve to fuel their determination to fight me every step of the way.

On May 6, 1969 The Canandaigua Lake Area Association, lead by leaders of "group" who met in the Pittsford home, asked if I would consent to a public meeting with my sanitary engineer to answer questions about the Health Departments approval of our $250,000 sewerage treatment plant. Over a hundred people attended. The engineer made a very professional slide show presentation showing what the plant would look like and how the three stages of treatment would result in water cleaner than the lake water itself. He also explained the Department of Health's intensive review and approval of the plans. In the question and answer period, someone asked, *"Mr. Sarkis, would you allow your children to swim at the mouth of the creek when the so called treated water is coming into the lake?"* I replied, *"Yes, based on the professional input you've heard today and the approval of the State Department of Health, I would."* His response, *"Mr. Sarkis, you would do anything to make a buck even if meant letting your children swim in raw sewage".* The meeting failed to convince many of those in attendance. They did not want not to listen to facts. They just wanted me to go away. The hostility of certain uncontrolled members of the audience caused great concern to my brother Joe and Larry Demarse who were in the audience. They actually feared for my safety. Gathering the support of two others, they escorted me out of the meeting and to my car to prevent me from being harmed.

This unruly meeting is best described in a letter to the editor in the Daily Messenger:

Prisoner of the Truck - Chapter 23

Hard Work, Creativity and Financial Miracles

At age 54, in the summer of 1970, to protect our *"initial plan"*, I needed the dollars to begin construction. The local banking institutions considered Bristol Harbour Village a public relations hot potato. Under the first and new South Bristol Town regulations, there was a clause in the zoning that would allow existing plans to remain in effect as long as there was a substantial start in construction. Based on the advise of our attorneys, I had to commit my dwindling personal funds to clear the site for the sewer plant, construct a road to the first building and build the concrete shell of this building on the edge of the cliff, the "skeleton". The skeleton had no roof, no balcony railings and no stairway. We then had an aerial photo taken, with the date of the photo certified. That was accepted by the Town of South Bristol as *"substantial commencement"* and all of our costly approvals remained intact and legally protected while we searched for funding.

Shortly thereafter, the Wall Street Journal reported that hundreds of businessmen throughout the United States were swindled by a Cleveland Venture Capital firm that was giving fraudulent commitment letters to prominent banks throughout the United States. The article stated that business men, desperate for financing, were required to submit a sum equal to 1% of the loan application, refundable if a commitment letter was not received. The bank in Florida had issued a commitment letter subject to funding from this Cleveland firm. The Florida bank relied on falsified financial statements from the Cleveland firm. I was one of the victims. I lost the $20,000 deposit and the loan commitment.

In October of 1969, the timing of the Bristol Mountain Enterprises, Inc. missed the hot market by two months. Commitments received for all of the shares of a $2.5 million offering faded into the dust. I was in deep trouble. The cost of engineers, architects, attorneys and the "substantial commencement" consumed almost all of my funds.

Here's how I felt. Since 1963, I tried to develop a successful ski area for the community with a limit on the amount of cash I wanted to invest. That failed.

It was supposed to be super ski area for the novice and intermediate skier. That failed.

Among the community leaders and the affluent people who lived on Canandaigua Lake, I went from being a respected successful entrepreneur of food, vending and skiing to a despised real estate developer. The news articles and letters to the editor filled several scrap books that are over two feet high, including letters that I wrote defending the quality of our plans and our commitment to prevent any detrimental effect on the lake environment. Armed with data prepared by our scientific engineers, I tried to make peace with opponents by meeting with them and addressing their concerns in a positive manner.

That failed.

Since I was blackballed in the Rochester financial community, I had to seek a lender outside of the area. That failed with a fraudulent lender.

I tried to go public with substantial assets: the ski area, the lake property and the master plan approvals from all the New York State governmental authorities. The timing was bad and that failed.

There was one more option. Surrender.

A short time after the October 1969 failure of the public offering, I received a call from Wallace Ely, the President of Security Trust Company. Mr. Ely was President of the Chamber of Commerce. I worked under him as Chairman of the Chamber's Membership Campaign. We met in his office. He asked me how everything was going with my Bristol Harbour Village plans. I asked if he was asking me as a banker interested in giving me a loan or for other reasons. He said he was not speaking as a banker. He was speaking as a middleman between the *"Seneca Point group"* and me. Since the Group did not see any further progress on the *"skeleton"* of the first building for six months, they assumed that I had run into financial difficulties. Mr. Ely said that they wanted to know if I would consider an offer for the actual cost of the land and the actual master plan approvals. I told him that there were other interested parties but I would think about such an offer. I also said that I spent most of my life making friends and I was not having any fun making enemies. For a full week, I deliberated on the offer. I discussed it with a few key advisors. We considered the following as it related to the Seneca Point's Group offer.

The Cliffside frontage was listed for several years before my interest. That was the Group's first chance to buy it for $46,000. It was reasonable to estimate the combined wealth of 50 owners in the Seneca Point Group at $50 million or more. If each owner pitched in only $1,000, they would have controlled this land and waterfront and preserved it as their green belt.

When they heard that I was going to purchase the Cliffside frontage, they should have contacted the seller through the broker to offer more than the list price. Again, $1,000 from each would have accomplished this. I would not have tried to outbid them.

They should have purchased the 165 acres and single family home on the Cliffside. Instead, they asked the owner not to sell it to me. This would have cost the Group $3,000 each. This would have made it impossible to install a sewer treatment plant and limit the 24 acre, 2,000 foot parcel to a few homes. This 165 acre parcel and home, with beautiful lakes views, could have become a rental property or a Seneca Point Group party house with tennis facilities etc..

The Group's proposal, through Mr. Ely, would be their fourth opportunity. Certainly, we reasoned, with most of our master plan approvals in hand, the Seneca Point Group would not risk the chance of having the property fall into the hands of a major developer with ample cash - a Developer not dedicated to the quality that I sought. This was their 4th chance to act. My advisors and I believed that they would not pass up this last opportunity to prevent the development of Bristol Harbour Village. At this stage, my investment in all of the land and professional fees was close to $500,000. I was emotionally and psychologically ready to throw in the towel. This would cost the Group $10,000 each to control the size and scope of the development. For their investment, they would control 2,600 feet of frontage, 292 acres and the master plan approvals. They could have spun off the land on the west of the Seneca Point Road that had no waterfront and preserved the 27 acre, 2600 feet of Cliffside frontage as a greenbelt.

A week later, I set up a meeting with Mr. Ely. I presented the actual cost of the land and the cost of the master plan approvals and litigation. This was my flag of surrender. Mr. Ely said he would present this to the *"Group"* and get back to me. Two weeks went by. I heard nothing from Mr. Ely. Instead, I received a phone call from my friend, Jack Carey, who as with Connecticut Mutual Life Insurance Company. He said, *"Freddie, I was invited to a party on Seneca Point over the weekend. I was shocked. They heard you were out of cash. They were celebrating your pending corporate and personal bankruptcy."* Jack and his associate Van Albanese tried to get Connecticut Mutual Life interested. Conn-Mutual looked at the master plan, the approvals and the economic model and turned it down.

I reflected on the impact of our opponent's strategy. They caused serious delays in our various approval processes. They damaged our public relations. They caused us to spend over $100,000 (over a million in today's dollars) in legal fees, far greater than would have been normal without their intense opposition at each stage of the approval process. In the end, in spite of winning all of our approvals, my financial plan failed. They had cause to celebrate.

A few months later, after this charade, on a cold winter evening in early December of 1970, after night skiing at Bristol Mountain, I drove to the lake property. I found a ladder to climb up the skeleton to the top balcony of the fourth floor. I sat on this balcony, without railings, huddled with my knees against my chest, with my back up against the concrete wall. No, I was not thinking about suicide. I did not want to return to my Ambassador Drive home office and the piles of investor proposal papers that surrounded me. It was a clear night. The moon was resting on the top of the snow covered mountain on the other side of the lake. There I sat in the bowel of the skeleton, the equivalent of 14 stories high from the lake water. As I looked at the reflection of the moon on the pure waters of Canandaigua Lake, I thought of the guide boat that would take tourist from the north shore down past the west and east side of the lake, highlighting historical homes and marked locations where boats would bring provisions and supplies to the few dwellings that were then on the lake. As the guide boat came down the West Side of the lake, I could see the guide pointing up to the white concrete skeleton on the edge of the cliff and saying into the loudspeaker on the boat, *"Now at the Cottage that we are passing, that's the skeleton of the start of a project that was supposed to be a master planned community of condominiums, a hotel, golf course and marina. A guy by the name of Sarkis spent five years and his personal fortune putting the land package together and fighting for approvals. His affluent neighbors, in great numbers, fought him every step of the way. When he finally got the approvals, he ran out of money and went bankrupt. That's why it is called the 'The Skeleton of Sarkis's Dream'. Now next to the skeleton is Seneca Point. The Seneca Point area is considered the most affluent of lakeside homes on the lake.*

On this winter evening, overlooking the lake, with lakeside homes closed for the winter, shivering from the cold in the belly of the concrete skeleton that I had created, I talked to God. I asked Him to help me to find the funds to finish Phase One. I told Him that material gain was not what I sought. I said that Phase One would prove that my plan would not harm the beauty of Canandaigua Lake nor would it have an adverse impact on my neighbor opponents. God knew that I did not want that summer boat guide to refer to my skeleton as "The Skeleton of Sarkis's Dream".

I calculated the last time I sent a check to the Carmelites Sisters. I determined the cost of eggs per day since my last check plus the cost of a dozen eggs for the next twelve months and sent them a check for the total with a short note, "Dear Sisters: Here I am again asking for your prayers. I am on the financial edge of a cliff. I ask you to pray for the success of my mission." The check was dated December 7, 1970, the date of the anniversary of the Japanese attack on Pearl Harbour.

After I mailed the check to the Carmelites in the oak paneled study of my Ambassador Drive home that I feared losing, while my patient and dedicated wife tended to our flock of five children and fired with enthusiasm gifted by the Lord, I began a strategy to find a Real Estate Investment Trust. I made one phone call after another. I found an interested REIT in Maryland.

My timing was perfect. They were looking for projects. On December 15, 1970, Colonel Hal Eichen, from General Mortgage Investments flew in to inspect the site and government approvals on December 15. He was familiar with neighborhood oppositions and attempts to stop a well planned development. They had no ties to the emotions of a community. He was impressed with me, the property, the master plan approvals that he knew were extremely difficult to get and the fact that there was no mortgage on the entire property. On December 28, 1970 we received a commitment for $2 million for Phase One. This would cover the cost of the sewer treatment plant, the conversion of the skeleton into our first 14 unit building on the edge of the cliff, the erection of the gondola and stairway to the beach as well as the sitework for the lots, six townhomes, tennis courts, single family phase one lot developments, two tennis courts and a recreation area for children. I phoned and thanked the Carmelites. I pondered on the Seven Gifts. I came to the conclusion that the Gifts sometimes don't work when you work with people who hate your mission.

In the spring of 1971, after the ski area closed, Larry Demarse came to the rescue with his construction experience. Larry supervised the construction of Phase One. His low cost idea for a bridge and gondola were unique and solidly built. He finished Phase One in time for the spring marketing season of 1971. We learned that the vertical rise of the gondola, equal to ten stories high, was the highest vertical cable gondola in the world. When one cabin reached the top and other cabin touched the bottom. Each gondola held four passengers and was self operated.

We sold the 14 condominium units. One of the first buyers was Jim O'Neill, the vice president of finance for Xerox. Mr. O'Neill told me that he was shocked when a middle-management executive at Xerox, who was an opponent to the development from the beginning, told him he would be foolish to buy at Bristol Harbour. This Xerox executive said that a Kodak engineer, who also resided on Canandaigua Lake, was concerned about the construction of the condominium. The Kodak engineer said that based on his evaluation, within a few years, the 14 unit building would be in danger of falling into the lake.

Larry Demarse reviewed with Mr. O'Neill the qualifications of the engineer who designed the footings for both the condominium building and the steel bridge that supported the gondola. The motive of the Xerox executive was clear. He believed that if Mr. O'Neill, the number 3 executive at Xerox, purchased in this first 14 unit building, it would trigger sales from other prominent executives in the Rochester area. Mr. O'Neill resented this interference and in support of our plans, allowed us to use his name as a reference to any prospective future buyer. Mr. O'Neill had the integrity and sense of fair play inherent in Joe Wilson, his Xerox boss; he saw me as a determined and honest entrepreneur. He did not respect the unfair tactics used by the middle management Xerox executive.

Franz Mittlemayer, the head of our Bristol Mountain Ski School, provided major assistance to the summer marketing effort. However, in spite of a good marketing and sales effort, lot sales did not materialize as expected. We faced another failure. The payback of our $2 million loan was dependent on the cash flow from the sale of lots and the presale of condominium units for buildings 2 and 3.

We knew we would have difficulty in making a payment on our loan in June of 1972. Both Bristol Harbour and Bristol Mountain were collateralized to the Real Estate Investment Trust. In spite of this crises, God had answered my prayer. The tourist boat guide could never point to the skeleton on the edge of the cliff. I had my miracles of owning the coffee vending, of getting Kodak for a customer and the miracle of completing Phase One of Bristol Harbour Village. I wondered how many more miracles should I expect? Is struggling for development money what God wants me to do the rest of my life? I began to feel that my mission was materialistic. I began to think about the less fortunate, the poor, the hungry and thirsty. TV documentaries and pictures of emaciated children in Africa touched my heart. It seemed that the miracle that I should be praying for would be the miracle of getting aid to these people, to these children.

I knew that I created my own Prison, the Prisoner of a Dream that had turned into a nightmare. Nevertheless, I thanked God for the support of my family and children. I found joy and comfort in their love, their morning and evening hugs, the prayers said for me on their knees and their cheerful spirit. I was determined to find an equity partner to pay off the $2 million and provide working capital for the continuation of the project. I had several leads, made many phone calls and sent informational packages without much success.

1972 - At age 45, in March of 1972, I received a phone call from Mother Nesser who was involved with ecumenical meetings at the Cenacle. The Cenacle was a retreat house for ladies located on East Avenue about ten minutes from where I lived. In addition to retreats, they held weekly prayer meetings. My sister Betty knew that I was having difficulties again. She did not know to what extent. Mother Nesser wanted me to attend one of the ecumenical meetings. I said, *"Mother Nesser, we both went to St. Joseph's school. I do not need to go to prayer meetings. When I get up in the morning, I do what the good Sisters of Notre Dame taught me. I offer my work up as a prayer and believe me it ends up being one big prayer."* Mother Nesser said,

"Look, maybe if you take a mini-vacation of two hours from whatever stress you are facing, it will be good for you. At least come to one evening meeting. You are not that far away." I sang with Mother Nesser in our St. Nicholas church choir for years. She was living Saint. I decided to attend a meeting.

I just sat and listened and observed. The group, numbered about 25, was indeed ecumenical – Protestants, Catholics and Jews. It was very informal and relaxed. Anyone could speak. Some shared experiences that they thanked God for. Others talked about loved ones who were having difficulties in marriage or in health or on drugs. Some asked for prayers to assist with these problems. Someone asked to be prayed over. I cannot remember what for. Some of those in attendance would put their hands on the person who was sitting in a chair and pray for their specific intention. One young enthusiastic young man, who told his story of helping drug addicts in a coffee shop in the inner city, was praying in a strange manner. It was not the *"gift of tongues"* that Jesus gave to his apostles when he appeared to them after His death. It was gibberish. I said nothing and left the meeting.

A week later, my curiosity about the young man's strange language got the best of me. I went again to see what I could learn. A lady talked about her experience that morning. She said her husband had gone off to work and the children were sent off to school. She said their combined income made it difficult to make ends meet. She had to go to work but the sink was plugged. Hand pumping failed. She thought, *"We can't afford a plumber Lord."* All of a sudden the water in the sink drained quickly on its own. The group said *"Praise the Lord"*. That was, as she described, *"a miracle."*

Again, I said nothing and could not wait to get out of this setting. On the ten minute drive home, I began to think about this lady's plugged sink. I realized that I had formed two judgments in two meetings in which I said nothing. One judgment was that the young man, who prayed in gibberish, was kind of crazy; the other judgment was that to treat an unplugged sink as a miracle was ridiculous.

Then I began to feel that I had lost my common touch. I was so obsessed with my own *"huge crises"*, that I overlooked the reality that in many lives what I considered "small" problems for other humans, were in fact *"huge crises"* in their lives. I thought of people with financial problems, scraping enough dollars to buy food & clothing or to pay the rent for fear of eviction, or losing their homes in a mortgage foreclosure, or having their cars, refrigerators, washing machines repossessed for lack of payment. I thought of the financial crises associated with helping a loved one with a drug, alcohol or gambling addiction or medical care that they could not afford or a marriage falling apart. I thought of my childhood and my Prison. In many ways, many people were in Prisons without bars. Prisons of financial stress, sickness, addictions, divorce or separation and the sad impact these Prisons had on children.

I thought people's crises were like a high-rise building with many people hanging onto the windowsills for their dear lives - by the tips of their fingers. If they were on the fifth floor or the twentieth floor, the fear of the fall was the same and the consequences of the fall were the same. The prayers to prevent the fall, no matter how far, were all equally important in the eyes of God.

These thoughts lead me to the third meeting prayer meeting. I felt that I had something to learn. I especially wanted to question the 21 year old young man who worked with young people who were addicted to drugs and alcohol. A few minutes after the meeting began, in this third meeting, I spoke my first words. I said to the young man. *"I have been to two meetings. I have said nothing. At each meeting your prayers sound like a lot of gibberish to me when you pray over someone. The Holy Spirit did not give the gift of gibberish. He gave the gift of a language so that the word of the gospel could be spread throughout the world. If it is gibberish, why can't you just speak in English and share your outpouring of prayer with others?"* He simply replied, *"Yes it would sound to you like gibberish. Here's how I feel. When I try to comprehend God and his Greatness, I cannot find the English words to praise him. What I do is a simple outpouring of my soul in praise for Him. Gibberish is what comes out of my mouth. It is my way of praising the Lord. That's just me."* Feeling a bit humbled and less judgmental, I sincerely thanked him for explaining his feelings. I came to realize that I must respect the differences in the way people praise the Lord.

A few minutes later, a lady asked us if we would pray for her boss. Someone said, "Is he sick?" She said, *"No, he is a businessman and a good Christian. He needs $3 million dollars to help save his business. He is sending packages about his business to all kinds of lenders and venture capital people. Within six months, if he doesn't find the $3 million he will be out of business. I said to him, you should pray for help. He said that you pray for the poor, the hungry, the thirsty, you do not pray for $3 million dollars. I am asking this group to pray that my boss will totally surrender his crises to the Lord"*, with her eyes suddenly focused on mine, she continued, *"and in that surrender he will find peace. In that peace, he will become less panic stricken, more relaxed, more creative and in that creativity he will find his $3 million."*

I was emotionally hit by her words. It was as if the Holy Spirit was sending me a message through her soft and sincere voice. She had described the exact sum that I was seeking and, at this particular point in my life, like her boss, I felt the same way he did about prayer. Yes, I would write a check for the Carmelites to pray for my intentions and or I could to talk to God and ask for help. However, the thought of *"totally surrendering"* my problem to the Lord and becoming more creative had never entered my mind, in spite of my spirituality.

I kept my business very confidential. No one knew that I was seeking a $2 million dollar partner, not even my family. Everyone remained where they were seated and said a group prayer for her boss. Then I heard someone say, *"Does anyone want to be prayed over."* To this day, I cannot explain it. As if I was in a hypnotic stage, I found myself going to that seat in the middle of the room and sitting down. The group surrounded me. Hands were touching my head, shoulders and arms. A voice said, *"What is it you want us to pray for?"* I could not say $2 million dollars. I found myself saying, *"Peace of Mind"*. It was as if every person touching me could feel the struggle I was living with. My eyes were closed. I heard their prayers. Many were in English. Others were in different languages, including the young man who spoke gibberish. Tears flooded my eyes. I felt as if a great burden had been lifted from my shoulders. I left the meeting and got into my car. I felt intoxicated with joy. If someone had been in the back seat, they would have concluded that I was drunk. I had this overwhelming sense of peace. I surrendered my crises to the Lord. I thanked Him for granting this tired and weary Prisoner of a Problem with *"Peace of Mind"*.

I woke up the next morning refreshed. My spirits were high. I felt that the Holy Spirit sent an Angel who spoke to me through the lady at Cenacle gathering. I spoke of this experience to my wife. She was glad it gave me peace. My kids came into the study that was surrounded by packages to be mailed to financial leads outside of Rochester. They gave me a hug and kiss and went off to school. How precious they were. How blessed I was to have such and understanding and supportive family. Gina had turned 14 and was helping her mom around the house and with her younger brothers. Greg was 11 and enjoyed his new role of replacing the gardener and handling snow shoveling in the winter. Wade was nine, Fritz was seven and Josh was three. I was truly a blessed man. They were all such a great joy and comfort to me.

After they left for school, the phone rang. It was Van Albanese from Connecticut Mutual. He wanted to know why I was tardy in the payment of my life insurance premium. I said, *"Van, I can trust you. I just don't have the money."* He said, *"Fred, only a few months ago, I read the success story of the sale of your first building."* I said, *"Van, they call that public relations."* He said he wanted to help me. I reminded him that we had sent a package to Conn-Mutual a few years ago. He said, *"Yes, but there's a new guy at the helm in the real estate investment department"* I calmly and creatively said, *"OK, but this time around I am going to send him pictures of the completion of Phase One, dramatic lake photographs from the balcony of building one and a description of the master plan approvals. If they want to see the economic model, they will have to sit with me on the balcony of our first 14-unit condominium building for a comprehensive review."*

A week later a mortgage broker, an expert in resort properties, was sitting on the balcony of the condominium with me reviewing the economic model. He had already driven around the entire lake, talked with the

Chamber of Commerce regarding the history of Bristol Harbour, visited Bristol Mountain, checked my references and interviewed two or three owners in the condominium building. He said, *"Fred, I cannot believe what you have accomplished in the approval process. To obtain the master plan approvals for 874 units, a 200-unit hotel, a golf course, and a 124-slip marina and to have the first Homeowners Association Offering Plan ever approved by the Attorney General's Office is a remarkable feat. You have been totally undercapitalized with a great location. What ideas do you have in structuring the deal?"*

Within six weeks, we signed papers that made the Connecticut Mutual Life Insurance Company our partner. They valued the project at $1,000,000. ($6.000,000 rounded in 2019 dollars) I would receive $500,000 ($3,000.000 rounded in 2019 dollars in cash that could be used for the ski area. I would leave $500,000 ($3,000,000) in the joint venture for a 50% ownership and they would make a loan to the joint venture for $6 million dollars for the purpose of paying of the REIT buying more land to equal 454 acres, retain Robert Trent Jones to build the golf course and commence construction on buildings 2, 3, 4 and 5 for a total of 176 new condominium units on the edge of the cliff. Jack Britton, the mortgage broker, who put the deal together said, *"Fred, I have been in this business for 25 years. I have never seen a deal go so quickly and smoothly as this one and do you what Fred, I can't explain it."*

I said, *"I can explain it Jack. It was a miracle and let me tell you why."* Jack was fascinated with the story of the Cenacle and said, *"I believe it was a miracle."*

I sold my prestigious 6,000 sq. ft. home on Ambassador Drive. We moved to a 1,200 sq. ft. prefabricated vacation home at Bristol Harbour within walking distance of my office. With mixed emotions, we had a garage sale. Moving was not a happy experience for any of us. However, my family took it in good stride and quickly made the adjustment to our new surroundings in the Naples School District and closer proximity to the lake and ski area.

The opponents to the project found some satisfaction in knowing that there would be a prestigious Robert Trent Jones Golf Course and Restaurant in their back yard. The pressure was off, I had an insurance company for a partner. My thanksgiving prayer was simple, *"Thank you Lord for this miracle. I will give it my best effort. If this Joint Venture fails, I will continue to be ever grateful for helping me to bring this dream to reality in a manner that will please Bristol Harbour residents and their neighbors."*

Then sings my soul, my Savior God, to thee;

How great thou art! How great thou art!

June 16, 1969. *"To the Editor:*

Considering the multitude of letters to the editor relative to the Bristol Harbour Village project and Fred Sarkis, I trust one more letter will not be a burden to you.

With one or two exceptions, most of the letters have come from those people who have not taken the time and effort to obtain the facts about modern sewage disposal systems recently developed through scientific research and engineering.

At the meeting held on May 6, 1969 at the Trenholm East by the Canandaigua Lake Association, Paul Russell, a sanitary engineer for Mr. Sarkis, tried in vain to present the facts about the new systems that will be used at the Bristol Harbour development.

Unfortunately, this meeting took on the atmosphere of an inquisition directed at Mr. Russell and Mr. Sarkis rather than a meeting to properly hear the facts. I was at this meeting and felt that the chairman should have stopped the discussion until some in attendance stopped acting like hoodlums at a barroom brawl.

I feel confident that the New York State Department of Health, which has approved of Mr. Sarkis' plans for sewage treatment, are in a better position to judge this project than many of the laymen who own property on Canandaigua Lake.

Eventually the State may insist on an inspection of all septic and sewage disposal systems along the lake and request that they meet modern standards along similar plans proposed by Bristol Harbour Village.

I think the real objection to Bristol Harbour Village, by some who own property in the vicinity, is based upon their desire to keep this entire area as a private preserve for their own enjoyment.

In years past the residents of the area had an opportunity to establish zoning. Apparently, for their own reasons, they were not interested. Now that a new development is underway, they suddenly have taken steps to establish zoning regulations.

As a footnote regarding the land purchased by Bristol Mountain Enterprises, all of this property was for sale over a period of years at a much lower price than Bristol Mountain Enterprises paid for it. Many of the residents now opposed to this project were aware of the fact that this land was for sale but did not choose to purchase it.

Herbert M. Ellinwood, West Lake Road, Canandaigua, N.Y."

Note: Mr. Ellinwood was the broker who sold this property to me on behalf of Bristol Mountain Enterprises, Inc. He was not a close friend. I did not ask him to write the letter. Any member of the "group" who resented this letter would never retain Mr. Ellinwood as their Broker. He jeopardized his business interests as a broker with all lake residents. Mr. Ellinwood passed away many years ago. I am saddened that I never took the time to write him a letter thanking him for his gift of Fortitude.

The controversy and extensive publicity over the sewerage treatment plant was a wake up call for all sources of pollution on Canandaigua Lake. We received our approvals because the treated water that would be discharged into the lake from Seneca Point Creek, would be purer than the lake water itself. In addition, the Department of Environmental Conservation required periodic samples and inspections to insure proper treatment. (In 30 years of operation, this plant has passed every inspection. It has never been cited for pollution).

In June of 1969, I wrote a letter to the editor titled *"Easy Pure Waters Test"*. The idea was taken from the Citizens Committee to save Cayuga Lake in NY State. Packets of a fluorescent dye called Pylam would be distributed free to each of more than 2,300 cottages and residences along both shores of Cayuga Lake. The test consisted of flushing the harmless dye through septic systems. If the system does not meet compliance standards, the dye will appear in the water or on the surface of the ground. A few weeks after this letter was published, the Canandaigua Lake Association in cooperation with the Canandaigua Chamber of Commerce offered the Dye Packs free of charge to about 2,000 cottages and homes on Canandaigua Lake. The Daily Messenger confirmed that this action was a result of my letter.

A few years later, thanks to the Daily Messenger, Dr. Joe Guattery, the President of the Canandaigua Chamber of Commerce and the reawaked Canandaigua Lake Pure Waters Association and objective political leaders, a public sewer system was installed along the lake in heavy residential areas, eliminating the many inadequate septic systems that were the cause of serious pollution. I thought to myself, many of those who opposed our plans for a state-approved pollution control system were ironically polluters themselves. I recalled what Jesus said when he was defending Mary Magdalene – "Let he who is without sin cast the first stone."

Ironically, in their highly publicized opposition to our plans, the "group" created the media storm that caused objective sources to focus on major sources of real pollution – the inadequate septic systems of many lakeside residences.

A Summary of Attempts to stop Bristol Harbour Village

In spite of Governmental Approvals

We thought we were home free when we received the Health Departments approval for the Sewage Treatment Plant. However, *actual* headlines thereafter read:

June 18, 1969 – "Canandaigua Lake Association Fight Sewage Plant Plan." The Canandaigua Lake Association retained a lawyer-conservationist who found fault with the plans.

June 20, 1969 – "Petition Asks Project Denial." "A petition reportedly bearing 5,300 signatures has been sent to Governor Rockefeller requesting that he and 'all other public officials responsible for health and purity of our water,' deny permission for construction of Bristol Harbour Village near Seneca Point on Canandaigua Lake." This release was sent to the Daily Messenger by the same lady of the "group", as vice president of Canandaigua Lake Association.

July 25, 1969 – "Controversial Sewer Plant OK'd. Bids are due August 5, 1969."

September 30, 1969 – "Seneca Point Suit is Filed" – An immediate neighbor takes us to court with the argument that our beach frontage was an illegal landfill.

October 18, 1969 – "Bristol Dropping Stock Offering. However, first building of 14 units is under construction."

October 24, 1969 – "Injunction Sought to Block Bristol Harbour Project." An attempt to prevent the discharge of water for the sewerage treatment plant that had not yet been constructed.

March 6, 1970 – "Lake Mooring Hearing Delayed." Opponents found a technical error in the application for a 128 slip marina.

April 17, 1970 – "Bristol Harbour Condominium of 14 units 35% complete."

April 30, 1970 – "Attorney General gives 56 Unit OK for Bristol Harbour."

May 21, 1970 – "Start of Dock Hearing for 128 slips."

May 26, 1970 – "End of five day dock hearing."

August 6, 1970 – "Sarkis Says Apartment Work Halted – due to tough money market."

October 6, 1970 – "Suit started over Apartments." – Pertaining to the injunction to prevent the docking facility.

October 7, 1970 – "Seneca Point Landfill Alleged in Supreme Court. Brought before the State Supreme Court."

October 16, 1970 – "Suit on Lake Project Opens." Pertaining to the charge of an illegal land fill at the beach area.

November 13, 1970 – "Bristol Harbour Sewer Loan Try Supported." – Ontario County supported a plan to obtain federal funding to build the treatment plant.

November 15, 1970 – "Dock Plan Opponents Ask Decision Delay" – Another attempt by opponents to delay final approval of the docks.

December 28, 1970 – "Sarkis Project is Resuming." Sarkis announces a loan in excess of $2 million from General Mortgage Investments in Maryland.

December 30, 1970 – "Sarkis Winner in Civil Suit"- Neighbor's lawsuit on regarding landfill of beach area loses.

January 1, 1971 – "Controversial Piers Nearer." The State Department of Environmental Conservation gives "notice of intent" to approve docks subject to clearance by another governmental agency.

April 14, 1971 – "Annulment Sought for Dock Site." The Canandaigua Lake Pure Waters Association instituted action in Supreme Court seeking to annul the permits granted for the docks.

September 29, 1971 – "Condominium at Bristol to be Occupied by November 1." Sarkis announces successful sales effort.

October 31, 1971 – "Suite to bar 100 foot dock lost by Canandaigua Lake Group. Dismissed by the State Supreme Court."

The Infamous One Week Dock Hearing in May of 1970

Mr. Dineen presided. I was hopeful that Mr. Dineen represented the people of the State of NY who own the lake rather than the landowners who live around it. Many residents who own property bordering the Canandaigua Lake, resent the State operated marinas on the north and south of the lake.

When the first day of the hearing commenced, I was outnumbered 110 to 3. The opposition included almost every major law firm in Rochester as well as many citizens from Seneca Point and the surrounding area. (See appendix I) I was accompanied by two lawyers retained for the purpose of seeking approval. Any law firm or resident who gave proper and timely notice could cross-examine any witness. The dock was one of the final attempts to block the Bristol plans. Without the docks, the planned Bristol Harbour Village development would be crippled. The "group", knowing I was in deep financial trouble, was united and well organized to put a final bullet in the heart of our plan. No docks in the Bristol Harbour Plan would cripple the sales of condominiums or homes. This would lead to our financial failure. Our opponents knew that we were blackballed by every local bank. They knew that I was exhausting my personal funds. They knew our public offering failed. Their goal was to bankrupt the plan.

We did our homework. On a mid-summer Saturday, in anticipation of the dock hearing, my brother Joe and I rented a boat on Canandaigua Lake. We counted every dock and mooring on the lake. We determined that by the addition of 128 slips for one-half mile of frontage, the average number of boats slips and moors per hundred feet for Bristol Harbour was less than the average number of slips and moorings on the lake per hundred feet. We gave this information to our attorneys. On two of the hottest days in the preceding summer, I had aerial photographs taken of the lake. The photos proved that the north shore was very active with boating activity, the south shore was not as active and the middle of the lake was very inactive. These were also provided to our attorneys.

Experts who testified at this included a Lymnologist, an expert on plant and animal life in fresh waters, the dock installers, representatives from the State of New York responsible for the evaluation of boating activity on lakes under the jurisdiction of NY State and others whom I cannot recall.

The hearing lasted for five full days. Attorneys for Seneca Point residents and residents who applied in a timely manner, were allowed to cross examine any witness. One young man from Seneca Point, who was not an attorney, walked back and forth with his hands behind his back, like the lawyer in a TV weekly series. He was questioning the installer of the docks. He asked if he was familiar with the testimony given by previous witnesses. The installer replied, *"No."* He then said, *"Now sir, in your testimony you have stated that there would be aluminum members used to support the 128 docking system, is that correct?"* *"Yes",* was the response.

"Would you tell the Hearing Officer and this room of people how many of these aluminum members would be installed to support the docking facility?" The installer said, "565". The young man swung around to the 100 people in the chamber and with his back turned to the witness and to the Hearing Officer, and with a voice that sounded like he had caught a criminal in the act, he said, *"Five hundred and sixty-five aluminum members to be installed in Canandaigua Lake."* With his hands still behind his back, he turned quickly to the witness and said, *"Now tell me sir, what harm will this do to the fish life in Canandaigua Lake?"* The response was, *"I am sure that when we are installing these supporting members, the fish will move."* The entire chamber, friend and foe alike, for the first time in five days, were in unison with their laughter.

When I took the stand, I was asked by an attorney who lived on Seneca Point, *"Mr. Sarkis, you do plan a hotel at BHV?"* "Yes". *"You do have dances for kids who are supposed to be 18 and over at Bristol Mountain in the off season."* "Yes". *"Will you rent hotel rooms to these young people when the dances are concluded."* My attorney to the Hearing Officer, *"Sir, this is not relevant to the application for docks".* Hearing officer, *"Agreed".*

Other questions for me. *"Do you have the funds to install 128 slips."* Answer, *"No".* Why do you take the time of all of us if you do not have the funding for such docks?" Answer, *"One can only seek investment capital or a loan when one has the approvals in hand."*

During the hearing, I poked our lawyers on a few occasions and said, *"Aren't you guys going to say anything?"* The response was *"Why say anything when their question are winning for us."*

Each day was reported in the newspaper. As the hearing reached an end, a major headline stated that a State Official responsible for monitoring the waters of New York State, supported the application for the docks on the basis that the middle of the lake where the docks were to be built was uncrowded even on the hottest of summer days; that all boats at Bristol Harbour, like other marinas, do not go out at the same time; that there would be no adverse impact on safety; that the people who did not have property on the lake and who used the state launching sites at the north and south of the lake, would find refuge in a storm or emergency in the middle of this 17 mile lake where the Bristol Harbour marina would be located. I thought, *"God Bless the State of New York for allowing citizens, other than lakefront property owners to have access to Canandaigua, the Gem of the Finger Lakes."*

At the break in the last day of the hearing, exhausted from a full week of hearings and the expected legal costs involved, I rushed to the phone to see how my alternate plan for a search for capital outside of Rochester was doing? My contact reminded me of my visit to the officers of the Florida bank who worked with a firm in Cleveland, Ohio. He said, *"Your $20,000 good faith deposit is in the safe hands of the lenders in Cleveland who are supplying the $2 million in funds to the Florida bank for a loan to Bristol Harbour with all your assets including the ski area as collateral. You have the letter of intent. The closing should be soon."*

The hearing officer heard everyone who had asked in advance to be heard. He called an end to the hearing. The delays in final approval are outlined above.

In spite of the combined wealth and influence of those who participated on Seneca Point; in spite of the local banks that found us out of favor because of board members and customers who owned lakeside homes on Canandaigua Lake; in spite of all of this united and powerful opposition to break my piggy bank, this former dark skinned, skinny, bow-legged, pigeon-toed, knocked-kneed boy Prisoner of the Truck who believed and fought for democracy around the world, discovered that the democratic process works, if you are persistent enough to make it work. Although it took months and thousands of dollars for professionals and attorneys, we won the right to install 128 slips.

The day after the hearing closed, an opponent to our application called the Editor of the Democrat and Chronicle to complain that the reporter, Marge Van Iseghem, who covered the daily news of this five-day hearing was my cousin and was therefore biased in her reporting. The opponents considered factual reporting as bias. I would be proud to call Marge Van Iseghem my cousin.

(Note: A bit of diversion. On Board the USS Guam, I served as a Yeoman 3rd Class, comparable to a Sargent in the US Army. My skill in shorthand and typing led me to working in the ship's office. My responsibilities included dictation from the ship's Commanding Officer as well as maintaining and the records of 2,000 enlisted men on board our ship. In addition, I would stand by the Executive Officer each week to record major and minor penalties in the records of the sailors involved. Minor penalties never became a permanent record on the sailor's record.

In writing this book, I thought that if there was a World Leader, who would hear the legitimate wrong doings of a particular leader of a Nation, and I was the note taker, our President Donald J. Trump would be sent to the brig for his lies and wrong doings.

As a World War II Veteran, I took the following oath when I enlisted in the Navy.

"Description

Upon enlisting in the United States Armed Forces, each person enlisting in an armed force (whether a soldier, sailor, coast guardsman, airman, or Marine) takes an oath of enlistment required by federal statute in 10 U.S.C. § 502. That section provides the text of the oath and sets out who may administer the oath:

(a) Enlistment Oath.— Each person enlisting in an armed force shall take the following oath:

"I, (state name of enlistee), do solemnly swear (or affirm) that I will support and defend the Constitution of the United States against all enemies, foreign and domestic; that I will bear true faith and allegiance to the same; and that I will obey the orders of the President of the United States and the orders of the officers appointed over me, according to regulations and the Uniform Code of Military Justice. So help me God."

And indeed, I was honored to then serve President Franklin D. Roosevelt and President Harry S. Truman.

And, speaking of oaths, on January 20, 2017

Donald Trump placed his left hand on an old Bible, raised his right hand and repeated 35 words (plus his full name) read by Chief Justice John G. Roberts Jr. from the Constitution.

"I, Donald John Trump, do solemnly swear that I will faithfully execute the Office of President of the United States, and will to the best of my ability, preserve, protect and defend the Constitution of the United States," he promised the American people, as prescribed by Article II, Section 1 of the Constitution, just as the presidents before him have done.
Definitions of the words in this oath:

Ability - *capacity, fitness, or tendency to act or be acted on in a (specified) way.*

Preserve - an activity that only one person or a particular type of person does or is responsible for.

Protect – keep safe from harm or injury

Defend - to drive danger or attack away from

Fact Checking our President's leadership follows.

Chapter One

How does one objectively and factual check on the Loose Lips of our President, Donald Trump? This WWII Veteran sincerely thanks, stands and salutes Fact Check Organization for allowing me to copy these full reports for the months of April and May 2019.

FACT CHECK

THE WIRE

Trump Wrong About Tax Law

By Robert Farley

Posted on April 11, 2019

Asked whether he believes federal law requires him to give Congress his tax returns, President Donald Trump responded, "There's no law whatsoever." He's wrong about that.

There is, in fact, a federal tax law that specifically states if the chairman of the House Ways and Means Committee makes a written request for an individual's tax returns — as Rep. Richard Neal has done seeking Trump's — the Treasury secretary "shall furnish" those returns. The law says those returns would be reviewed confidentially in an executive session.

Some Republicans have argued that Neal needs to demonstrate a legitimate legislative purpose in order to review the president's returns, and there is disagreement about whether he has. That is a debate that seems likely to end up in federal court.

That legal dispute led a reporter to ask Trump on April 10, "Do you believe federal law requires you to give Congress your tax returns?"

Trump responded, "No, there is no law. As you know, I got elected last time with this same issue. And while I'm under audit, I won't do it. If I'm not under audit, I would do it. I had no problem with it. But while I'm under audit, I would not give my taxes. There's no law whatsoever."

As we have written, there is no law that compels presidential candidates or presidents to publicly release their tax returns, though it has been a custom for them to do so for more than 30 years. Trump was the first major party presidential nominee not to release any tax returns, dating back to 1976, when President Gerald Ford released a summary of his tax returns, rather than the complete returns. Every major party nominee since then has released complete tax returns.

But the reporter's question wasn't whether Trump was legally obligated to release his tax returns *publicly*, it was whether federal law required they be turned over *to Congress*.

According to Joseph J. Thorndike, a historian at Tax Analysts, "Despite what the president said, there is a law."

In his April 3 letter to the IRS commissioner requesting Trump's returns for the tax years 2013 through 2018, Neal cited the authority granted to him through an arcane provision in the IRS Code section 6103(f).

IRS law generally requires that tax returns be kept confidential. But the section cited by Neal states, "Upon written request from the chairman of the Committee on Ways and Means of the House of Representatives, the chairman of the Committee on Finance of the Senate, or the chairman of the Joint Committee on Taxation, the Secretary shall furnish such committee with any return or return information specified in such request, except that any return or return information which can be associated with, or otherwise identify, directly or indirectly, a particular taxpayer shall be furnished to such committee only when sitting in closed executive session unless such taxpayer otherwise consents in writing to such disclosure."

"There is a law directly on point," Edward Kleinbard, a professor at the University of Southern California Gould School of Law and chief of staff for Congress' Joint Committee on Taxation from 2007 to 2009, told us via email.

Some legal scholars, including Kleinbard, believe that Neal needs to demonstrate a legitimate legislative purpose for requesting the president's returns. In his letter, Neal notes that the Ways and Means Committee is tasked with ensuring the IRS "is enforcing the laws in a fair and impartial manner." Neal explains that he has requested the president's returns to make sure the IRS is doing a good job in its mandated review of the president's tax returns.

> ***Neal letter, April 3***: *Consistent with its authority, the Committee is considering legislative proposals and conducting oversight related to our Federal tax laws, including, but not limited to, the extent to which the IRS audits and enforces the Federal tax laws against a President. Under the Internal Revenue Manual, individual income tax returns of a President are subject to mandatory examination, but this practice is IRS policy and not codified in the Federal tax laws. It is necessary for the Committee to determine the scope of any such examination and whether it includes a review of underlying business activities required to be reported on the individual income tax return.*

Kleinbard believes that meets the threshold of proving a bona fide purpose for the request.

"The Chairman's request here was carefully written to explain his reasons, which include, wearing his oversight hat, ensuring that the IRS is doing its job auditing the President," Kleinbard said. "Further, the President is the Taxpayer in Chief. We have a tax system in which we each assess tax against ourselves – that's what you do when you file a return. The Taxpayer in Chief needs to set a standard of compliance to which we all should aspire. For him to abdicate that responsibility threatens the integrity of the income tax system, which surely is something that should concern W&M [the Ways and Means committee]. So there's no doubt that W&M has more than met any standard that might be read into the statute."

In a phone interview, Thorndike agreed that Neal appears to have framed a legitimate request within the scope of his committee's oversight responsibilities.

The last time Congress looked into the IRS audit of a president's returns was during the Richard Nixon administration. In that case, Nixon voluntarily provided his returns. A congressional committee concluded there were several items incorrectly reported on Nixon's returns, finding he owed about $477,000 in additional taxes.

"So there is good historical reason to be concerned" that the IRS is doing its job properly with review of presidential returns, Thorndike said.

Thorndike said that while it seems Neal's request is on solid legal footing, "it remains to be seen" how a court might rule.

Republican Pushback

Treasury missed Neal's deadline to produce the returns by April 10. In a letter sent to Neal that day, Treasury Secretary Steven Mnuchin said the request "raises serious issues concerning the constitutional scope of Congressional investigative authority, the legitimacy of the asserted legislative purpose, and the constitutional rights of American citizens."

"Given the seriousness of these issues, Mnuchin said Treasury has consulted with the Department of Justice "to ensure that our response is fully consistent with the law and the Constitution."

Mnuchin noted that Republican Sen. Chuck Grassley, who as chairman of the Senate Finance Committee has the same authority as Neal from IRS Code section 6103 (f), blasted Neal's efforts as politically motivated. Grassley said the request was "a pretext to bring this president down."

The IRS statute states that if the returns were provided to Neal, they would be viewed confidentially in "closed executive session" of the Ways and Means Committee. But legal scholars said depending on what lawmakers find, it is possible the committee could conclude it has a constitutional responsibility to release the returns publicly.

In a speech from the Senate floor, Grassley said the IRS is only required to turn over tax records under the law if the request is tied to "a legitimate legislative purpose in asking for them."

Although Neal said the aim is to make sure the IRS review of the president's tax returns is being done fully, appropriately and impartially, Grassley contended, "There is no reason to believe the IRS is doing any less due diligence in its review of President Trump's taxes than it has for any other president in our memory."

Jay Sekulow, an attorney for Trump, made similar arguments in an appearance on ABC's "This Week" on April 7. Sekulow questioned what legitimate legislative purpose the request served.

"This idea that you can use the IRS as a political weapon, which is what is happening here, is incorrect both as a matter of statutory law and constitutionally," Sekulow said.

As for Trump's claim that "there is no law," George K. Yin, a professor of law and taxation at the University of Virginia School of Law, who served as chief of staff of the Joint Committee on Taxation from 2003 to 2005, suspects Trump was referring to the custom — but not the law — that has been followed by presidents for the last four decades to release copies of their tax returns to the public.

"I doubt that [Trump] has even heard of the law now being invoked by Chairman Neal," Yin told us via email. "Since the question focused on giving <u>Congress</u> his returns, his answer is wrong but not egregiously wrong because of his likely confusion."

The IRS statute cited by Neal "contains no limits," Yin said. "The chairman can request anyone's returns and the Treasury Secretary is directed to furnish them." Yin said there may be "an implicit condition" that Neal's request have a "legitimate legislative purpose" such as oversight of the IRS. "But there is no specific precedent on this point because to my knowledge, the authority Mr. Neal is invoking has never been challenged," Yin said.

"Neal's request stated two purposes that would qualify as legitimate legislative purposes," Yin said, adding that Sekulow's counterargument is that "the stated purposes are not the real purpose, and that the real purpose is simply to make a political attack."

Again, those are questions that would need to be settled in federal court. And that's where the issue seems likely to be headed. "If it has to be litigated, it will be litigated," Sekulow said on ABC's "This Week."

Share The Facts

Donald Trump
President of the United States

April 2019 - Full report - Update

Statistical measures of how things have changed since the president took office.

By [Brooks Jackson](#)

Posted on April 11, 2019

Summary

Since President Donald Trump took office:

- Attempted unauthorized crossings at the U.S.-Mexico border soared to the highest levels in over a decade.
- The trade deficit rose by more than $100 billion — 23.5 percent.
- The economy added 5.1 million jobs; unemployment fell to the lowest rate in nearly half a century.
- Economic growth picked up, but fell short of what Trump promised.
- The number of restrictions in the federal rulebook stopped growing, and fell a bit.
- After-tax corporate profits hit record levels. Stock prices rose.
- Carbon emissions, which had been falling, rose 2 percent.
- At least 1 million fewer people have health insurance (7 million according to Gallup).
- One-fifth of the judges on federal appeals courts have been installed by Trump.

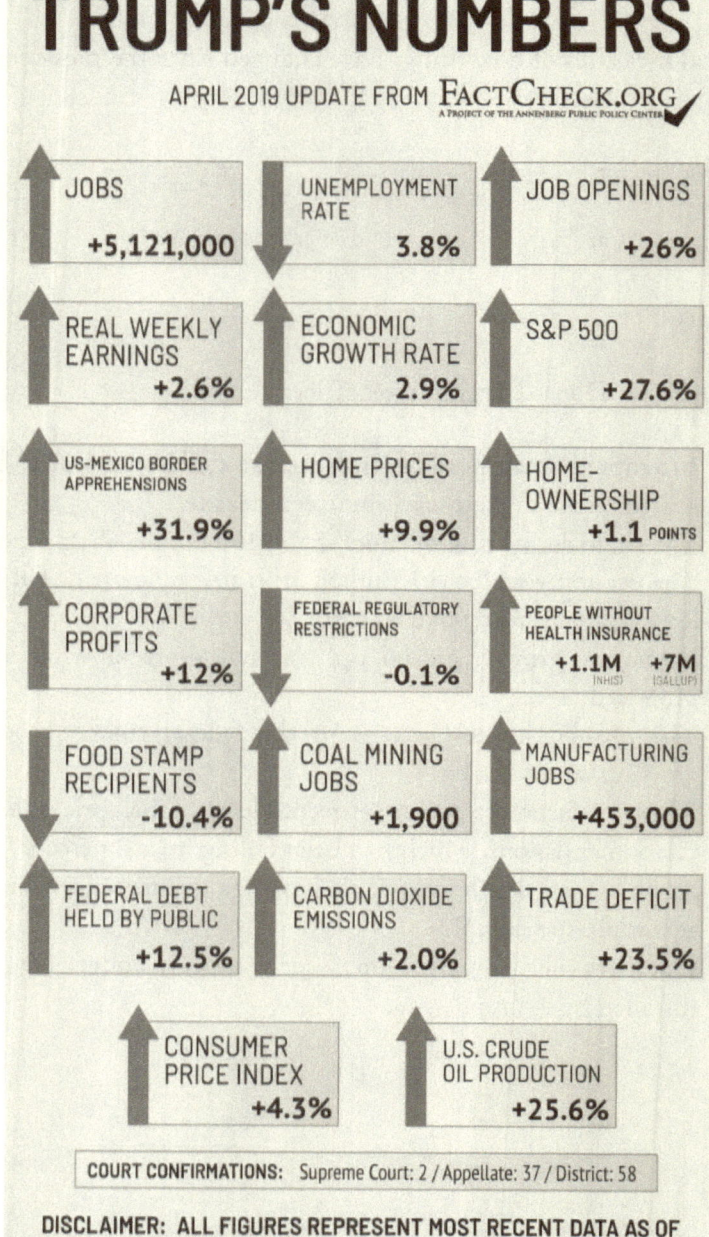

Analysis

This is our fifth quarterly update of the "Trump's Numbers" scorecard that we posted in January 2018 and have updated every three months, most recently on Jan. 16. We'll publish additional updates every three months, as fresh statistics become available.

Here we've included statistics that may seem good or bad or just neutral, depending on the reader's point of view. That's the way we did it when we posted our first "Obama's Numbers" article more than six years ago — and in the quarterly updates and final summary that followed. And we've maintained the same practice under Trump.

Then as now, we make no judgment as to how much credit or blame any president deserves for things that happen during his time in office. Opinions differ on that.

Jobs and Unemployment

Job growth slowed a bit under Trump, but unemployment dropped to the lowest level in nearly half a century.

Employment — Total nonfarm employment grew by 5,121,000 during the president's first 26 months in office, according to the most recent figures available from the Bureau of Labor Statistics.

That continued an unbroken chain of monthly gains in total employment that started in October 2010.

The average monthly gain under Trump so far is 197,000 — compared with an average monthly gain of 217,000 during Obama's second term.

Trump will have to pick up the pace if he is to fulfill his campaign boast that he will be "the greatest jobs president that God ever created."

Unemployment — The unemployment rate, which was well below the historical norm when Trump took office, has continued to fall even lower.

The Bureau of Labor Statistics now figures the rate was 4.7 percent when he was sworn in. The most recent rate, for March, is 3.8 percent.

It had been as low as 3.7 percent in September and November of last year. That was the lowest since December 1969.

The jobless rate has been at or below 4 percent for the most recent 13 months on record. It hasn't been that low for that long since a 50-month streak ending in January 1970.

The historical norm is 5.6 percent, which is the median monthly rate for all the months since the start of 1948.

Job Openings — Another reason employment growth has slowed is a shortage of qualified workers.

The number of unfilled job openings hit more than 7.6 million in November, the highest in the 18 years the BLS has tracked this figure.

As of the last day of February, 2019 the most recent figure on record, it was still nearly 7.1 million. That's a gain of 1,463,000 unfilled job openings — or 26.0 percent — since Trump took office.

For the first time on record the number of job openings exceeded the number of unemployed people looking for work in March of last year, and in every month since.

Labor Force Participation — Despite the abundance of jobs, the labor force participation rate — which went down 2.8 percentage points during the Obama years — has remained little changed under Trump.

The labor force participation rate is the portion of the entire civilian population age 16 and older that is either employed or currently looking for work in the last four weeks. Republicans often criticized Obama for the decline during his time, even though it was due mostly to the post-World War II baby boomers reaching retirement age, and other demographic factors beyond the control of any president.

Since Trump took office, the rate has fluctuated in a narrow range between 63.2 percent and 62.7 percent. It was 63.0 percent in March — up just 0.1 percentage point from where it was the month Trump took office.

Manufacturing Jobs — Manufacturing jobs increased under Trump, just at a rate slightly faster than total employment.

The number rose by 453,000 between Trump's inauguration and March. That followed a net decrease of 192,000 under Obama.

The increase since January 2017 amounts to 3.7 percent, compared with the 3.5 percent increase in overall employment. The number of manufacturing jobs is still 920,000 below where it was in December 2007, at the start of the Great Recession.

Economic Growth

The economy grew somewhat faster under Trump — but not at the rate he promised. Gross domestic product was 2.9 percent higher in 2018 than the year before, according to the U.S. Commerce Department's Bureau of Economic Analysis.

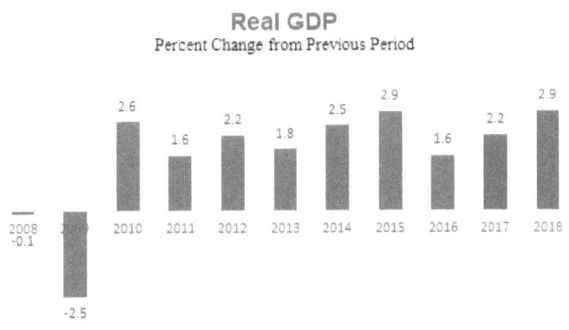

Growth under Trump has averaged far less than the 4 percent to 6 percent per year that he promised repeatedly, both when he was a candidate and also as president.

The economy grew only 2.2 percent during his first year, and 2.9 percent for all of 2018, according to the BEA. It spurted briefly to a 4.2 percent annual rate in the second quarter of 2018, prompting Trump to proudly claim credit. But it then fell back to a 3.4 percent rate in the third quarter and a 2.2 percent rate in the final quarter.

And growth seems to have slowed even further since then. BEA's first official estimate of growth in the first quarter of 2019 isn't scheduled to be released until April 26. However, the "GDPNow" forecast produced by the Federal Reserve Bank of Atlanta projects that the first-quarter growth rate will come in at 2.3 percent — despite the 35-day partial government shutdown that ended Jan. 25. (The Congressional Budget Office has estimated that the shutdown shaved 0.4 percentage points off the annualized rate of first-quarter growth.)

Most economists believe this year's growth will be less than last year's. CBO's most recent economic outlook, issued Jan. 28, projects real GDP growth falling to 2.7 percent this year and 1.9 percent next year. And the even more recent median forecast of the Federal Reserve Board members and Federal Reserve Bank presidents, issued on March 20, projects only 2.1 percent growth this year and 1.9 percent in 2020.

Other leading economists tend to agree that economic growth is slowing. For the business and university economists who offered an annual GDP forecast to the *Wall Street Journal's* monthly economic survey in March, the average prediction was for 2.1 percent growth this year and 1.7 percent next year. The National Association for Business Economics' March survey was only a little more optimistic, producing a median forecast of 2.4 percent growth for this year and 2.0 percent in 2020.

Trump's GDP Spin

The White House website proclaimed: "Economic Growth Has Reached 3 Percent for the First Time in More than a Decade." But that's not true.

As we've said, growth fell just short of 3 percent when measured by the usual economic yardstick. And even using Trump's measure, it grew faster than 3 percent less than four years ago.

The White House Council of Economic Advisers issued a carefully worded explanation that growth was 3.1 percent (later revised down to 3.0 percent) — *if* measured by comparing the final three months of 2018 with the same quarter a year earlier. That's correct, as far as it goes. And it is also the first time since 2005 that this final-quarter to final-quarter measure was 3 percent or better, as far as *that* goes.

But year-to-year economic growth is normally measured by comparing the GDP for all of 2018 with the GDP for all of 2017. That change was 2.9 percent, as we have said, and was just equal to the growth in 2015, only three years earlier.

Furthermore, the White House claim that growth was the best in 13 years rests on cherry-picking only the *final* quarters of each year from BEA's Table 1.1.11, which gives the 12-month change in real GDP ending in each quarter. And by that measure the economy grew faster — 3.4 percent — as recently as the 12 months ending in the second quarter of 2015, just three-and-a-half years earlier.

Regulations

The growth of federal regulation has stopped under Trump.

It wasn't exactly the "sudden, screeching and beautiful halt" Trump prematurely claimed back in December 2017, when in fact the number of federal restrictions was still growing. But over the next several months the rise decelerated, and then reversed. The number of restrictions has now dropped to just below where it was when Trump was sworn in.

The number of restrictive words and phrases (such as "shall," "prohibited" or "may not") contained in the Code of Federal Regulations went up by 0.73 percent during Trump's first 15 months, reaching a peak of nearly 1.09 million on April 6, 2018, according to daily tracking done by the QuantGov project at George Mason University's Mercatus Center.

But as of April 9, 2019, the number had dropped back below 1.08 million — 864 fewer than on Jan. 20, 2017, the day Trump took office. In percentage terms, the drop is less than one-tenth of 1 percent.

That small drop is a big change from the past. Restrictions grew at an average of 1.5 percent per year during both the Obama years and the George W. Bush years, according to annual QuantGov tracking.

The Mercatus count of restrictions doesn't attempt to assess the cost or benefit of any particular rule — such assessments require a degree of guesswork and are sensitive to assumptions. But it does track the sheer volume of federal rules with more precision than we have found in other metrics.

Some of the recent changes are just clearing deadwood. In March, for example, the Internal Revenue Service removed 296 regulations that it said "are no longer necessary because they do not have any current or future applicability." And last year the Treasury Department scrapped an entire chapter of zombie-like regulations issued by the old Office of Thrift Supervision, which oversaw the savings-and-loan industry before being abolished in 2011. S&Ls have since fallen under other federal banking regulators, but the obsolete OTS rules remained on the books.

However, many of the rules Trump has eliminated are quite significant. Within a month of taking office, for example, Trump signed a law nullifying an Obama-era rule prohibiting coal mining companies from dumping waste into streams and waterways. Last year his administration withdrew Obama's edict requiring automakers to double the fuel efficiency of new cars and light trucks to 54.5 miles per gallon by the year 2025. Instead, the requirement will be capped at 37 mpg starting in 2020. And in May, Trump signed a massive rollback of banking regulations, easing rules for all but the largest banks.

Crime

Crime declined during Trump's first year, and the downward trend accelerated in the first half of 2018.

Preliminary FBI statistics, released Feb. 25, show the number of violent crimes went down 4.3 percent in the first half of last year, compared with the same period in 2017. The number of property crimes declined even more, 7.2 percent.

That followed a 0.2 percent decline in violent crimes and a 3 percent drop in property crimes during all of 2017, according to the FBI's annual Crime in the United States report. Nationwide FBI figures for 2018, which include crime rates per 100,000 inhabitants, won't be released until later this year, likely in September.

Crime had been rising during the two years before Trump took office, a trend he greatly exaggerated when he was a candidate. During his campaign, Trump repeatedly and falsely claimed that the murder rate was "the highest it's been in 45 years." In fact, the murder rate had dropped to the lowest on record in 2014 — 4.4 murders per 100,000 inhabitants. And while it did rise for the next two years, it was still only 5.4 per 100,000 in 2016, far below the peak rate of 10.2 reached in 1980.

Coal and Environment

Coal Mining Jobs — As a candidate, Trump promised to "put our [coal] miners back to work," but so far not many have regained their jobs.

A revised total of 35,600 coal mining jobs disappeared during the Obama years, but as of February, only 1,900 of them had come back since Trump took office, according to BLS figures.

The outlook for coal miners remains bleak. The Energy Information Administration currently estimates that U.S. coal production fell 2 percent last year and will fall 9 percent this year and by another 6 percent in 2020. EIA expects natural gas will continue to displace coal for the generation of electricity.

Carbon Emissions — Carbon dioxide emissions from energy consumption are now going up under Trump, after falling for years.

Figures from the Energy Information Administration show CO2 emissions fell by a total of 14.5 percent between 2007 and 2017, due mainly to electric utilities shifting away from coal-fired plants in favor of cheaper, cleaner natural gas, as well as solar and wind power.

After Trump took office, CO2 emissions fell more slowly at first — by 0.8 percent in 2017, half the 1.8 percent decline in Obama's final year. And the trend has now reversed entirely. Emissions during the most recent 12 months on record, ending in December 2018, were 2.0 percent higher than in all of 2016.

EIA figures put the increase in CO2 emissions at 2.8 percent for all of 2018, compared with 2017. (Earlier, the Rhodium Group, a private research firm, grabbed headlines with a "preliminary" estimate that the 2018 increase would be 3.4 percent. But that was not supported by later EIA data.)

EIA said the 2018 rise is due mainly to a hotter summer and colder winter that resulted in higher natural gas consumption. It predicted that CO2 emissions would fall by 1.6 percent in 2019 and 1.0 percent in 2020, if temperatures return to normal as forecast. But even if those future reductions materialize, it would leave a net gain in total carbon emissions since Trump took office.

Border Security

Illegal border crossings are surging under Trump, to the highest levels in over a decade.

Last month more than 92,000 people were apprehended trying to cross the U.S.-Mexico border without permission — the highest monthly total since April 2007.

That number dropped during Trump's first few months in office, hitting a low of 11,127 in April 2017. But the trend has been strongly upward since then, and has lately accelerated.

For the most recent 12 months on record, the monthly average was 48,672 which is 31.9 percent higher than the monthly average of 36,912 in 2016. We use this rolling monthly average for our chart, because these monthly figures are subject to wide seasonal variations.

In the last three months, however, the number of unauthorized crossings has spiked even higher — beyond anything seen in nearly a dozen years. The monthly average so far this year is over 69,000, higher than the monthly average for any full year since 2007.

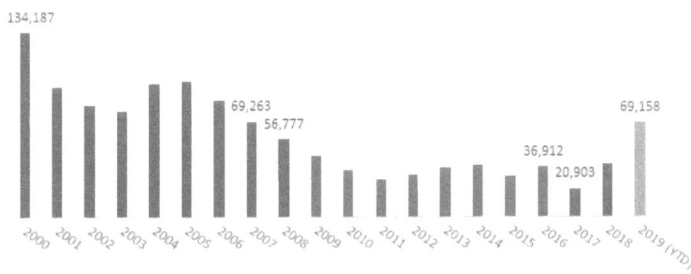

Of those apprehended in March, less than one-third were single adults. Rather, 57 percent were part of "family units" made up of a child under

18 accompanied by a parent or guardian, and nearly 10 percent were unaccompanied children. Border Patrol officials said they are coming primarily from Guatemala, Honduras and El Salvador, and many are seeking asylum. It's a big change from the days when most such attempted border crossings were made by Mexican males seeking work.

"The Border Patrol is facing an <u>unprecedented humanitarian and border security crisis</u>," said Brian Hastings, the Border Patrol's chief of law enforcement operations. "We've arrived at the breaking point."

Hastings told reporters in a conference call April 9 that more than 11,000 detainees — none of them with criminal records — had been released into the U.S. because the Border Patrol lacks space to house them. They were given notices to appear for court dates. That could bring even more unauthorized border crossings in the coming months, he said. "[W]ord of mouth and social media have spread news," Hastings said. "And more immigrants are emboldened to make the dangerous journey."

Corporate Profits

After-tax corporate profits are running at record levels under Trump. During 2018, they hit $1.95 trillion, eclipsing the previous annual record set under Obama.

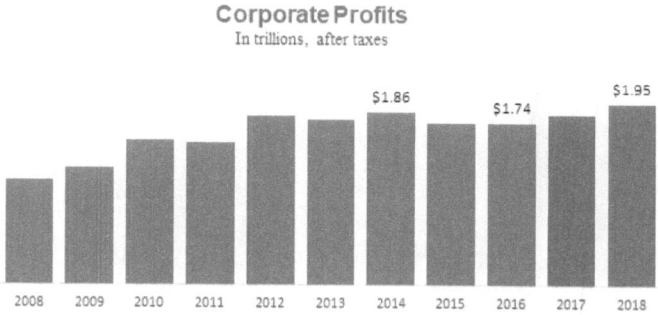

Last year's after-tax profits were 12 percent higher than the full-year figure for 2016, the year before Trump took office. They also were 4.9 percent above the best previous full-year figure, which was $1.86 trillion in 2014.

These annual (and also quarterly) estimates originate with the Bureau of Economic Analysis (see line 45).

After-tax profits got a boost in 2018 from the tax cut Trump signed into law Dec. 22, 2017, dropping the top federal tax rate on corporate income to 21 percent, from 35 percent. Profits *before* taxes (line 43) actually edged down by about one-tenth of 1 percent last year, and were 3.7 percent below the 2014 level.

Stock Market

Stock prices continued their long rise with Trump in office — though it's been a bumpy ride.

Market indexes set record after record last year — only to see much of the gain erased in the worst December since 1931. But that was followed this year by the best first quarter in a decade.

At the close on April 10, the Standard & Poor's 500-stock average was just 1.5 percent below the record high set on Sept. 20, 2018, and 27.6 percent higher than it was on the last trading day before Trump's inauguration.

Other indexes took similar rebounds. At the April 10 close, the Dow Jones Industrial Average, made up of 30 large corporations, was up 32.6 percent under Trump. And the NASDAQ composite index, made up of more than 3,000 companies, was 43.8 percent higher than before Trump took office.

The bull market began its rise in the depths of the Great Recession in 2009, and became the longest in history last year. This year it passed its 10th anniversary in March.

Wages and Inflation

The upward trend in real wages continued under Trump, and inflation remained in check.

CPI —The Consumer Price Index rose 4.3 percent during Trump's first 26 months, continuing a long period of historically low inflation.

In the most recent 12 months, ending in March, the CPI rose 1.9 percent. The CPI rose an average of 1.8 percent each year of the Obama presidency (measured as the 12-month change ending each January), and an average of 2.4 percent during each of George W. Bush's years.

Wages — Paychecks continued to grow faster than prices.

The average weekly earnings of all private-sector workers, in "real" (inflation-adjusted) terms, rose 2.6 percent during Trump's first 26 months (ending in March) after going up 3.9 percent during the previous four years.

Those figures are for all private-sector workers, including managers and supervisors.

For rank-and-file production and nonsupervisory workers (who make up 82 percent of all private-sector workers), real weekly earnings have gone up 2.5 percent so far under Trump, after rising 4.9 percent during Obama's last four years in office.

Consumer Sentiment

Consumer confidence in the economy rose under Trump, then dropped back again.

The University of Michigan's Surveys of Consumers reported that its Index of Consumer Sentiment hit 101.4 in March of last year, which was the highest in more than 15 years. For all of 2018 the level averaged 98.4, which was the best full-year average since 2000.

But from there it slid to 91.2 in January — exactly where it had been in September 2016, before Trump was elected.

However, the level bounced back in the most recent survey, covering March, hitting 98.4. That eased concerns of a future recession. The survey's chief economist, Richard Curtin, said: "Overall, the data do not indicate an emerging recession but point toward slightly lower unit sales of vehicles and homes during the year ahead."

Home Prices and Ownership

Home Prices — Home prices soared to record levels under Trump, but recently have slipped back a bit.

The most recent sales figures from the National Association of Realtors show the national median price of an existing, single-family home sold in February was $251,400.

Earlier, in June 2018, the median monthly price peaked at $276,500 — the highest ever recorded. The median for all of 2018 was $261,600, the highest full-year figure on record.

But even though prices fell back in subsequent months, the February median is still $22,700 higher than the median price of $228,700 for homes sold during the month Trump took office — a gain in value of 9.9 percent. The rise in the Consumer Price Index during the same period was 3.8 percent.

Frederick W. Sarkis

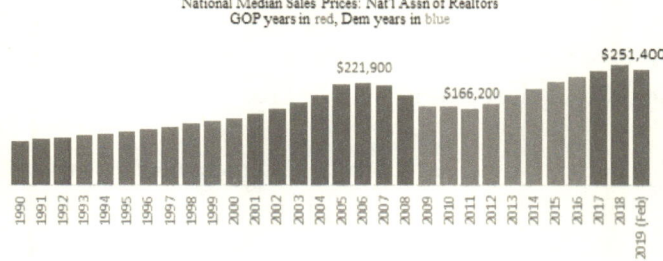

The Realtors' figures reflect raw sales prices without attempting to adjust for such factors as variations in the size, location, age or condition of the homes sold in a given month or year. Even so, a similar pattern emerges from the S&P CoreLogic Case-Shiller U.S. National Home Price Index, which compares sales prices of similar homes and seeks to measure changes in the total value of all existing single-family housing stock.

The Case-Shiller index for January sales (the most recent available) was 10.5 percent higher than where it stood in the month Trump took office.

Whichever way you measure it, homeowners have seen the value of their houses rise substantially since Trump took office.

Homeownership — Meanwhile, the percentage of Americans who own their homes has continued to recover from a years-long slide, gaining 1.1 percentage points since Trump took office.

The homeownership rate began to slide after peaking at 69.2 percent of households for two quarters in 2004. It hit bottom in the second quarter of 2016 at 62.9 percent — the lowest point in more than half a century, and tied for the lowest on record.

The rate recovered 0.8 points before Trump took office, and has gone up another 1.1 points since then, reaching 64.8 percent in the fourth quarter of 2018, according to the most recent Census Bureau figures.

But it is still 4.4 points below the peak level of 15 years earlier.

Trade

The trade deficit that Trump promised to reduce grew much larger instead.

The most recent government figures show that the total U.S. trade deficit in goods and services during the most recent 12 months on record (ending in January) was $622 billion. That's an increase of $118 billion, or 23.5 percent, compared with 2016.

China — The goods-and-services trade deficit with China grew at a similar pace, up by 22.8 percent between 2016 and the most recent 12 months on record, ending in December, when it hit nearly $379 billion.

Trump last year initiated a full-scale trade conflict with China, imposing tariffs on $250 billion worth of Chinese goods. China has retaliated with its own tariffs on $110 billion of U.S. goods. Trump tweeted Jan. 8 that talks to strike a new trade deal with China are going "very well," but so far no deal has been announced.

Mexico — Meanwhile, the much smaller trade deficit in goods and services with Mexico totaled $78 billion during the 12 months ending in December, an increase of 25.8 percent compared with 2016.

Canada — The trade *surplus* that the U.S. runs with Canada has practically disappeared under Trump. The trade balance was positive by a scant $1.2 billion during the 12 months ending in December. That surplus is 83.6 percent smaller than it was in 2016.

On Nov. 30 Trump and the leaders of Canada and Mexico signed a new trade agreement to replace the 25-year-old North American Free Trade Agreement, which Trump had promised to scrap during his campaign. The new agreement will be called the United States-Mexico-Canada Agreement, or USMCA. The new agreement still requires approval by Congress before it can take effect.

Health Insurance Coverage

The number of people lacking health insurance has risen by more than 1 million under Trump, and millions more are expected to drop or lose coverage this year.

The rise compared with 2016 was about 1.1 million as of the first nine months of 2018, according to the most recent report from the National Health Interview Survey, issued Feb. 27. The NHIS said 9.2 percent of the population lacked coverage during the period, up from 9.0 percent in 2016.

A much greater rise was reported by a Gallup survey covering the final quarter of 2018. Gallup on Jan. 23 put the rise in uninsured adults at about 7 million, compared with the last half of 2016. Gallup put the percentage of uninsured adults at 13.7 percent in the October-December quarter.

The two surveys aren't strictly comparable. Besides the differing time periods, Gallup covers only adults age 18 and over, while the NHIS covers all ages, including children. NHIS said the 1.1 million increase it found was not statistically significant. But taken together, both surveys point to an upward trend that seems to have accelerated during the latter part of last year. (For more on these differing estimates, see our Feb. 12 story, "Did the Uninsured Increase by 7 Million?")

The NHIS figure took a big jump from the data we reported in January, when 100,000 *fewer* people were listed as lacking covering during the first *six* months of last year, compared with 2016. The NHIS doesn't break out the total number of uninsured people for each quarter, but clearly there was a very large increase in the third quarter of 2018. The NHIS estimate for all of 2018 is expected sometime in May, and we will cover it in our next update.

Trump failed to "repeal and replace" the Affordable Care Act as he promised to do, but did slash advertising and outreach aimed at enrolling people in Obamacare plans. In December 2017 he signed a tax bill that ended the ACA's tax penalty for people who fail to obtain coverage, effective this year. And in March the Trump administration joined an effort by GOP state attorneys general seeking a court decision to overturn the entire act.

The nonpartisan Congressional Budget Office estimated in May 2018 that with the end of the mandate penalty 3 million people will drop or lose coverage this year, and another 2 million in 2020.

Food Stamps

The number of food stamp recipients has gone down since Trump's inauguration.

As of January, the most recent month for which figures are available, 38.1 million people were receiving the aid. The number has gone down 4.4 million, or 10.4 percent, since January 2017, when Trump took office.

The number generally has been going down since peaking at nearly 47.8 million in December 2012, as the economy recovered from the Great Recession of 2007-2009.

In December, the Trump administration issued a proposed rule that would tighten work requirements for able-bodied adults between the ages of 18 and 49, with no dependents. Generally, the rules limit aid to three months for such adults, but many states secured waivers to that rule during the 2007-2009 recession and still have them in place, despite a booming economy. Trump's proposal would affect only a fraction of all food stamp recipients, however. Less than 9 percent of all people getting food stamps are classified as able-bodied adults living in households without children, and 26 percent of those are already working, according to the U.S. Department of Agriculture.

Judiciary Appointments

Trump is putting his mark on the federal appeals courts more quickly than Obama was able to do in his time in office.

Supreme Court — So far Trump has won Senate confirmation for two Supreme Court nominees, Justice Neil Gorsuch and Justice Brett M. Kavanaugh.

Obama also was able to fill two high court vacancies during his first two years in office, with Justice Sonia Sotomayor and Justice Elena Kagan. But the Kavanaugh nomination to fill the vacancy created by Justice Anthony Kennedy's retirement is significant because Kavanaugh may move the court to the right. He is considered more conservative than Kennedy, who sometimes sided with the liberal justices to provide deciding votes on issues including gay rights, abortion, capital punishment and affirmative action.

However, Kavanaugh disappointed abortion foes when he sided with the court's liberals on one of his first votes, against taking up a case about whether citizens should be allowed to sue states that cut off Medicaid funding for Planned Parenthood health clinics.

Court of Appeals — Trump also won confirmation of 37 U.S. Court of Appeals judges (30 during his first two years and another seven in the current Congress as of April 9). That's more than double the total for Obama, who won confirmation for only 18 as of the same point in his first term (14 during his first two years and two more in the 112th Congress as of April 8, 2011).

Trump has now installed nearly 21 percent of all the 179 appellate court judges authorized by federal law.

District Court — When it comes to the lower courts, Trump has just pulled ahead of Obama. With the confirmation of the latest two judges on April 10– to seats on federal courts in Texas and Indiana — he has won confirmation for 58 of his nominees to be federal District Court judges (nearly 9 percent of the 677 authorized district judges), while Obama had won confirmation for 57 at the same point in his presidency.

Trump must share responsibility for this record with the Republican majority in the Senate. Republicans not only refused to consider Obama's appointment of Merrick Garland to fill the Supreme Court vacancy eventually filled by Gorsuch, but they also blocked confirmation of dozens of Obama's nominees to lower courts. Trump inherited 17 Court of Appeals vacancies, for example, including seven that had Obama nominees pending but never confirmed.

Federal Debt and Deficits

Trump inherited rising federal debt and deficits, and his tax cut and spending increases are making both rise faster.

The federal debt held by the public stood at over $16.2 trillion at the last count on April 9 — $1.8 trillion higher than when he took office. That's a 12.5 percent increase under Trump. And that figure will go up even more quickly in coming years unless Trump and Congress impose massive spending cuts, or reverse course and increase taxes.

Trump's cuts in corporate and individual income tax rates — as well as the bipartisan spending deal he signed Feb. 9, 2018 — are causing the red ink to gush even faster than it did before. The annual federal deficit for fiscal year 2018, which ended Sept. 30, was $779 billion, up from nearly $666 billion the year before.

That's an increase of $113 billion. Much of the increase was due to reduced receipts from corporate income taxes, which fell by $92 billion.

CBO's latest Budget and Economic Outlook, issued Jan. 28, estimates that under current law, the deficit will continue rising for the foreseeable future, exceeding $1 trillion annually starting in fiscal year 2022. (Baseline deficit projections are in Table 1-1, line 30.)

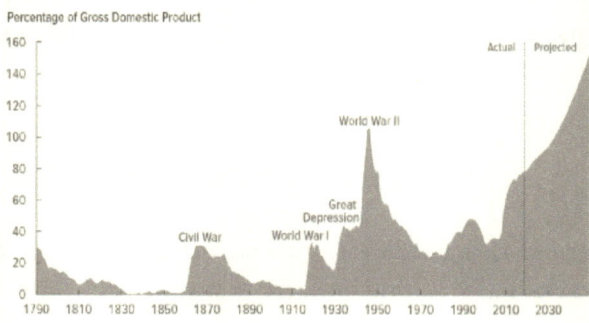
CBO Chart

Further, CBO said that over the next 10 years annual deficits would run "well above the average over the past 50 years" at between 4.1 percent and 4.7 percent of the nation's entire economic output. CBO projected that the national debt would reach 93 percent of GDP by 2029 — the highest since just after World War II — and reach 150 percent of GDP in 2049 — "far higher than it has ever been."

Oil Production and Imports

U.S. crude oil production resumed its upward trend under Trump, rising 25.6 percent during the most recent 12 months on record (ending in January), compared with all of 2016.

Domestic oil production has increased every year since 2008, except for a 6.1 percent drop in 2016 after prices plunged to below $30 a barrel, from more than $100 in 2014. The price returned to more than $50 a barrel by the end of 2016, prompting increased drilling and production. The price has averaged over $57 since Trump took office.

As a result of this rising production, the trend to reduced reliance on foreign oil also resumed. The U.S. imported an estimated 11.4 percent of its oil and petroleum products last year — less than half of the 24.4 percent figure for all of 2016. And in January, the EIA projected that the

U.S. would likely be exporting more petroleum than it imports by the end of 2020.

Dependence on imports peaked in 2005, when the U.S. imported 60.3 percent of its petroleum, and it has declined every year since except for 2016, when it ticked up by 0.3 percentage points.

Sources

Bureau of Labor Statistics. "Employment, Hours, and Earnings from the Current Employment Statistics survey (National); Total Nonfarm Employment, Seasonally Adjusted." Data extracted 10 Apr 2019.

Bureau of Labor Statistics. "Labor Force Statistics from the Current Population Survey; Unemployment Rate, Seasonally Adjusted." Data extracted 10 Apr 2019.

Bureau of Labor Statistics. "Job Openings and Labor Turnover Survey: Job Openings, Seasonally Adjusted." Data extracted 10 Apr 2019.

Bureau of Labor Statistics. "Labor Force Statistics from the Current Population Survey; Labor Force Participation Rate." Data extracted 10 Apr 2019.

Bureau of Labor Statistics. "Labor Force Statistics from the Current Population Survey; All employees, thousands, manufacturing, seasonally adjusted." Data extracted 10 Apr 2019.

U.S. Bureau of Economic Analysis. "Table 1.1.1. Percent Change From Preceding Period in Real Gross Domestic Product." Interactive data extracted 10 Apr 2019.

Wall Street Journal. "WSJ Economic Survey January 2019."

National Association of Business Economists. "NABE Outlook Survey – March 2019."

McLaughlin, Patrick A., and Oliver Sherouse. RegData US 3.0 Daily (dataset). QuantGov, Mercatus Center at George Mason University, Arlington, VA. Daily Summary tracking of restrictions in the eCFR (Electronic Code of Federal Regulations). Downloaded 15 Jan 2018.

McLaughlin, Patrick A. and Oliver Sherouse. 2017. "QuantGov—A Policy Analytics Platform." "RegData 3.0 Restrictions by Year." Downloaded 15 Jan 2018.

Federal Bureau of Investigation. "Crime in the United States 2017;" Table 1. 24 Sep 2018.

Federal Bureau of Investigation. "Crime in the United States, Jan-Jun 2018, Preliminary Semiannual Uniform Crime Report." 25 Feb 2019.

Bureau of Labor Statistics. "Labor Force Statistics from the Current Population Survey; All employees, thousands, coal mining, seasonally adjusted." Data extracted 10 Apr 2019.

U.S. Energy Information Administration. Short Term Energy Outlook. 9 Apr 2019.

U.S. Border Patrol. "U.S. Border Patrol Apprehensions FY2019" Undated. Accessed 10 Apr 2019.

U.S. Border Patrol. "Total Illegal Alien Apprehensions By Month Fiscal Years 2000-2018." Undated. Accessed 10 Apr 2019.

U.S. Bureau of Economic Analysis. Corporate Profits After Tax (without IVA and CCAdj) [CP], retrieved from FRED, Federal Reserve Bank of St. Louis. 10 Apr 2019.

Yahoo! Finance. "Dow Jones Industrial Average." Accessed 10 Apr 2019.

Yahoo! Finance. "S&P 500." Accessed 10 Apr 2019.

Yahoo! Finance. "NASDAQ Composite." Accessed 10 Apr 2019

Smith, Adam. "Wall Street's Bull Market Celebrates Its 10th Anniversary." The Street. 10 Mar 2019.

Eagan, Matt. "Market milestone: This is the longest bull run in history." CNN.com. 22 Aug 2018.

Bureau of Labor Statistics. "Consumer Price Index – All Urban Consumers." Data extracted 10 Apr 2019.

Bureau of Labor Statistics. "Employment, Hours, and Earnings from the Current Employment Statistics survey (National); Average Weekly Earnings of All Employees, 1982-1984 Dollars." Data extracted 10 Apr 2019.

Bureau of Labor Statistics. "Employment, Hours, and Earnings from the Current Employment Statistics survey (National); Average Weekly Earnings of production and nonsupervisory employees, 1982-1984 Dollars." Data extracted 10 Apr 2019.

University of Michigan Surveys of Consumers. "The Index of Consumer Sentiment." Mar 2019.

National Association of Realtors. "Sales Price of Existing Single-Family Homes." 22 Mar 2019.

S&P Dow Jones Indices. "S&P CoreLogic Case-Shiller U.S. National Home Price NSA Index." Data extracted 10 Apr 2019.

U.S. Census Bureau. "Time Series: Not Seasonally Adjusted Home Ownership Rate." Data extracted 10 Apr 2019.

U.S. Bureau of Economic Analysis. "U.S. International Trade in Goods and Services, January 2019." 27 Mar 2019.

U.S. Bureau of Economic Analysis. "Table 1, U.S. Trade in Goods and Services, 1992-present." 27 Mar 2019.

U.S. Bureau of Economic Analysis. "Table 3. U.S. International Trade by Selected Countries and Areas: Balance on Goods and Services." 27 Mar 2019.

Centers for Disease Control and Prevention; National Health Interview Survey. "Health Insurance Coverage: Estimates From the National Health Interview Survey, January – September 2018." 27 Feb 2019.

Witters, Dan. "U.S. Uninsured Rate Rises to Four-Year High." Gallup. 27 Jan 2019.

Congressional Budget Office. "Federal Subsidies for Health Insurance Coverage for People Under Age 65, 2018 to 2028." May 2018.

U.S. Department of Agriculture, Food and Nutrition Service. "Supplemental Nutrition Assistance Program (Data as of Apr 5, 2019)." Data extracted 10 Apr 2019.

U.S. Department of Agriculture, Food and Nutrition Service. Supplemental Nutrition Assistance Program (SNAP) data, fiscal years 1968-2018.

Administrative Office of the U.S. Courts. "Judicial Confirmations for January 2019," archived web listing of confirmations in 115th Congress. Accessed 10 Apr 2019.

Administrative Office of the U.S. Courts. "Confirmation Listing" web listing of confirmations in 116th Congress. Accessed 10 Apr 2019.

Administrative Office of the U.S. Courts. "Judicial Confirmations for January 2011," archived web listing of confirmations in 110th Congress. Accessed 10 Apr 2019.

Administrative Office of the U.S. Courts. "Judicial Confirmations for January 2013," archived web listing of confirmations in 111th Congress. Accessed 10 Apr 2019.

U.S. Treasury. "The Debt to the Penny and Who Holds It." Data extracted 10 Apr 2019.

U.S. Treasury. "Final Monthly Treasury Statement of Receipts and Outlays of the United States Government For Fiscal Year 2017 Through September 30, 2017." 20 Oct 2017.

U.S. Treasury. "Final Monthly Treasury Statement of Receipts and Outlays of the United States Government For Fiscal Year 2018 Through September 30, 2018." 15 Oct 2018.

Congressional Budget Office. "The Budget and Economic Outlook: 2019 to 2029" 28 Jan 2019.

Hall, Keith. "The 2019 Budget and Economic Outlook; Presentation to the American Business Conference, Washington, D.C." 2 Apr 2019.

U.S. Energy Information Administration. "U.S. Field Production of Crude Oil." Data accessed 10 Apr 2019.

U.S. Energy Information Administration. "Weekly Cushing OK WTI Spot Price FOB." Weekly oil price data. Accessed 10 Apr 2019.

U.S. Energy Information Administration. "Table 3.3a Petroleum Trade: Overview." Monthly Energy Review. 26 Mar 2019.

Chapter Two

FEATURED POSTS › THE WIRE

Did Barr Mislead Congress?

By Lori Robertson

Posted on May 1, 2019

Democrats claim Attorney General William Barr misled Congress last month when asked if he was aware of concerns that special counsel Robert S. Mueller's team may have had with his March 24 memo summarizing the Mueller report. We'll lay out the facts about Mueller's letter to Barr, Barr's April testimony to Congress, and what the attorney general said about it in his May 1 testimony.

On March 24, Barr issued a four-page memo about the Mueller report, which wouldn't be released, in redacted form, until April 18. We now know that Mueller had concerns about Barr's memo, which he expressed in a March 27 letter. That letter says the special counsel's office also had "communicated" concerns on March 25.

The *Washington Post* and *New York Times* reported on the existence of the March 27 letter on April 30, and the Justice Department released it the following day, before Barr was set to testify before the Senate Judiciary Committee.

In his letter, Mueller told Barr that the attorney general's March 24 summary "did not fully capture the context, nature, and substance of this Office's work and conclusions," a point Mueller said his office made to the Department of Justice on March 25. Mueller asked that Barr publicly release redacted introductions and executive summaries from the special counsel report, which Mueller included with his letter, saying, "Release at this time would alleviate the misunderstandings that have arisen and would answer congressional and public questions about the nature and outcome of our investigation."

> ***Mueller, letter to Barr, March 27:*** *As we stated in our meeting of March 5 and reiterated to the Department early in the afternoon of March 24, the introductions and executive summaries of our two-volume report accurately summarize this Office's work and conclusions. The summary letter the Department sent to Congress and released to the public late in the afternoon of March 24 did not fully capture the context, nature, and substance of this Office's work and conclusions. We communicated that concern to the Department on the morning of March 25. There is now public confusion about critical aspects of the results of our investigation. This threatens to undermine a central purpose for which the Department appointed the Special Counsel: to assure full public confidence in the outcome of the investigations.*

Once that letter came to light, Democrats said Barr had misled Congress and should resign. In the May 1 hearing, Sen. Mazie Hirono said Barr had "lied." Democrats pointed to two exchanges on April 9 and 10 between Barr and Democratic Rep. Charlie Crist and Sen. Chris Van Hollen.

Prior to those hearings, on April 3, the *Times*, and the following day the *Post*, reported that members of Mueller's team were concerned that Barr's memo didn't adequately reflect their findings, in particular that the evidence on possible obstruction of justice by President Donald Trump was more damaging than Barr's memo indicated.

On April 9, when Barr testified before a House appropriations subcommittee, Crist asked him about those media reports.

> **Crist, April 9:** *Reports have emerged recently ... that members of the special counsel's team are frustrated at some level with the limited information included in your March 24th letter, that it does not adequately or accurately, necessarily, portray the report's findings. Do you know what they're referencing with that?*
>
> **Barr:** *No, I don't. I think, I think, I suspect that they probably wanted, you know, more put out. But in my view, I was not interested in putting out summaries or trying to summarize, because I think any summary regardless of who prepares it not only runs the risk of, you know, being under-inclusive or over-inclusive but also, you know, would trigger a lot of discussion and analysis that really should await everything coming out at once.*

On April 10, Barr was before a Senate appropriations subcommittee when Van Hollen asked him about his conclusion in the March 24 memo that "the evidence developed during the Special Counsel's investigation is not sufficient to establish that the President committed an obstruction-of-justice offense."

> **Van Hollen, April 10:** *Did Bob Mueller support your conclusion?*
>
> **Barr:** *I don't know whether Bob Mueller supported my conclusion.*

We don't know what Mueller thought of Barr's conclusion on whether the president had committed obstruction of justice. Mueller doesn't say anything about that in his March 27 letter to Barr. Instead, the special counsel took issue with what Barr's memo said about the conclusions of Mueller's investigation. Mueller wrote that Barr's memo "did not fully capture the context, nature, and substance of this Office's work and conclusions."

With the Crist exchange, however, we know that Barr was aware of Mueller's concerns about the March 24 memo. In May 1 testimony before the Senate Judiciary Committee, Barr drew a distinction between being asked about the concerns of "members of the special counsel's team," which was Crist's question, as opposed to being asked about Mueller himself. Barr also claimed that Crist's question was "a very different question" than one "related" to the Mueller letter.

Barr <u>said</u> in his opening statement — and this was part of the *Washington Post* <u>report</u> the day before — that he called Mueller after receiving the March 27 letter.

> ***Barr, May 1:*** *I asked [Mueller] if he was suggesting that the March 24th letter was inaccurate, and he said no, but that the press reporting had been inaccurate and that the press was reading too much into it. ... He said that his concern focused on his explanation of why he did not reach a conclusion on obstruction, and he wanted more put out on that issue. He wanted, he argued for putting out summaries of each volume, the executive summaries that had been written by his office, and if not that then other material that focused on the issue of why he didn't reach the obstruction question. But he was very clear with me that he was not suggesting that we had misrepresented his report.*

Sen. Patrick Leahy, a Democrat, <u>asked</u> Barr why he didn't reveal that Mueller had concerns when he was questioned by Crist in April.

> **Leahy, May 1:** *Why did you testify on April 9 that you didn't know the concerns being expressed by Mueller's team, when in fact you had heard those concerns directly from Mr. Mueller two weeks before?*
>
> **Barr:** *Well, as I said, I talked directly to Bob Mueller about his letter to me and specifically asked him, what exactly are your concerns, are you saying that the March 24th letter was misleading or inaccurate or what. He indicated that it was not. ...*
>
> *The question from Crist was, reports have emerged recently, press reports that members of the special counsel's team are frustrated at some level with the limited information included in your March 24th letter in that they don't adequately or accurately portray the report's findings [Barr emphasized the word "findings"]. I don't know what members he's talking about, and I certainly am not aware of any challenge to the accuracy of the findings.*
>
> **Leahy:** *... My question was why would you say you were not aware of concerns when weeks before your testimony Mr. Mueller had expressed concerns to you? ...*
>
> **Barr:** *Well, I answered a question. And the question was relating to unidentified members who were expressing frustration over the accuracy relating to findings. I don't know what that refers to at all. I talked directly to Bob Mueller, not members of his team. And even though I did not know what was being referred to, and Mueller had never told me that the expression of the findings was inaccurate, but I did then volunteer that I thought they were talking about the desire to have more information put out. But it wasn't my purpose to put out more information.*
>
> **Leahy:** *Mr. Barr, I feel your answer was purposefully misleading, and I think others do, too.*

Mueller's letter said Barr's March 24 memo "did not fully capture the context, nature, and substance of this Office's work and conclusions," while Crist asked about media reports that members of Mueller's team "are frustrated at some level with the limited information included in your March 24th letter, that it does not adequately or accurately, necessarily, portray the report's findings." Barr focused on the word "accurately," saying that Mueller never told him "the expression of the findings was inaccurate." But Mueller did say the Barr memo didn't "fully capture" Mueller's conclusions, and he asked Barr to release more information.

Later in the May 1 hearing, Sen. Sheldon Whitehouse accused Barr of "masterful hairsplitting" when Barr denied that Crist's question was "very related" to the Mueller letter.

> **Whitehouse:** *Would you concede that you had an opportunity to make this letter [Mueller letter] public on April 4 when Rep. Crist asked you a very related question?*
>
> **Barr:** *I don't know what you mean by related question, it seems to me it'd be a very different question.*
>
> **Whitehouse:** *I can't even follow that down the road. I mean, boy, that's some masterful hairsplitting.*

We'll leave it to readers to decide whether Crist's question was "very related" or "very different." But at the very least, the attorney general didn't give Congress the full story about what he knew regarding the special counsel's concerns about his March 24 memo.

Chapter Three

FactChecking Trump's Fox News Interview

By *Eugene Kiely*

Posted on May 22, 2019

President Donald Trump, in a lengthy interview on Fox News, made several statements that were false, misleading or not supported by the evidence:

- Trump claimed Joe Biden, as vice president, pressured Ukraine to fire a prosecutor who "was after his son," Hunter Biden. There's no evidence that Biden was under investigation, although he was a board member for a company whose owner was under investigation.
- Trump said of North Korea: "They haven't had any tests over the last two years — zero." It's true that they haven't had any nuclear tests or long-range missile tests, but North Korea has tested short-range missiles twice this month.
- The president said he will provide $15 billion in assistance to U.S. farmers hurt by the trade war, because that's "the most money that China has ever paid" for U.S. agricultural goods. But federal data show that China purchased nearly $27.2 billion in U.S. agricultural goods in 2012.
- Trump boasted that Honda is "coming in [to the U.S.] with $14.5 billion" in investments. A Michigan-based automotive research

group says that Honda has announced $1.7 billion in U.S. vehicle manufacturing investments over the last five years.
- The president said he has "tremendous poll numbers now." Trump's average approval rating is currently below 43 percent.

In a <u>wide-ranging interview</u> that aired May 19 on "The Next Revolution," Trump and the show's host, Steve Hilton, discussed foreign policy, international trade, the economy, politics and more.

Hunter Biden and Ukraine

At one point, Hilton raised Trump's campaign promise to "drain the swamp," asking the president whether former White House aides should be allowed to lobby for foreign companies. The president pivoted to 2020 — implying that a potential 2020 rival, Joe Biden, intervened while he was vice president to halt an investigation in Ukraine of his son, Hunter.

Trump twisted the facts when he said that the then-vice president threatened to withhold $2 billion in U.S. loan guarantees unless Ukraine dropped its investigation into Hunter and fired the prosecutor. There's no evidence that Hunter was under investigation.

> ***Trump:*** *Biden, he calls them and says, "Don't you dare prosecute, if you don't fire this prosecutor" — the prosecutor was after his son. Then he said, "If you fire the prosecutor, you'll be OK. And if you don't fire the prosecutor, we're not giving you $2 billion in loan guarantees," or whatever he was supposed to give. Can you imagine if I did that?*

Let's review what we know — and don't know — about the Bidens and Ukraine.

In March 2016, Biden went to Ukraine and told the government that the U.S. would withhold $1 billion in loan guarantees if Ukraine failed to address corruption and remove its prosecutor general, Viktor Shokin. We know this because Biden boasted about it last year during an appearance at the Council on Foreign Relations.

The former vice president, who is now running for president, said the incident occurred during a visit to Kiev.

> ***Biden, Jan. 23, 2018:*** *I was supposed to announce that there was another billion-dollar loan guarantee. And I had gotten a commitment from [then-Ukraine President Petro] Poroshenko and from [then-Ukraine Prime Minister Arseniy] Yatsenyuk that they would take action against the state prosecutor. And they didn't.*
>
> *So they said they had — they were walking out to a press conference. I said, nah, I'm not going to — or, we're not going to give you the billion dollars. They said, you have no authority. You're not the president. The president said — I said, call him. I said, I'm telling you, you're not getting the billion dollars. I said, you're not getting the billion. I'm going to be leaving here in, I think it was about six hours. I looked at them and said: I'm leaving in six hours. If the prosecutor is not fired, you're not getting the money. Well, son of a bitch. He got fired.*

The U.S. wasn't the only one critical of Ukraine's anti-corruption efforts. A month earlier, the International Monetary Fund threatened to withhold $40 billion unless Ukraine undertook "a substantial new effort" to fight corruption.

At the time, Hunter Biden was a board member for the Burisma Group, one of the biggest private gas companies in Ukraine. He joined the board in May 2014, instantly raising concerns about a potential conflict of interest. An Associated Press article called Biden's hiring "politically awkward."

"Hunter Biden's employment means he will be working as a director and top lawyer for a Ukrainian energy company during the period when his father and others in the Obama administration attempt to influence the policies of Ukraine's new government, especially on energy issues," the AP wrote.

However, there is no evidence that Hunter Biden was under investigation or that his father pressured Ukraine on his behalf.

A few days before Fox News aired the Trump interview, Yuriy Lutsenko, Ukraine's current prosecutor general, gave his own interview to Bloomberg News and said: "Hunter Biden did not violate any Ukrainian laws at least as of now, we do not see any wrongdoing."

Lutsenko told Bloomberg that the prosecutor general's office in 2014 — before Shokin took office — opened a corruption investigation against Mykola Zlochevsky, the owner of Burisma, and numerous others. He said the probe's focus was Serghi Kurchenko, who owned a number of gas companies, and a transaction that occurred in November 2013, months before Biden joined Burisma.

> ***Bloomberg News, May 16:*** *As part of the 5-year-old inquiry, the prosecutor general's office has been looking at whether Kurchenko's purchase of an oil storage terminal in southern Ukraine from Zlochevksy in November 2013 helped Kurchenko launder money. Lutsenko said the transaction under scrutiny came months before Hunter Biden joined the Burisma board.*
>
> *"Biden was definitely not involved," Lutsenko said. "We do not have any grounds to think that there was any wrongdoing starting from 2014."*

The investigation is still active, he said.

North Korea and Nuclear Tests

The president also spoke about North Korea and its nuclear weapons program. Trump met with North Korea dictator Kim Jong Un in June of last year, and the two leaders agreed to "promote the denuclearization of the Korean Peninsula."

During Kim's reign, North Korea has conducted numerous nuclear tests and missile launches — including four nuclear weapons tests and three test launches of intercontinental ballistic missiles, or ICBMs.

> ***Trump:*** *But, they haven't had any tests over the last two years — zero. There's a chart and it shows 24 tests, 22 tests, 18 tests. Then I come, and once I'm there for a little while you know, we went through a pretty rough rhetorical period. Once I'm there for a little while, no tests, no tests, no tests.*

It's true that North Korea has not conducted a nuclear test since Sept. 3, 2017, and it hasn't launched an ICBM since Nov. 29, 2017. (See details in the Arms Control Association timeline.) But North Korea has conducted short-range missile tests twice this month, and it continues to actively pursue a nuclear weapons program.

The U.S. intelligence community released a threat assessment report in January that said, "We continue to observe activity inconsistent with full denuclearization."

The report didn't detail what kind of activity. But a week earlier, the Center for Strategic and International Studies in Washington issued a report that said it found "approximately 20 undeclared missile operating bases," including one that serves as a missile headquarters.

A month later, three Stanford University researchers issued a report that said North Korea "continued to operate and, in some cases, expand the nuclear weapons complex infrastructure. It continued to operate its nuclear facilities to produce plutonium and highly enriched uranium that may allow it to increase the number of nuclear weapons in its arsenal from roughly 30 in 2017 to 35-37."

China and Trade

Another subject that the president addressed was the ongoing trade war with China.

The Trump administration last year <u>imposed</u> tariffs on $250 billion worth of Chinese goods, and China responded with tariffs on $110 billion of U.S. goods. The trade dispute escalated this month. First, the Trump administration on May 10 <u>raised</u> tariffs from 10 percent to 25 percent on about $200 billion worth of Chinese goods. China <u>responded</u> three days later when it announced that it would increase tariffs from 10 percent to 25 percent on roughly $60 billion worth of U.S. goods, beginning June 1.

The dispute has hurt U.S. agricultural exports in particular, and the administration responded by authorizing <u>up to $12 billion</u> in aid to U.S. farmers. Trump said he would increase financial assistance to $15 billion and explained how he arrived at that number.

> ***Trump:*** *I said to Sonny Perdue, Department of Agriculture — secretary of Agriculture – "Sonny, what's the most money that China has ever paid toward agriculture, toward buying food product?" He said $15 billion a number of years ago. I said "Is that the most?" He said "Yes." Some people will say close to (inaudible) but $15 billion was about the most. I said "Good. I'm going to take $15 billion out of the $100 billion, and I'm going to give that to our farmers."*

Trump told a <u>similar story</u> in a recent speech to the National Association of Realtors.

> ***Trump, May 17:*** *So I called Sonny Perdue, our great Secretary of Agriculture, and I said, "Sonny…" — (applause) — I said, "Sonny, what's the biggest amount they've ever spent in this country?" He said, "About $15 billion. People could say 18, 19. But basically $15 billion." And I said, "So let's take $15 billion, set it aside out of the 100 or 125 billion [in annual tariffs imposed on all imports]."*

We asked the White House and the Department of Agriculture about this conversation. Neither responded. The Office of the U.S. Trade Representative referred us to the White House.

But this much we know based on available data and emails from two federal agencies: $15 billion isn't "the biggest amount" that China has spent on U.S. agricultural exports.

In its annual reports on shifts in U.S. merchandise trade, the United States International Trade Commission reported that China purchased $27.2 billion in U.S. agricultural products in 2012 – the most in one year from 2010 to 2017.

The most recent USITC report covers 2013 to 2017, and a commission spokeswoman told us a new report covering 2018 would not be released until November. However, according to the Department of Agriculture, agricultural exports to China fell dramatically to $9.2 billion in 2018. That was "almost all due to retaliatory tariffs" imposed by China, Wallace E. Tyner, who teaches agricultural economics at Purdue University, told us in an email.

We also know that, as of the morning of May 20, the U.S. has paid $8.54 billion to farmers through three aid programs, a USDA spokesperson said.

The Market Facilitation Program — the largest of the three programs — can provide up to $10 billion to producers of corn, cotton, sorghum, soybean, wheat, dairy, hogs, almonds and sweet cherries, according to a December report by the Congressional Research Service on the trade aid programs. The top five commodities that received assistance through the program were soybeans, corn, wheat, cotton and sorghum, the USDA spokesperson told us.

We found that, from 2009 through 2018, the most that China imported of those five commodities in any one year totaled nearly $20 billion, according to Census Bureau export data. That occurred in 2012, when China's agricultural purchases included nearly $14.9 billion in soybeans,

$3.4 billion in raw cotton and $1.3 billion in corn, according to Census data.

As we said, we don't know what the president meant when he said that $15 billion was "the biggest amount they've ever spent in this country." We will update this item if the White House responds.

Honda and U.S. Investments

In talking about the U.S. economy, Trump boasted about companies coming to the United States — singling out one car company in particular.

> **Trump:** *Well, really very simply, we have companies coming in here, as you know, by the dozens and by the hundreds and big ones, car companies, Honda's coming in with $14.5 billion.*

We don't know how many companies have relocated to the U.S. or have left the U.S. But the president overestimates Honda's future investment in the U.S.

On its website, Honda said that its total capital investment in the U.S. (not just auto manufacturing) has been $21 billion over the last 60 years, including $5.6 billion in the last five years. We could not find any new automotive investments that would equal $14.5 billion, so we reached out to the Michigan-based Center for Automotive Research Group, which tracks new investments in the United States.

Kristin Dziczek, vice president of industry, labor and economics, told us that she, too, could not match the $14.5 billion figure cited by Trump, and "we try to keep very close tabs on these things." She said Honda has announced auto manufacturing investments totaling $1.7 billion over the last five years.

In February, Honda announced that it would close a manufacturing plant in Swindon, England, in 2121, when it stops production of its current

Civic model. Honda Chief Executive Officer Takahiro Hachigo told Automotive News that the next generation Civic will be manufactured in North America, but the company has yet to say where the plant or plants will be located.

Honda currently has five vehicle manufacturing plants in the United States, including one in Indiana that builds the current Civic models. It also manufactures Civic models in Ontario, Canada.

We reached out to Honda, but did not hear back. We will update this article if we do.

Trump's Approval Rating

The president also boasted that he has "tremendous poll numbers now."

It's subjective, of course, to describe one's poll numbers as "tremendous." But Trump's average job approval rating — based on polling data assembled from dozens of polls by Real Clear Politics and FiveThirtyEight — is currently below 43 percent.

As of May 22, Trump's average job approval rating on Real Clear Politics was 42.5 percent, and FiveThirtyEight put it at 41.1 percent. By contrast, those who disapproved of Trump's job performance averaged 53.7 percent, according to Real Clear Politics, and 53.8 percent, according to FiveThirtyEight.

As for individual polls taken this month, Trump's job approval rating reached a peak of 51 percent in the Zogby Poll, which was conducted May 2 to May 9 and had a margin of error of plus or minus 3.4 percent. The low point was a Morning Consult poll, which showed the president at 37 percent. That poll was taken May 17 to 19, and had an error margin of plus or minus 2 percent.

Trump Repeats

As we often find, the president also repeated some false claims that we have previously debunked:

China Trade Deficit: The president said, "We have a trade deficit with China of $500 billion." That's false. As we have written before, the U.S. trade deficit with China in goods and services was a record $378.7 billion in 2018, according to the Bureau of Economic Analysis (see table 3). The U.S. had a $419.3 billion deficit with China in goods (table 6) and a $40.5 billion surplus in services (table 9).

Tariff Revenue: Trump said that, as a result of tariffs he has placed on Chinese goods, "we are going to be taking in possibly $100 billion, possibly more than that in tariffs. We never took in 10 cents from China." It's not true, as we have previously said, that the U.S. has never collected tariffs on Chinese goods. The amount of tariff revenue has increased, but the U.S. did collect billions of dollars each year since at least 2000. For example, the U.S. collected about $13.4 billion in 2016, according to the U.S. International Trade Commission database. As we also wrote, tariffs are taxes paid by U.S. importers in the form of customs duties, not by the Chinese government or its companies.

Liquefied Natural Gas Exporting. The president said, "I was in Louisiana opening up a $10 billion LNG plant that would've never been approved under another type of administration, never," and, "They've been trying for years to get it built, but we got approvals very quickly for the big LNG." That's false. As we wrote before, the plant in question, Sempra Energy's Cameron LNG plant, was approved in 2014 by the Obama administration, a fact Sempra Energy confirmed.

Chapter Four

THE WIRE

FactChecking Trump's Fox News Interview

By *Eugene Kiely*

Posted on May 22, 2019 | Updated on May 24, 2019

President Donald Trump, in a lengthy interview on Fox News, made several statements that were false, misleading or not supported by the evidence:

- Trump claimed Joe Biden, as vice president, pressured Ukraine to fire a prosecutor who "was after his son," Hunter Biden. There's no evidence that Biden was under investigation, although he was a board member for a company whose owner was under investigation.
- Trump said of North Korea: "They haven't had any tests over the last two years — zero." It's true that they haven't had any nuclear tests or long-range missile tests, but North Korea has tested short-range missiles twice this month.
- The president said he will provide $15 billion in assistance to U.S. farmers hurt by the trade war, because that's "the most money that China has ever paid" for U.S. agricultural goods. But federal data show that China purchased nearly $27.2 billion in U.S. agricultural goods in 2012.

- Trump boasted that Honda is "coming in [to the U.S.] with $14.5 billion" in investments. A Michigan-based automotive research group says that Honda has announced $1.7 billion in U.S. vehicle manufacturing investments over the last five years.
- The president said he has "tremendous poll numbers now." Trump's average approval rating is currently below 43 percent.

In a wide-ranging interview that aired May 19 on "The Next Revolution," Trump and the show's host, Steve Hilton, discussed foreign policy, international trade, the economy, politics and more.

Hunter Biden and Ukraine

At one point, Hilton raised Trump's campaign promise to "drain the swamp," asking the president whether former White House aides should be allowed to lobby for foreign companies. The president pivoted to 2020 — implying that a potential 2020 rival, Joe Biden, intervened while he was vice president to halt an investigation in Ukraine of his son, Hunter.

Trump twisted the facts when he said that the then-vice president threatened to withhold $2 billion in U.S. loan guarantees unless Ukraine dropped its investigation into Hunter and fired the prosecutor. There's no evidence that Hunter was under investigation.

> ***Trump:*** *Biden, he calls them and says, "Don't you dare prosecute, if you don't fire this prosecutor" — the prosecutor was after his son. Then he said, "If you fire the prosecutor, you'll be OK. And if you don't fire the prosecutor, we're not giving you $2 billion in loan guarantees," or whatever he was supposed to give. Can you imagine if I did that?*

Let's review what we know — and don't know — about the Bidens and Ukraine.

In March 2016, Biden went to Ukraine and told the government that the U.S. would withhold $1 billion in loan guarantees if Ukraine failed to address corruption and remove its prosecutor general, Viktor Shokin. We know this because Biden boasted about it last year during an appearance at the Council on Foreign Relations.

The former vice president, who is now running for president, said the incident occurred during a visit to Kiev.

> ***Biden, Jan. 23, 2018:*** *I was supposed to announce that there was another billion-dollar loan guarantee. And I had gotten a commitment from [then-Ukraine President Petro] Poroshenko and from [then-Ukraine Prime Minister Arseniy] Yatsenyuk that they would take action against the state prosecutor. And they didn't.*
>
> *So they said they had — they were walking out to a press conference. I said, nah, I'm not going to — or, we're not going to give you the billion dollars. They said, you have no authority. You're not the president. The president said — I said, call him. I said, I'm telling you, you're not getting the billion dollars. I said, you're not getting the billion. I'm going to be leaving here in, I think it was about six hours. I looked at them and said: I'm leaving in six hours. If the prosecutor is not fired, you're not getting the money. Well, son of a bitch. He got fired.*

The U.S. wasn't the only one critical of Ukraine's anti-corruption efforts. A month earlier, the International Monetary Fund threatened to withhold $40 billion unless Ukraine undertook "a substantial new effort" to fight corruption.

At the time, Hunter Biden was a board member for the Burisma Group, one of the biggest private gas companies in Ukraine. He joined the board in May 2014, instantly raising concerns about a potential conflict of interest. An Associated Press article called Biden's hiring "politically awkward."

"Hunter Biden's employment means he will be working as a director and top lawyer for a Ukrainian energy company during the period when his father and others in the Obama administration attempt to influence the policies of Ukraine's new government, especially on energy issues," the AP wrote.

However, there is no evidence that Hunter Biden was under investigation or that his father pressured Ukraine on his behalf.

A few days before Fox News aired the Trump interview, Yuriy Lutsenko, Ukraine's current prosecutor general, gave his own interview to Bloomberg News and said: "Hunter Biden did not violate any Ukrainian laws at least as of now, we do not see any wrongdoing."

Lutsenko told Bloomberg that the prosecutor general's office in 2014 — before Shokin took office — opened a corruption investigation against Mykola Zlochevsky, the owner of Burisma, and numerous others. He said the probe's focus was Serghi Kurchenko, who owned a number of gas companies, and a transaction that occurred in November 2013, months before Biden joined Burisma.

> ***Bloomberg News, May 16:*** *As part of the 5-year-old inquiry, the prosecutor general's office has been looking at whether Kurchenko's purchase of an oil storage terminal in southern Ukraine from Zlochevksy in November 2013 helped Kurchenko launder money. Lutsenko said the transaction under scrutiny came months before Hunter Biden joined the Burisma board.*
>
> *"Biden was definitely not involved," Lutsenko said. "We do not have any grounds to think that there was any wrongdoing starting from 2014."*

The investigation is still active, he said.

North Korea and Nuclear Tests

The president also spoke about North Korea and its nuclear weapons program. Trump met with North Korea dictator Kim Jong Un in June of last year, and the two leaders <u>agreed</u> to "promote the denuclearization of the Korean Peninsula."

During Kim's reign, North Korea has <u>conducted</u> numerous nuclear tests and missile launches — including four nuclear weapons tests and three test launches of intercontinental ballistic missiles, or ICBMs.

> ***Trump:*** *But, they haven't had any tests over the last two years — zero. There's a chart and it shows 24 tests, 22 tests, 18 tests. Then I come, and once I'm there for a little while you know, we went through a pretty rough rhetorical period. Once I'm there for a little while, no tests, no tests, no tests.*

It's true that North Korea has not conducted a nuclear test since Sept. 3, 2017, and it hasn't launched an ICBM since Nov. 29, 2017. (See details in the Arms Control Association <u>timeline</u>.) But North Korea has <u>conducted</u> short-range missile tests twice this month, and it continues to actively pursue a nuclear weapons program.

The U.S. intelligence community released a <u>threat assessment report</u> in January that said, "We continue to observe activity inconsistent with full denuclearization."

The report didn't detail what kind of activity. But a week earlier, the Center for Strategic and International Studies in Washington <u>issued a report</u> that said it found "approximately 20 undeclared missile operating bases," including one that serves as a missile headquarters.

A month later, three Stanford University researchers <u>issued a report</u> that said North Korea "continued to operate and, in some cases, expand the nuclear weapons complex infrastructure. It continued to operate its nuclear facilities to produce plutonium and highly enriched uranium that may allow it to increase the number of nuclear weapons in its arsenal from roughly 30 in 2017 to 35-37."

China and Trade

Another subject that the president addressed was the ongoing trade war with China.

The Trump administration last year <u>imposed</u> tariffs on $250 billion worth of Chinese goods, and China responded with tariffs on $110 billion of U.S. goods. The trade dispute escalated this month. First, the Trump administration on May 10 <u>raised</u> tariffs from 10 percent to 25 percent on about $200 billion worth of Chinese goods. China <u>responded</u> three days later when it announced that it would increase tariffs from 10 percent to 25 percent on roughly $60 billion worth of U.S. goods, beginning June 1.

The dispute has hurt U.S. agricultural exports in particular, and the administration responded by authorizing <u>up to $12 billion</u> in aid to U.S. farmers. Trump said he would increase financial assistance to $15 billion and explained how he arrived at that number.

> ***Trump:*** *I said to Sonny Perdue, Department of Agriculture — secretary of Agriculture – "Sonny, what's the most money that China has ever paid toward agriculture, toward buying food product?" He said $15 billion a number of years ago. I said "Is that the most?" He said "Yes." Some people will say close to (inaudible) but $15 billion was about the most. I said "Good. I'm going to take $15 billion out of the $100 billion, and I'm going to give that to our farmers."*

Trump told a <u>similar story</u> in a recent speech to the National Association of Realtors.

> ***Trump, May 17:*** *So I called Sonny Perdue, our great Secretary of Agriculture, and I said, "Sonny…" — (applause) — I said, "Sonny, what's the biggest amount they've ever spent in this country?" He said, "About $15 billion. People could say 18, 19. But basically $15 billion." And I said, "So let's take $15 billion, set it aside out of the 100 or 125 billion [in annual tariffs imposed on all imports]."*

We asked the White House and the Department of Agriculture about this conversation. Neither responded. The Office of the U.S. Trade Representative referred us to the White House.

But this much we know based on available data and emails from two federal agencies: $15 billion isn't "the biggest amount" that China has spent on U.S. agricultural exports.

In its annual reports on shifts in U.S. merchandise trade, the United States International Trade Commission reported that China purchased $27.2 billion in U.S. agricultural products in 2012 – the most in one year from 2010 to 2017.

The most recent USITC report covers 2013 to 2017, and a commission spokeswoman told us a new report covering 2018 would not be released until November. However, according to the Department of Agriculture, agricultural exports to China fell dramatically to $9.2 billion in 2018. That was "almost all due to retaliatory tariffs" imposed by China, Wallace E. Tyner, who teaches agricultural economics at Purdue University, told us in an email.

We also know that, as of the morning of May 20, the U.S. has paid $8.54 billion to farmers through three aid programs, a USDA spokesperson said.

The Market Facilitation Program — the largest of the three programs — can provide up to $10 billion to producers of corn, cotton, sorghum, soybean, wheat, dairy, hogs, almonds and sweet cherries, according to a December report by the Congressional Research Service on the trade aid programs. The top five commodities that received assistance through the program were soybeans, corn, wheat, cotton and sorghum, the USDA spokesperson told us.

We found that, from 2009 through 2018, the most that China imported of those five commodities in any one year totaled nearly $20 billion, according to Census Bureau export data. That occurred in 2012, when China's agricultural purchases included nearly $14.9 billion in soybeans,

$3.4 billion in raw cotton and $1.3 billion in corn, according to Census data.

As we said, we don't know what the president meant when he said that $15 billion was "the biggest amount they've ever spent in this country." We will update this item if the White House responds.

Honda and U.S. Investments

In talking about the U.S. economy, Trump boasted about companies coming to the United States — singling out one car company in particular.

> **Trump:** *Well, really very simply, we have companies coming in here, as you know, by the dozens and by the hundreds and big ones, car companies, Honda's coming in with $14.5 billion.*

We don't know how many companies have relocated to the U.S. or have left the U.S. But the president overestimates Honda's future investment in the U.S.

On its website, Honda said that its total capital investment in the U.S. (not just auto manufacturing) has been $21 billion over the last 60 years, including $5.6 billion in the last five years. We could not find any new automotive investments that would equal $14.5 billion, so we reached out to the Michigan-based Center for Automotive Research Group, which tracks new investments in the United States.

Kristin Dziczek, vice president of industry, labor and economics, told us that she, too, could not match the $14.5 billion figure cited by Trump, and "we try to keep very close tabs on these things." She said Honda has announced auto manufacturing investments totaling $1.7 billion over the last five years.

In February, Honda announced that it would close a manufacturing plant in Swindon, England, in 2121, when it stops production of its current

Civic model. Honda Chief Executive Officer Takahiro Hachigo told Automotive News that the next generation Civic will be manufactured in North America, but the company has yet to say where the plant or plants will be located.

Update, May 24: "We have not provided any further detail other than we are considering production of Civic for North America in North America," Honda corporate spokesman Chris Abbruzzese told us in an email. He provided us with a list of $712 million worth of vehicle manufacturing investments that Honda had made in the United States in 2017 and 2018.

"We do not disclose our future investment plans publicly," Abbruzzese said.

Honda currently has five vehicle manufacturing plants in the United States, including one in Indiana that builds the current Civic models. It also manufactures Civic models in Ontario, Canada.

Trump's Approval Rating

The president also boasted that he has "tremendous poll numbers now."

It's subjective, of course, to describe one's poll numbers as "tremendous." But Trump's average job approval rating — based on polling data assembled from dozens of polls by Real Clear Politics and FiveThirtyEight — is currently below 43 percent.

As of May 22, Trump's average job approval rating on Real Clear Politics was 42.5 percent, and FiveThirtyEight put it at 41.1 percent. By contrast, those who disapproved of Trump's job performance averaged 53.7 percent, according to Real Clear Politics, and 53.8 percent, according to FiveThirtyEight.

As for individual polls taken this month, Trump's job approval rating reached a peak of 51 percent in the Zogby Poll, which was conducted May 2 to May 9 and had a margin of error of plus or minus 3.4 percent. The low point was a Morning Consult poll, which showed the president at 37 percent. That poll was taken May 17 to 19, and had an error margin of plus or minus 2 percent.

Trump Repeats

As we often find, the president also repeated some false claims that we have previously debunked:

China Trade Deficit: The president said, "We have a trade deficit with China of $500 billion." That's false. As we have written before, the U.S. trade deficit with China in goods and services was a record $378.7 billion in 2018, according to the Bureau of Economic Analysis (see table 3). The U.S. had a $419.3 billion deficit with China in goods (table 6) and a $40.5 billion surplus in services (table 9).

Tariff Revenue: Trump said that, as a result of tariffs he has placed on Chinese goods, "we are going to be taking in possibly $100 billion, possibly more than that in tariffs. We never took in 10 cents from China." It's not true, as we have previously said, that the U.S. has never collected tariffs on Chinese goods. The amount of tariff revenue has increased, but the U.S. did collect billions of dollars each year since at least 2000. For example, the U.S. collected about $13.4 billion in 2016, according to the U.S. International Trade Commission database. As we also wrote, tariffs are taxes paid by U.S. importers in the form of customs duties, not by the Chinese government or its companies.

Liquefied Natural Gas Exporting. The president said, "I was in Louisiana opening up a $10 billion LNG plant that would've never been approved under another type of administration, never," and, "They've been trying for years to get it built, but we got approvals very quickly for the big LNG." That's false. As we wrote before, the plant in question, Sempra Energy's Cameron LNG plant, was approved in 2014 by the Obama administration, a fact Sempra Energy confirmed.

Chapter Five

FEATURED POSTS › THE WIRE

FactChecking Trump's Response to Mueller

By Eugene Kiely, Robert Farley and D'Angelo Gore

Posted on May 30, 2019

In an impromptu press conference and on Twitter, President Donald Trump responded to special counsel Robert Mueller's remarks about the Russia investigation with several false and questionable claims:

- Trump suggested that he could not be impeached because he hasn't been charged with a crime. "I can't imagine the courts allowing it," he added. But constitutional scholars tell us a statutory crime is not a necessary predicate to impeachment, and impeachment is not reviewable by the courts.
- Trump claimed that he could not be charged with obstruction of justice because he was not guilty of an underlying crime. But Mueller, in his report, and again in his public statement, explained that it is possible to be guilty of obstruction even if one has been cleared of the underlying crime that gave rise to an investigation.
- Trump said that, unlike him, President Bill Clinton was found "guilty, guilty, guilty, guilty, guilty" by a "special prosecutor." Kenneth Starr, the independent counsel who investigated Clinton, did tell Congress that there was evidence to impeach Clinton. But

that was an authority given to independent counsels — not special counsels, such as Mueller.
- Trump repeated his claim that Mueller was "totally conflicted" — a charge that even one of Trump's own advisers told him was "ridiculous."
- Trump claimed, "Russia did not help me get elected." The Mueller report, however, says the Russians carried out a social media campaign and targeted cyberattacks against Hillary Clinton and the Democratic party committees to damage Clinton and help Trump.

Mueller spoke publicly on May 29 for the first time about the special counsel's investigation. The former FBI director reiterated the key findings of his report, which was issued on April 18, and elaborated a bit on why he did not make a determination on whether Trump had obstructed the federal investigation.

The Mueller report said investigators "found multiple acts by the President that were capable of exerting undue influence over law enforcement investigations, including the Russian-interference and obstruction investigations." However, the report said it could not make a "traditional prosecutorial judgment," because the department's Office of Legal Counsel had issued an opinion that states an "indictment or criminal prosecution of a sitting President" would be unconstitutional.

"Because we determined not to make a traditional prosecutorial judgment, we did not draw ultimate conclusions about the President's conduct," the report said. "The evidence we obtained about the President's actions and intent presents difficult issues that would need to be resolved if we were making a traditional prosecutorial judgment. At the same time, if we had confidence after a thorough investigation of the facts that the President clearly did not commit obstruction of justice, we would so state. Based on the facts and the applicable legal standards, we are unable to reach that judgment. Accordingly, while this report does not conclude that the President committed a crime, it also does not exonerate him."

In his May 29 remarks, Mueller reiterated that his report did not clear the president on the issue of obstruction. "[A]s set forth in the report after that investigation, if we had had confidence that the president clearly did not commit a crime, we would have said so," Mueller said.

Trump responded to questions about Mueller's remarks shortly before leaving the White House for Colorado to deliver a commencement address at the Air Force Academy.

High Crimes and Misdemeanors

Trump was asked about the possibility of the Democratic-controlled House seeking to impeach him based on Mueller's report, which detailed 11 "key events" of possible obstruction of justice. Trump suggested that he could not be impeached because he hasn't been charged with a crime and the courts may not allow it.

> ***Reporter, May 30:*** *Do you think they're going to impeach you? Do you think they're –.*
>
> ***Trump:*** *I don't see how. They can, because they're possibly allowed, although I can't imagine the courts allowing it. I've never got into it. I never thought that would even be possible to be using that word. To me, it's a dirty word, the word impeach. It's a dirty, filthy, disgusting word and it had nothing to do with me.*
>
> *So, I don't think so, because there was no crime. You know it's high crimes and, not with or or, it's high crimes and misdemeanors. There was no high crime and there was no misdemeanor, so how do you impeach based on that?*

Trump was referring to Article 2, Section 4 of the U.S. Constitution, which states in full: "The President, Vice President and all civil Officers of the United States, shall be removed from Office on Impeachment for, and Conviction of, Treason, Bribery, or other high Crimes and Misdemeanors."

Constitutional scholars told us that Trump is wrong to suggest that a statutory crime is required for the House to bring impeachment charges and it is very unlikely that the courts would get involved in impeachment proceedings.

"The President is wrong on both counts," Neil Kinkopf, a professor of law at Georgia State University's College of Law.

First it is worth nothing that Mueller said "charging the president with a crime was ... not an option we could consider," because of the OLC opinion — which states that an "indictment or criminal prosecution of a sitting President" would be unconstitutional."

Regardless, Kinkopf and others we consulted with said that the framers of the Constitution meant impeachment to serve as a political remedy to remove federal officials from office for subverting the system of government — not necessarily for violating criminal statutes.

"The phrase 'treason, bribery or other high crimes and misdemeanors' does not refer to statutorily codified crimes," Kinkopf said. "Rather, the catchall 'other high crimes and misdemeanors' is meant to be open-ended and to refer to all misconduct that is harmful to the nation in a manner similar to 'treason and bribery' even if it does not meet the technical requirements of the current version of the federal criminal code."

Philip Bobbitt, a law professor at the University of Texas, referred us to Alexander Hamilton's Federalist No. 65, which states that the subjects of impeachments "are of a nature which may with peculiar propriety be denominated POLITICAL, as they relate chiefly to injuries done immediately to the society itself." (The Federalists Papers were published in New York to urge the state to ratify the proposed Constitution.)

"The president seems to be confusing 'High Crimes' which are political offenses, see Federalist #65, with ordinary crimes and perhaps also confusing the term 'misdemeanor' with the common understanding of this as a minor offense," Bobbitt said.

After President Richard Nixon resigned in the wake of Watergate, the Senate Judiciary Committee in 1974 published a report on the grounds for presidential impeachment that said the phrase "high Crimes and Misdemeanors ... has a special historical meaning different from the ordinary meaning of the terms 'crimes' and 'misdemeanors.'"

"'High Misdemeanors' referred to a category of offenses that subverted the system of government," the committee report said. "Since the fourteenth century the phrase 'high Crimes and Misdemeanors' had been used in English impeachment cases to charge officials with a wide range of criminal and non-criminal offenses against the institutions and fundamental principles of English government."

As for Trump's claim that the courts would bar Congress from impeaching him, Princeton University political professor Keith E. Whittington called it "very unlikely."

"The precise question of whether a court could review a congressional judgment that a particular offense is within the scope of the constitutional impeachment power has never been tested," Whittington told us. "The U.S. Supreme Court has held that other aspects of the impeachment power are political questions entrusted to the sole discretion of Congress to resolve, and it seems very unlikely that the Court would intervene in the context of a presidential impeachment."

Whittington referred us to an essay he wrote after Trump made a similar claim last month. In his essay, Whittington referred to a Supreme Court ruling involving the impeachment and conviction of Federal District Judge Walter Nixon. The U.S. Supreme Court rejected his appeal.

"The parties do not offer evidence of a single word in the history of the Constitutional Convention or in contemporary commentary that even alludes to the possibility of judicial review in the context of the impeachment powers," the court said in its opinion.

Obstruction Without Conspiracy?

Trump also claimed that he could not be guilty of obstruction of justice because he was not guilty of an underlying crime — specifically the special counsel's office found that Trump did not conspire with Russian efforts to influence the 2016 election.

But Mueller, in his report, and again in his public statement on May 29, explained that it is possible to be guilty of obstruction even if one has been cleared of the underlying crime that gave rise to an investigation.

According to Trump, Mueller "said, essentially, 'You're innocent.' I'm innocent of all charges. And, you know, the thing that nobody brings up: There was no crime. They're saying 'he's obstructing something' and there was no crime. And nobody brings it up."

Trump made similar arguments shortly before his press conference, when he tweeted: "It was a crime that didn't exist. So now the Dems and their partner, the Fake News Media …. say he fought back against this phony crime that didn't exist, this horrendous false accusation, and he shouldn't fight back, he should just sit back and take it. Could this be Obstruction? No, Mueller didn't find Obstruction either."

In his comments, Mueller said his investigation concluded there was "insufficient evidence to charge a broader conspiracy" between the Russians who sought to influence the election and the Trump campaign. But he did not clear Trump on obstruction of justice.

"If we had had confidence that the president clearly did not commit a crime, we would have said so," Mueller said in his remarks. "We did not, however, make a determination as to whether the president did commit a crime."

Mueller also explained the importance of an obstruction investigation.

"The matters we investigated were of paramount importance," he said. "It was critical for us to obtain full and accurate information from every person we questioned. When a subject of an investigation obstructs that investigation or lies to investigators, it strikes at the core of their government's effort to find the truth and hold wrongdoers accountable."

In the written special counsel report, Mueller explained that proof of an underlying crime is "not an element of an obstruction offense."

Mueller cited the case <u>United States vs. Greer</u>, in which a federal circuit judge concluded, "obstruction of a criminal *investigation* is punishable even if the prosecution is ultimately unsuccessful or even if the investigation ultimately reveals no underlying crime."

So why would someone obstruct an investigation if they had done nothing illegal? And if they did, why would investigators care?

"Obstruction of justice can be motivated by a desire to protect non-criminal personal interests, to protect against investigations where underlying criminal liability falls into a gray area, or to avoid personal embarrassment," the Mueller report states. "The injury to the integrity of the justice system is the same regardless of whether a person committed an underlying wrong."

"In this investigation," the report states, "the evidence does not establish that the President was involved in an underlying crime related to Russian election interference. But the evidence does point to a range of other possible personal motives animating the President's conduct. These include concerns that continued investigation would call into question the legitimacy of his election and potential uncertainty about whether certain events — such as advance notice of WikiLeaks's release of hacked information or the June 9, 2016 meeting between senior campaign officials and Russians — could be seen as criminal activity by the President, his campaign, or his family."

Although Attorney General William Barr <u>concluded</u> after reading Mueller's report that "the evidence developed during the Special Counsel's investigation is not sufficient to establish that the President committed an obstruction-of-justice offense," it is something that Congress could consider in impeachment hearings. In his remarks May 29, Mueller said that one reason for laying out the evidence for obstruction is that the Constitution provides "a process other than the criminal justice system to formally accuse a sitting president of wrongdoing."

Bill Clinton Found 'Guilty'?

At one point, Trump made an apples-to-oranges comparison of his situation to that of former President Bill Clinton.

> ***Trump, May 30:*** *There were no charges. None. If you look at — if you look at Bill Clinton, that very nice gentleman who's been so much on my side, as you know, his special prosecutor — it was guilty, guilty, guilty, guilty, guilty. So many guiltys. With me, there was no guilty.*

Trump is referring to independent counsel Kenneth Starr, who led a four-year investigation of Clinton, including the president's sexual affair with White House intern Monica Lewinsky. Starr did not issue a criminal indictment of Clinton; in the report on his investigation, Starr said there was "substantial and credible information supporting … eleven possible grounds for impeachment" by Congress, including several examples of perjury and obstruction of justice.

Clinton was impeached by the House of Representatives, but he was acquitted by the Senate — meaning he was ultimately not found "guilty."

The impeachment recommendation to Congress, however, was an authority specifically granted to independent counsels, such as Starr, under the Ethics in Government Act of 1978. The independent counsel statute of that law expired in June 1999.

Mueller was appointed as "special counsel" in 2017. In that role, he did not have the same authority, Kimberly Wehle, a University of Baltimore law professor, told us in an email.

"Starr was under a separate statute, which expired," she said. "Mueller was under an internal DOJ regulation. Totally different legal regimes. Starr was required to report to Congress. Mueller was required to report to Barr."

Kinkopf told us the "regs setting up the position of Special Counsel and defining the report that the Special Counsel would produce were specifically in response to the perceived abuses of the Starr Report — particularly its partisan tone and gratuitous forays into salacious detail."

The Justice Department regulation covering special counsels says they have "the authority to investigate and prosecute federal crimes committed in the course of, and with intent to interfere with, the Special Counsel's investigation, such as perjury, obstruction of justice, destruction of evidence, and intimidation of witnesses; and to conduct appeals arising out of the matter being investigated and/or prosecuted."

But, on the matter of obstruction, Mueller said in his report that he decided not to make "a traditional prosecutorial judgment" about Trump, in part, because of a DOJ legal opinion that says "the indictment or criminal prosecution of a sitting President would impermissibly undermine the capacity of the executive branch to perform its constitutionally assigned functions" in violation of "the constitutional separation of powers."

Still, in considering whether the president may have committed obstruction of justice, Mueller himself examined 11 "key events," which we have written about before.

"Our investigation found multiple acts by the President that were capable of exerting undue influence over law enforcement investigations, including the Russian-interference and obstruction investigations," Mueller wrote.

"The incidents were often carried out through one-on-one meetings in which the President sought to use his official power outside of usual channels. These actions ranged from efforts to remove the Special Counsel and to reverse the effect of the Attorney General's recusal; to the attempted use of official power to limit the scope of the investigation; to direct and indirect contacts with witnesses with the potential to influence their testimony."

In his public remarks on May 29, Mueller said that one reason for laying out the evidence for obstruction is that the Constitution provides "a process other than the criminal justice system to formally accuse a sitting president of wrongdoing."

That "tiptoes pretty close to an impeachment referral and is at the very least an invitation to further Congressional investigation," Bobbitt told us. "I think that is as far as the Special Counsel felt he could go; he certainly was not authorized by the governing regs to recommend an impeachment."

Mueller's Alleged Conflicts

Trump also repeated some false and misleading claims about Mueller and the investigation, including his insistence that the special counsel was "totally conflicted" — a charge that even one of Trump's own advisers warned him was "ridiculous."

Trump has long claimed that Mueller should not have been appointed special counsel due to alleged conflicts of interest — claims we most recently dealt with in our April 19 story, "Debunking Mueller's 'Conflicts.'" Trump's claim hinges on two main allegations: that Mueller wanted the job of FBI director but the president turned him down; and that Mueller had a "business dispute" over membership fees when Mueller left a country club owned by Trump. The special counsel report, however, undermines both of those claims.

Here's how the president put it on May 30:

> ***Trump, May 30***: *I think he's totally conflicted. Because, as you know, he wanted to be the FBI Director, and I said no. As you know, I had a business dispute with him. After he left the FBI, we had a business dispute. Not a nice one. He wasn't happy with what I did, and I don't blame him. But I had to do it because that was the right thing to do. But I had a business dispute.*
>
> *And he loves Comey. You look at the relationship with those two. So whether it's love or deep like, but he was conflicted.*
>
> *Look, Robert Mueller should've never been chosen because he wanted the FBI job and he didn't get it. And the next day, he was picked as Special Counsel. So you tell somebody, "I'm sorry, you can't have the job." And then, after you say that, he's going to make a ruling on you? It doesn't work that way. Plus, we had a business dispute. Plus, his relationship with Comey was extraordinary.*

Hours after his press conference, Trump also tweeted that Mueller "came to the Oval Office (along with other potential candidates) seeking to be named the Director of the FBI … I told him NO. The next day he was named Special Counsel — A total Conflict of Interest NICE!"

Chapter Six

FactChecking Trump's Response to Mueller

By Eugene Kiely, Robert Farley and D'Angelo Gore

Posted on May 30, 2019

Donald J. Trump

✓@realDonaldTrump

"Robert Mueller came to the Oval Office (along with other potential candidates) seeking to be named the Director of the FBI. He had already been in that position for 12 years, I told him NO. The next day he was named Special Counsel - A total Conflict of Interest. NICE!"

That doesn't jibe with the testimony of former White House Chief Strategist Steve Bannon who told investigators that it was the White House that invited Mueller to the Oval Office to "offer a perspective on the institution of the FBI." According to the special counsel report, "Bannon said that, although the White House thought about beseeching Mueller to become Director again, he did not come in looking for the job."

As for the alleged dispute over membership fees at the Trump National Golf Club in Sterling, Virginia, the special counsel report also addresses that. According to the report, Mueller informed the club in a letter on Oct. 12, 2011, that he would no longer be a member. The letter "noted that 'we live in the District and find that we are unable to make full use of the Club' and that inquired 'whether we would be entitled to a refund of a portion of our initial membership fee,' which was paid in 1994," the report said.

"About two weeks later, the controller of the club responded that the Muellers' resignation would be effective October 31, 2011, and that they would be 'placed on a waitlist to be refunded on a first resigned/first refunded basis' in accordance with the club's legal documents," the report said. "The Muellers have not had further contact with the club."

In July 2017, a spokesman for the special counsel said, "Mr. Mueller left the club in October 2011 without dispute."

As for Trump's claim that Mueller was conflicted because he has an "extraordinary" relationship with fired FBI Director James Comey — "He loves Comey," Trump said — we note that Comey testified before a congressional committee in December that while he admires Mueller, "We're not friends in any social sense." Added Comey, "I don't know his phone number, I've never been to his house, I don't know his children's names."

The special counsel report notes that when Trump initially laid out his claims about Mueller's alleged conflicts, several advisers recommended the president drop it.

According to the report, the president's advisers — including then-White House Chief of Staff Reince Priebus, then-White House counsel Don McGahn and Bannon — "pushed back on his assertion of conflicts, telling the President they did not count as true conflicts." Bannon told investigators that he "recalled telling the President that the purported conflicts were 'ridiculous' and that none of them was real or could come close to justifying precluding Mueller from serving as Special Counsel."

Russian Interference Helped Trump

Shortly before his press conference, Trump tweeted, "I had nothing to do with Russia helping me to get elected." It seemed to be the first time he acknowledged that Russian interference helped him in 2016. But when asked about his tweet, Trump took it back.

> **Reporter, May 30:** Do you believe that Russia helped you get elected?
>
> **Trump:** No, Russia did not help me get elected. You know who got me elected? You know who got me elected? I got me elected. Russia didn't help me at all. Russia, if anything, I think, helped the other side.

In fact, Russia did help Trump's campaign. Russian President Vladimir Putin denied that Russia interfered in the election, but admitted that he wanted Trump to win.

The Mueller report details how the Russians "carried out a social media campaign that favored presidential candidate Donald J. Trump and disparaged presidential candidate Hillary Clinton," and "conducted computer-intrusion operations against entities, employees, and volunteers working on the Clinton Campaign and then released stolen documents" to damage her presidential campaign.

In his remarks, Mueller said the public release of the stolen documents "were designed and timed to interfere with our election and to damage a presidential candidate," referring to Clinton.

Mueller's report also lays out how eager the Trump campaign was to use the stolen material to its political advantage, even after the Department of Homeland Security and the Office of the Director of National Intelligence issued a joint public statement on Oct. 7, 2016, that the Russian Government was behind the hacking.

Although investigators "did not establish" the Trump campaign "conspired or coordinated" with Russia's "election interference activities," Mueller's report said "the [Trump] Campaign expected it would benefit electorally from information stolen and released through Russian efforts." (See our story "Kushner Distorts Scope of Russia Interference" for more about Russian's efforts to help Trump.)

THE WIRE Kushner Distorts Scope of Russia Interference

By *Eugene Kiely* and *Lori Robertson*

Posted on April 24, 2019

Special counsel Robert Mueller's report concluded that "[t]he Russian government interfered in the 2016 presidential election in sweeping and systematic fashion" — contrary to Jared Kushner's claim that Russia's effort amounted to little more than "a couple Facebook ads."

The report details how the Russians "carried out a social media campaign that favored presidential candidate Donald J. Trump and disparaged presidential candidate Hillary Clinton," and "conducted computer-intrusion operations against entities, employees, and volunteers working on the Clinton Campaign and then released stolen documents" to damage the Democratic presidential nominee's campaign.

It also lays out how eager the Trump campaign was to use the stolen material to its political advantage, even after the Department of Homeland Security and the Office of the Director of National Intelligence issued a joint public statement on Oct. 7, 2016, "that the Russian Government directed the recent compromises of e-mails from US persons and institutions, including from US political organizations."

Although investigators "did not establish" the Trump campaign "conspired or coordinated" with Russia's "election interference activities," Mueller's report said "the [Trump] Campaign expected it would benefit electorally from information stolen and released through Russian efforts."

Kushner, the president's son-in-law and adviser, made his comments during an interview at the Time100 Summit (starting at the 3:57 mark). He said the "investigations and all of the speculation" over the past two years "has had a much harsher impact on our democracy than a couple Facebook ads."

> ***Kushner, April 23***: *And quite frankly, the whole thing is just a big distraction for the country. You look at what Russia did, you know, buying some Facebook ads to try to sow dissent and do it, it's a terrible thing. But I think the investigations and all of the speculation that's happened for the last two years has had a much harsher impact on our democracy than a couple Facebook ads. I think they said [Russians] spent about $160,000. I spent $160,000 on Facebook every three hours during the campaign. Now if you look at the magnitude of what they did and what they accomplished, I think the ensuing investigations have been way more harmful to our country.*

Kushner downplays the extensive social media influence campaign the Russians waged to help elect his father-in-law and ignores entirely the Russian cyberattack on Clinton and her supporters that was designed to undermine Clinton's campaign.

Here we recap what the Mueller report said about Russia's election interference efforts.

'Russian Hacking Operations'

The FBI's counterintelligence investigation of Russia began in late July 2016 — a few days after WikiLeaks began releasing emails that had been stolen from the Democratic National Committee. The investigation was sparked by a tip it received from a foreign government official who learned from George Papadopoulos, a Trump foreign policy adviser, "that the Trump Campaign had received indications from the Russian government that it could assist the Campaign through the anonymous release of information that would be damaging to Hillary Clinton," according to the Mueller report.

The federal investigation uncovered a sophisticated hacking operation by two units of the Main Intelligence Directorate, or GRU, which is responsible for intelligence collection for the Russian military. One unit was responsible for developing a "specialized" malware, while the other unit "conducted large-scale spearphishing campaigns," according to the Mueller report.

The targets, of course, were the DNC, the Democratic Congressional Campaign Committee and Clinton's presidential campaign committee.

The scope of the hacking operation: Beginning in March 2016, the GRU "hacked the computers and email accounts of organizations, employees, and volunteers supporting the Clinton Campaign, including the email account of campaign chairman John Podesta," the report said. The GRU gained access to 29 DCCC computers and more than 30 computers on the DNC network, including the DNC email server and shared file server.

"In total, the GRU stole hundreds of thousands of documents from the compromised email accounts and networks," the report says.

The groups behind the release of the stolen documents: The GRU publicly released emails and documents stolen from the Democrats "through two fictitious online personas that it created — DCLeaks and Guccifer 2.0 — and later through the organization WikiLeaks," the report said.

The *Washington Post* reported on June 14, 2016, that hackers had gained access to DNC servers — the first public disclosure of a cyberattack on a U.S. political committee.

A day later, Guccifer 2.0 — a "[f]ictitious online persona operated by the GRU" — took credit in a blog post for hacking the DNC computers and released a few documents, including the Democratic Party's 200-page opposition research report on Donald Trump. Guccifer falsely attributed the DNC hack "to a lone Romanian hacker."

"The main part of the papers, thousands of files and mails, I gave to Wikileaks. They will publish them soon," Guccifer 2.0 says in its blog post.

Julian Assange, the founder of WikiLeaks, opposed Clinton's candidacy. The Mueller report said that Assange, in November 2015, "wrote to other members and associates of WikiLeaks that '[w]e believe it would be much better for GOP to win … Dems+Media+liberals woudl [sic] then form a block to reign in their worst qualities. . . . With Hillary in charge, GOP will be pushing for her worst qualities., dems+media+neoliberals will be mute . … She's a bright, well connected, sadisitic sociopath.'"

The timing of the public release of the stolen documents: According to the Mueller report, "The release of the documents was designed and timed to interfere with the 2016 U.S. presidential election and undermine the Clinton Campaign."

About five weeks after Guccifer 2.0 took credit for hacking DNC servers, WikiLeaks released more than 20,000 stolen DNC emails and other documents. (It would eventually release more than 44,000 DNC emails and 17,000 attachments, WikiLeaks says on its website.) The first drop came on July 22, 2016 — three days before the Democratic National Convention in Philadelphia.

The timing proved damaging to party unity, and Clinton's attempts to use the convention to woo supporters of her top rival, Sen. Bernie Sanders. The released documents embarrassedparty officials who were seen as working behind the scenes at the DNC to undermine Sanders' campaign, and forced the DNC chairwoman, Debbie Wasserman-Schultz, to resignon the eve of the convention.

The timing was no coincidence.

The Mueller report said WikiLeaks sent a direct message on Twitter to Guccifer 2.0 on July 6, 2016, seeking information that would disrupt the DNC convention and Clinton's attempts at unity. "[I]f you have anything hillary related we want it in the next tweo [sic] days prefab le [sic] because the DNC is approaching and she will solidify bernie supporters behind her after," WikiLeaks wrote to Guccifer 2.0.

"[W]e think trump has only a 25% chance of winning against hillary … so conflict between bernie and hillary is interesting," WikiLeaks wrote.

On Oct. 7, 2016, WikiLeaks began releasing emails "the first set of emails stolen by the GRU from the account of Clinton Campaign chairman John Podesta." Those emails were released "less than an hour" after the *Washington Post* published a 2005 video that caught Trump on a hot mic during a filming of "Access Hollywood" bragging about grabbing and kissing women because "when you're a star, they let you do it."

Trump campaign's use of stolen documents: In downplaying Russia's interference in the election, Kushner ignored the campaign's interest in the stolen documents and Trump's extensive use of them to his advantage.

"The Trump Campaign showed interest in WikiLeaks's releases of hacked materials throughout the summer and fall of 2016," the Mueller report said.

After DNC emails were released in July, Trump tweeted, "The Wikileaks e-mail release today was so bad to Sanders that it will make it impossible for him to support her, unless he is a fraud!" At the same time, Paul Manafort, Trump's campaign manager, told Gates that he "wanted to be kept apprised of any developments with WikiLeaks," according to the Mueller report.

"According to [Deputy Campaign Chairman Rick] Gates, by the late summer of 2016, the Trump Campaign was planning a press strategy, a communications campaign, and messaging based on the possible release of Clinton emails by WikiLeaks," the report said.

The report also said that Trump and "other Campaign advisors privately sought information [redacted] about any further planned WikiLeaks releases."

Donald Trump Jr., exchanged direct messages on Twitter with WikiLeaks, expressing interest in any new document dumps. On Oct. 3, 2016, Trump Jr. asked WikiLeaks: "What's behind this Wednesday leak I keep reading about?" WikiLeaks did not respond, at least not on Twitter. Four days later, WikiLeaks released Podesta's emails.

After the first set of Podesta's emails was released, Trump took to Twitter on numerous occasions to draw attention to the stolen documents and away from the "Access Hollywood "video. Here are some of his tweets, which also came days after the U.S. intelligence community identified Russia as the source of the hacked emails:

Oct. 11, 2016: "I hope people are looking at the disgraceful behavior of Hillary Clinton as exposed by WikiLeaks. She is unfit to run."

Oct. 12, 2016: "Very little pick-up by the dishonest media of incredible information provided by WikiLeaks. So dishonest! Rigged system!"

Oct. 16, 2016: "We've all wondered how Hillary avoided prosecution for her email scheme. Wikileaks may have found the answer. Obama!"

In the closing weeks of the campaign, WikiLeaks became a big part of Trump's closing argument against Clinton.

On Oct. 21, 2016, Manafort — who had left the campaign at this point — "sent Kushner an email and attached a strategy memorandum proposing that the Campaign make the case against Clinton 'as the failed and corrupt champion of the establishment' and that 'Wikileaks provides the Trump campaign the ability to make the case in a very credible way — by using the words of Clinton, its campaign officials and DNC members,'" according to the Mueller report.

Trump often read from the stolen emails and other documents at his campaign rallies.

In many cases, Trump distorted the facts to fit his campaign message that Clinton supports "open borders," would harm Medicare and Social Security, was soft on terrorism, and was too cozy with big banks. (Read our item "Trump Twists Facts on WikiLeaks" for more information on how Trump distorted the facts on those and other topics.)

"In sum, the investigation established that the GRU hacked into email accounts of persons affiliated with the Clinton Campaign, as well as the computers of the

DNC and DCCC. The GRU then exfiltrated data related to the 2016 election from these accounts and computers, and disseminated that data through fictitious online personas (DCLeaks and Guccifer 2.0) and later through WikiLeaks," the Mueller report said. "The investigation also established that the Trump Campaign displayed interest in the WikiLeaks releases."

Russian 'Active Measures' Social Media Campaign

Russia's Internet Research Agency, an online propaganda operation, began social media operations in the United States as early as 2014, creating social media accounts using fictitious personas.

In the 2016 campaign, "Some IRA employees, posing as U.S. persons and without revealing their Russian association, communicated electronically with individuals associated with the Trump Campaign and with other political activists to seek to coordinate political activities, including the staging of political rallies," the report said. "By the end of the 2016 U.S. election, the IRA had the ability to reach millions of U.S. persons through their social media accounts."

The figures cited on the reach and amount of these social media accounts are significantly greater than "a couple Facebook ads," as Kushner said.

> **Mueller report:** *Multiple IRA-controlled Facebook groups and Instagram accounts had hundreds of thousands of U.S. participants. IRA-controlled Twitter accounts separately had tens of thousands of followers, including multiple U.S. political figures who retweeted IRA-created content. In November 2017, a Facebook representative testified that Facebook had identified 470 IRA-controlled Facebook accounts that collectively made 80,000 posts between January 2015 and August 2017. Facebook estimated the IRA reached as many as 126 million persons through its Facebook accounts. In January 2018, Twitter announced that it had identified 3,814 IRA-controlled Twitter accounts and notified approximately 1.4 million people Twitter believed may have been in contact with an IRA-controlled account.*

Much of the material in the report on the structure of the IRA and its social media operations is redacted, due to "harm to ongoing matter." In February 2018, the special counsel <u>indicted</u> 13 Russian nationals and three Russian entities, including the IRA. The group was funded by Yevgeniy Viktorovich Prigozhin, who was sanctioned by the U.S. in December 2016 and has reported ties to Russian President Vladimir Putin, and companies he controlled.

According to the indictment, the IRA's monthly budget was more than $1.25 million (U.S. dollars) by September 2016.

The U.S. social media operation was known as the "Translator" internally at the IRA, the Mueller report said. It included the creation of social media pages falsely claiming to be associated with U.S. political groups or mimicking them. For instance, the IRA Twitter account @TEN_ GOP suggested it was affiliated with the Tennessee Republican Party. "More commonly," the Mueller report said, "the IRA created accounts in the names of fictitious U.S. organizations and grassroots groups and used these accounts to pose as anti-immigration groups, Tea Party activists, Black Lives Matter protesters, and other U.S. social and political activists."

The operation was aimed at supporting Trump's candidacy and opposing Clinton. One of the directions to IRA operators included: "Main idea: Use any opportunity to criticize Hillary [Clinton] and the rest (except Sanders and Trump – we support them)."

As for Facebook ads, the IRA bought more than 3,500 of them, not just "a couple," spending about $100,000, the special counsel's report said, attributing those figures to Facebook.

The special counsel said the IRA bought its first known ad backing Trump's campaign on April 19, 2016 — an ad for an Instagram account called "Tea Party News" encouraging people to help "'make a patriotic team of young Trump supporters' by uploading photos with the hashtag '#KIDS4TRUMP.'" The IRA bought dozens of ads supporting the Trump campaign in the months that followed, "predominantly through the Facebook groups 'Being Patriotic,' 'Stop All Invaders,' and 'Secured

Borders.'" Other bogus Facebook groups created by the IRA included: "Black Matters," "LGBT United" and "United Muslims of America." These accounts "attracted hundreds of thousands of followers."

On Twitter, the IRA created fake accounts and also automated both accounts to spread its content. One IRA account — @march_for_trump — promoted rallies in support of the campaign. The IRA would organize rallies by direct messaging followers, asking them to attend, and finding a real U.S. person to agree to serve as the coordinator of the event. The special counsel's office identified "dozens" of such rallies, the first of which was a "confederate rally" in November 2015. Some rallies attracted just a few people, but others attracted hundreds. The Trump campaign actually posted on its Facebook page about an IRA-organized rally in Miami in August 2016.

One poster for IRA-organized rallies in Pittsburgh and Philadelphia used an image of a now-deceased West Virginia coal miner with the words, "Miners For Trump, Bring Back Our Jobs."

The bogus social media accounts were realistic enough to fool some U.S. media outlets, which quoted tweets they thought were from real U.S. people, and well-known figures who retweeted or responded to these accounts, including former Ambassador Michael McFaul, Fox News' Sean Hannity, Trump informal adviser Roger Stone and Michael Flynn Jr., son of the campaign's foreign policy adviser and later national security adviser in the administration.

The IRA also had interactions with the Trump campaign. On "multiple occasions, members and surrogates of the Trump Campaign promoted– typically by linking, retweeting, or similar methods of reposting–pro-Trump or anti-Clinton content published by the IRA through IRA-controlled social media accounts," the report said. For instance, posts from that @TEN_GOP Twitter account were cited or retweeted by Donald J. Trump Jr., Eric Trump, Kellyanne Conway, Brad Parscale and Michael T. Flynn.

Also, there were "a few instances" in which IRA employees asked members of the campaign for help with rallies the IRA had organized. The Mueller report concluded: "While certain campaign volunteers agreed to provide the requested support (for example, agreeing to set aside a number of signs), the investigation has not identified evidence that any Trump Campaign official understood the requests were coming from foreign nationals."

Kushner equates the Russian interference effort to "a couple Facebook ads" and $160,000. But as the Mueller report makes clear, it was a sophisticated, years long hacking and social media effort to influence an election.

FACTCHECK.ORG *A Project of The Annenberg Public Policy Center*

Kushner Distorts Scope of Russia Interference

By *Eugene Kiely* and *Lori Robertson*

Posted on April 24, 2019

Special counsel Robert Mueller's report concluded that "[t]he Russian government interfered in the 2016 presidential election in sweeping and systematic fashion" — contrary to Jared Kushner's claim that Russia's effort amounted to little more than "a couple Facebook ads."

The report details how the Russians "carried out a social media campaign that favored presidential candidate Donald J. Trump and disparaged presidential candidate Hillary Clinton," and "conducted computer-intrusion operations against entities, employees, and volunteers working on the Clinton Campaign and then released stolen documents" to damage the Democratic presidential nominee's campaign.

It also lays out how eager the Trump campaign was to use the stolen material to its political advantage, even after the Department of Homeland Security and the Office of the Director of National Intelligence issued a joint public statement on Oct. 7, 2016, "that the Russian Government directed the recent compromises of e-mails from US persons and institutions, including from US political organizations."

Although investigators "did not establish" the Trump campaign "conspired or coordinated" with Russia's "election interference activities," Mueller's report said "the [Trump] Campaign expected it would benefit electorally from information stolen and released through Russian efforts."

Kushner, the president's son-in-law and adviser, made his comments during an interview at the Time100 Summit (starting at the 3:57 mark). He said the "investigations and all of the speculation" over the past two years "has had a much harsher impact on our democracy than a couple Facebook ads."

> ***Kushner, April 23***: *And quite frankly, the whole thing is just a big distraction for the country. You look at what Russia did, you know, buying some Facebook ads to try to sow dissent and do it, it's a terrible thing. But I think the investigations and all of the speculation that's happened for the last two years has had a much harsher impact on our democracy than a couple Facebook ads. I think they said [Russians] spent about $160,000. I spent $160,000 on Facebook every three hours during the campaign. Now if you look at the magnitude of what they did and what they accomplished, I think the ensuing investigations have been way more harmful to our country.*

Kushner downplays the extensive social media influence campaign the Russians waged to help elect his father-in-law and ignores entirely the Russian cyberattack on Clinton and her supporters that was designed to undermine Clinton's campaign.

Here we recap what the Mueller report said about Russia's election interference efforts.

'Russian Hacking Operations'

The FBI's counterintelligence investigation of Russia began in late July 2016 — a few days after WikiLeaks began releasing emails that had been stolen from the Democratic National Committee. The investigation was sparked by a tip it received from a foreign government official who learned from George Papadopoulos, a Trump foreign policy adviser, "that the Trump Campaign had received indications from the Russian government that it could assist the Campaign through the anonymous release of information that would be damaging to Hillary Clinton," according to the Mueller report.

The federal investigation uncovered a sophisticated hacking operation by two units of the Main Intelligence Directorate, or GRU, which is responsible for intelligence collection for the Russian military. One unit was responsible for developing a "specialized" malware, while the other unit "conducted large-scale spearphishing campaigns," according to the Mueller report.

The targets, of course, were the DNC, the Democratic Congressional Campaign Committee and Clinton's presidential campaign committee.

The scope of the hacking operation: Beginning in March 2016, the GRU "hacked the computers and email accounts of organizations, employees, and volunteers supporting the Clinton Campaign, including the email account of campaign chairman John Podesta," the report said. The GRU gained access to 29 DCCC computers and more than 30 computers on the DNC network, including the DNC email server and shared file server.

"In total, the GRU stole hundreds of thousands of documents from the compromised email accounts and networks," the report says.

The groups behind the release of the stolen documents: The GRU publicly released emails and documents stolen from the Democrats "through two fictitious online personas that it created — DCLeaks and Guccifer 2.0 — and later through the organization WikiLeaks," the report said.

The *Washington Post* reported on June 14, 2016, that hackers had gained access to DNC servers — the first public disclosure of a cyberattack on a U.S. political committee.

A day later, Guccifer 2.0 — a "[f]ictitious online persona operated by the GRU" — took credit in a blog post for hacking the DNC computers and released a few documents, including the Democratic Party's 200-page opposition research report on Donald Trump. Guccifer falsely attributed the DNC hack "to a lone Romanian hacker."

"The main part of the papers, thousands of files and mails, I gave to Wikileaks. They will publish them soon," Guccifer 2.0 says in its blog post.

Julian Assange, the founder of WikiLeaks, opposed Clinton's candidacy. The Mueller report said that Assange, in November 2015, "wrote to other members and associates of WikiLeaks that '[w]e believe it would be much better for GOP to win … Dems+Media+liberals woudl [sic] then form a block to reign in their worst qualities. . . . With Hillary in charge, GOP will be pushing for her worst qualities., dems+media+neoliberals will be mute . … She's a bright, well connected, sadisitic sociopath.'"

The timing of the public release of the stolen documents: According to the Mueller report, "The release of the documents was designed and timed to interfere with the 2016 U.S. presidential election and undermine the Clinton Campaign."

About five weeks after Guccifer 2.0 took credit for hacking DNC servers, WikiLeaks released more than 20,000 stolen DNC emails and other documents. (It would eventually release more than 44,000 DNC emails and 17,000 attachments, WikiLeaks says on its website.) The first drop came on July 22, 2016 — three days before the Democratic National Convention in Philadelphia.

The timing proved damaging to party unity, and Clinton's attempts to use the convention to woo supporters of her top rival, Sen. Bernie Sanders. The released documents embarrassedparty officials who were seen as working behind the scenes at the DNC to undermine Sanders' campaign, and forced the DNC chairwoman, Debbie Wasserman-Schultz, to resignon the eve of the convention.

The timing was no coincidence.

The Mueller report said WikiLeaks sent a direct message on Twitter to Guccifer 2.0 on July 6, 2016, seeking information that would disrupt the DNC convention and Clinton's attempts at unity. "[I]f you have anything hillary related we want it in the next tweo [sic] days prefab le [sic] because the DNC is approaching and she will solidify bernie supporters behind her after," WikiLeaks wrote to Guccifer 2.0.

"[W]e think trump has only a 25% chance of winning against hillary … so conflict between bernie and hillary is interesting," WikiLeaks wrote.

On Oct. 7, 2016, WikiLeaks began releasing emails "the first set of emails stolen by the GRU from the account of Clinton Campaign chairman John Podesta." Those emails were released "less than an hour" after the *Washington Post* published a 2005 video that caught Trump on a hot mic during a filming of "Access Hollywood" bragging about grabbing and kissing women because "when you're a star, they let you do it."

Trump campaign's use of stolen documents: In downplaying Russia's interference in the election, Kushner ignored the campaign's interest in the stolen documents and Trump's extensive use of them to his advantage.

"The Trump Campaign showed interest in WikiLeaks's releases of hacked materials throughout the summer and fall of 2016," the Mueller report said.

After DNC emails were released in July, Trump tweeted, "The Wikileaks e-mail release today was so bad to Sanders that it will make it impossible for him to support her, unless he is a fraud!" At the same time, Paul Manafort, Trump's campaign manager, told Gates that he "wanted to be kept apprised of any developments with WikiLeaks," according to the Mueller report.

"According to [Deputy Campaign Chairman Rick] Gates, by the late summer of 2016, the Trump Campaign was planning a press strategy, a communications campaign, and messaging based on the possible release of Clinton emails by WikiLeaks," the report said.

The report also said that Trump and "other Campaign advisors privately sought information [redacted] about any further planned WikiLeaks releases."

Donald Trump Jr., exchanged direct messages on Twitter with WikiLeaks, expressing interest in any new document dumps. On Oct. 3, 2016, Trump Jr. asked WikiLeaks: "What's behind this Wednesday leak I keep reading about?" WikiLeaks did not respond, at least not on Twitter. Four days later, WikiLeaks released Podesta's emails.

After the first set of Podesta's emails was released, Trump took to Twitter on numerous occasions to draw attention to the stolen documents and away from the "Access Hollywood" video. Here are some of his tweets, which also came days after the U.S. intelligence community identified Russia as the source of the hacked emails:

Oct. 11, 2016: "I hope people are looking at the disgraceful behavior of Hillary Clinton as exposed by WikiLeaks. She is unfit to run."

Oct. 12, 2016: "Very little pick-up by the dishonest media of incredible information provided by WikiLeaks. So dishonest! Rigged system!"

Oct. 16, 2016: "We've all wondered how Hillary avoided prosecution for her email scheme. Wikileaks may have found the answer. Obama!"

In the closing weeks of the campaign, WikiLeaks became a big part of Trump's closing argument against Clinton.

On Oct. 21, 2016, Manafort — who had left the campaign at this point — "sent Kushner an email and attached a strategy memorandum proposing that the Campaign make the case against Clinton 'as the failed and corrupt champion of the establishment' and that 'Wikileaks provides the Trump campaign the ability to make the case in a very credible way — by using the words of Clinton, its campaign officials and DNC members,'" according to the Mueller report.

Trump often read from the stolen emails and other documents at his campaign rallies.

In many cases, Trump distorted the facts to fit his campaign message that Clinton supports "open borders," would harm Medicare and Social Security, was soft on terrorism, and was too cozy with big banks. (Read our item "Trump Twists Facts on WikiLeaks" for more information on how Trump distorted the facts on those and other topics.)

"In sum, the investigation established that the GRU hacked into email accounts of persons affiliated with the Clinton Campaign, as well as the computers of the DNC and DCCC. The GRU then exfiltrated data related to the 2016 election from these accounts and computers, and disseminated that data through fictitious online personas (DCLeaks and Guccifer 2.0) and later through WikiLeaks," the Mueller report said. "The investigation also established that the Trump Campaign displayed interest in the WikiLeaks releases."

Russian 'Active Measures' Social Media Campaign

Russia's Internet Research Agency, an online propaganda operation, began social media operations in the United States as early as 2014, creating social media accounts using fictitious personas.

In the 2016 campaign, "Some IRA employees, posing as U.S. persons and without revealing their Russian association, communicated electronically with individuals associated with the Trump Campaign and with other political activists to seek to coordinate political activities, including the staging of political rallies," the report said. "By the end of the 2016 U.S. election, the IRA had the ability to reach millions of U.S. persons through their social media accounts."

The figures cited on the reach and amount of these social media accounts are significantly greater than "a couple Facebook ads," as Kushner said.

> **Mueller report:** *Multiple IRA-controlled Facebook groups and Instagram accounts had hundreds of thousands of U.S. participants. IRA-controlled Twitter accounts separately had tens of thousands of followers, including multiple U.S. political figures who retweeted IRA-created content. In November 2017, a Facebook representative testified that Facebook had identified 470 IRA-controlled Facebook accounts that collectively made 80,000 posts between January 2015 and August 2017. Facebook estimated the IRA reached as many as 126 million persons through its Facebook accounts. In January 2018, Twitter announced that it had identified 3,814 IRA-controlled Twitter accounts and notified approximately 1.4 million people Twitter believed may have been in contact with an IRA-controlled account.*

Much of the material in the report on the structure of the IRA and its social media operations is redacted, due to "harm to ongoing matter." In February 2018, the special counsel indicted 13 Russian nationals and three Russian entities, including the IRA. The group was funded by Yevgeniy Viktorovich Prigozhin, who was sanctioned by the U.S. in December 2016 and has reported ties to Russian President Vladimir Putin, and companies he controlled.

According to the indictment, the IRA's monthly budget was more than $1.25 million (U.S. dollars) by September 2016.

The U.S. social media operation was known as the "Translator" internally at the IRA, the Mueller report said. It included the creation of social media pages falsely claiming to be associated with U.S. political groups or mimicking them. For instance, the IRA Twitter account @TEN_ GOP suggested it was affiliated with the Tennessee Republican Party. "More commonly," the Mueller report said, "the IRA created accounts in the names of fictitious U.S. organizations and grassroots groups and used these accounts to pose as anti-immigration groups, Tea Party activists, Black Lives Matter protestors, and other U.S. social and political activists."

The operation was aimed at supporting Trump's candidacy and opposing Clinton. One of the directions to IRA operators included: "Main idea: Use any opportunity to criticize Hillary [Clinton] and the rest (except Sanders and Trump – we support them)."

As for Facebook ads, the IRA bought more than 3,500 of them, not just "a couple," spending about $100,000, the special counsel's report said, attributing those figures to Facebook.

The special counsel said the IRA bought its first known ad backing Trump's campaign on April 19, 2016 — an ad for an Instagram account called "Tea Party News" encouraging people to help "'make a patriotic team of young Trump supporters' by uploading photos with the hashtag '#KIDS4TRUMP.'" The IRA bought dozens of ads supporting the Trump campaign in the months that followed, "predominantly through the Facebook groups 'Being Patriotic,' 'Stop All Invaders,' and 'Secured Borders.'" Other bogus Facebook groups created by the IRA included: "Black Matters," "LGBT United" and "United Muslims of America." These accounts "attracted hundreds of thousands of followers."

On Twitter, the IRA created fake accounts and also automated bot accounts to spread its content. One IRA account — @march_for_trump — promoted rallies in support of the campaign. The IRA would organize rallies by direct messaging followers, asking them to attend, and finding a real U.S. person to agree to serve as the coordinator of the event. The special counsel's office identified "dozens" of such rallies, the first of which was a "confederate rally" in November 2015. Some rallies attracted just a few people, but others attracted hundreds. The Trump campaign actually posted on its Facebook page about an IRA-organized rally in Miami in August 2016.

One poster for IRA-organized rallies in Pittsburgh and Philadelphia used an image of a now-deceased West Virginia coal miner with the words, "Miners For Trump, Bring Back Our Jobs."

The bogus social media accounts were realistic enough to fool some U.S. media outlets, which quoted tweets they thought were from real U.S. people, and well-known figures who retweeted or responded to these accounts, including former Ambassador Michael McFaul, Fox News' Sean Hannity, Trump informal adviser Roger Stone and Michael Flynn Jr., son of the campaign's foreign policy adviser and later national security adviser in the administration.

The IRA also had interactions with the Trump campaign. On "multiple occasions, members and surrogates of the Trump Campaign promoted–typically by linking, retweeting, or similar methods of reposting–pro-Trump or anti-Clinton content published by the IRA through IRA-controlled social media accounts," the report said. For instance, posts from that @TEN_GOP Twitter account were cited or retweeted by Donald J. Trump Jr., Eric Trump, Kellyanne Conway, Brad Parscale and Michael T. Flynn.

Also, there were "a few instances" in which IRA employees asked members of the campaign for help with rallies the IRA had organized. The Mueller report concluded: "While certain campaign volunteers agreed to provide the requested support (for example, agreeing to set aside a number of signs), the investigation has not identified evidence that any Trump Campaign official understood the requests were coming from foreign nationals."

Kushner equates the Russian interference effort to "a couple Facebook ads" and $160,000. But as the Mueller report makes clear, it was a sophisticated, yearslong hacking and social media effort to influence an election.

Share The Facts

Jared Kushner
Senior adviser to the president

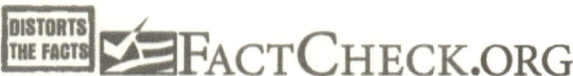

"You look at what Russia did, you know, buying some Facebook ads to try to sow dissent and do it, it's a terrible thing. But I think the investigations and all of the speculation that's happened for the last two years has had a much harsher impact on our democracy than a couple Facebook ads."

Time100 Summit – Tuesday, April 23, 2019

Chapter Seven

I love the word Freedom, especially Freedom of the Press. Our president refers to the press, such as CNN, ABC, NBC as fake news. He wants to build that wall on our southern border because he says, *"Sorry, people want border security and extreme vetting"*. I say to him, *"Why don't you creatively focus on building bridges of peace with Mexico? Delegate this authority to the right person. Possibly work on a 50-50 cost effort with Mexico, one which assists Mexico with the issue it faces with immigration from countries south of it where mothers, fathers and children are escaping extremely difficult times"*. (Note: In June of 2019 our president began a bridge of peace with Mexico. I pray that it will work in the interests of all those involved. Will he stop talking about the wall?

Our President said that he watched protests yesterday but was under the impression that we just had an election! Why didn't these people vote? Celebs hurt cause badly."

Why couldn't he have just said, *"We just had an election? The people spoke. For those who didn't vote for me, I will work hard to earn their respect"*. Young and old alike, Democrats and Republicans would have respected this kind of presidential comment.

He said, *"We are going to have an unbelievable, perhaps record-setting turnout for the inauguration, and there will be plenty of movie and entertainment stars. All the dress shops are sold out in Washington. It's hard to find a great dress for this inauguration."*

I was born in Rochester, NY where photography was invented by George Eastman, founder of Eastman Kodak. Photography was used in Obama's election as well as our President. These photos proved that there were close to 1.8 million who attended Obama's inauguration in 2009, and close to 1 million who attended his second inauguration in 2013 according to District of Columbia officials. These government officials estimated 700,000 to 900,000 people attended your inauguration. You did not have a record-setting turnout. (On this issue and in many others, he ignores or refused to accept the facts that rule)

In 2017, he said, *"Happy New Year to all, including to my many enemies and those who fought me and lost so badly they just don't know what to do. Love!"*

I say this is sarcastic which is *"The use of irony to mock or convey contempt: "his voice, hardened by sarcasm, could not hide his resentment".*

Synonyms of sarcastic, derision, mockery, ridicule, scorn, sneering, scoffing, irony, cynicism.

Possibly his advisors, like Kelly Ann Conway, and Attorney General William Barr should have made him familiar with the following leadership quotations, if indeed, they had the courage of their convictions.

"Leaders who seek power and control end up losing both." **Dr. Henry Cloud**

"A leadership position is one that requires many different skills. It is an activity that is sometimes hard to measure, but the results of the team will determine the leader's success." Catherine Pulsifer

"An accepted leader has only to be sure of what it is best to do, or at least to have made up his mind about it." Winston Churchill

"Effective leaders inspire and motivate people to follow their visions willingly and eagerly, not out of fear." Keith and Maya Traver

"Your values are who you are, and they represent how you will lead." Kristina Diviny-MacBury, Principal Pro

"My leadership style was one that I needed to involve staff members in a much stronger role as their own change agents where they not only clearly understood the issues but also took it upon themselves to recommend strategies for change that would improve service yet maintain the same staffing model." Byron Pulsifer

Our President said, *"A very credible source has called my office and told me that Barack Obama's birth certificate is a fraud."*

He was determined to 'expose' President Obama's birthplace back in 2012, and even claimed to have sent investigators to Hawaii in the hopes of proving Obama wasn't born in the United States. This was not true. George Washington said, *"Truth will ultimately prevail where there are pains to bring it to light".*

He said, *"Robert Pattinson should not take back Kristen Stewart. She cheated on him like a dog & will do it again – just watch. He can do much better!"*

I try to think of a past US President who engaged in such public trash talk. I cannot find one.

He said, *"Ariana Huffington is unattractive, both inside and out. I fully understand why her former husband left her for a man – he made a good decision."*

He stooped particularly low with this comment about the Huffington Post founder.

He said, *"Meryl Streep, one of the most over-rated actresses in Hollywood, doesn't know me but attacked me last night at the Golden Globes. She is a Hillary flunky who lost big. For the 100th time, I never "mocked" a disabled reporter (would never do that) but simply showed him "groveling" when he totally changed a 16 year old story that he had written in order to make me look bad. Just more very dishonest media!"*

Is this response by our President truly presidential? And the record shows he did mock a disabled reporter. (As a 10 year old boy, growing up in the inner city, when one lied, we would say, *"Liar, liar, your pants are on fire").* And I think there is a cartoon somewhere where President Trump's pants are on fire).

He said, "I will build a great wall – and nobody builds walls better than me, believe me – and I'll build them very inexpensively. I will build a great, great wall on our southern border, and I will make Mexico pay for that wall. Mark my words."

Our president says he is a Christian. Then he should recall Jesus saying, *"Blessed are the Peacemakers because they will be called the children of God."* And those of Jewish Faith, *"The work of righteousness shall be peace"* Isiah. And those of Muslim faith, *"O You who believe! Enter absolutely into peace (Islam). Do not follow in the footsteps of satan. He is an outright enemy to you." (Holy Quran: 2, 208)*

And further, he should dwell on this quote. *The "tear down this wall" speech was not the first time Reagan had addressed the issue of the Berlin Wall. On a visit to West Berlin in June 1982, he'd stated 'I'd like to ask the Soviet leaders one question. Why is the wall there?', and in 1986, <u>25 years</u> after the construction of the wall, in response to a West German newspaper asking when he thought the wall could be 'torn down', Reagan said, "I call upon those responsible to dismantle it today".*

And our President inhumanly said, *"When Mexico sends its people, they're not sending the best. They're sending people that have lots of problems and they're bringing those problems with us. They're bringing drugs. They're bringing crime. They're rapists… And some, I assume, are good people."*

As a self-proclaimed Christian, he should be aware of this biblical quotation. *"Whatsoever you do for the least of my brethren, that you do unto me".* In my view, his comment is a *"Loose Lips"* racially offensive slur.

He said, *"If I were running the View, I'd fire Rosie O'Donnell. I mean, I'd look at her right in that fat, ugly face of hers, I'd say Rosie, you're fired."*

I recall this quote from the media. *"Trump has infamously hated on Rosie O'Donnell, making crude, sexist and misogynistic remarks about her on multiple occasions".*

I say to this to our President. *"Mr. President: From age 12 to age 18, I served as an altar boy in the Catholic Church. On board our ship, the USS Guam, in WWII, I was the Chaplain's assistant for two years, until the war ended. Your bar-room-base and all of your other supporters may not find fault with your slanderous words but I do and I believe God does too".*

And in regard to many other negative published remarks, I say to our President and his supporting base, who profess to be Christians, why not consider and practice the following biblical beatitudes in your personal, business and political life and actions?

"Blessed are the poor in spirit, for theirs is the kingdom of heaven. Blessed are those who mourn, for they will be comforted. Blessed are the meek, for they will inherit the earth. Blessed are those who hunger and thirst after righteousness, for they will be filled. Blessed are the merciful, for they shall be shown mercy. Blessed are the pure in heart, for they will see God. Blessed are the peacemakers, for they will be called the children of God. Blessed are those who are persecuted because of righteousness, for theirs is the kingdom of heaven. Blessed are you when people insult you, persecute you and falsely say all kinds of evil against you because of me. Rejoice and be glad, because great is your reward in heaven, for in the same way they persecuted the prophets who were before you".

Our President said, *"One of the key problems today is that politics is such a disgrace. Good people don't go into government."*

I say to him, *"Good people do go into government. Sadly, if you do not agree with good people, you either build a wall against them or you fire them".*

Our President said, *"The beauty of me is that I'm very rich."*

I say that he should be concerned about his arrogance. The quote from the Bible he placed his hands on when he was inaugurated as our President reads" *"Then Jesus said to His disciples, "Truly I tell you, it is difficult for a rich man to enter the kingdom of heaven. Again, I tell you. It is easier for a camel to pass through the eye of a needle than a rich man to enter the Kingdom of God".*

In my view, there are many rich men who will not have difficulty entering the Kingdom of God because *"By their good works, they will be known".* And, indeed, there are many, many rich men with outstanding "good works".

And regarding his illusive tax returns, it is time that Congress should change the law so that any elected official, including the President, can no longer be illusive from the American people. And I ask his base, what is it that our President is hiding?

Our President said, *"It's freezing and snowing in New York – we need global warming!"*

He ignores the written opinions of the global warming scientists. And his book "Art of the Deal", it is obvious that he should have studied silence as well as science in college rather than his *"Art of the Deal".*

Our President said, *"I've said if Ivanka weren't my daughter, perhaps I'd be dating her."*

Instead, he should graciously say, *"I've said if Ivanka weren't my daughter, I would feel as if I were deprived of a great blessing".*

He said, *"My fingers are long and beautiful, as, it has been well documented, as are various other parts of my body."*

As far as our President's applauding supporting base is concerned, I often wonder, *"Would they applaud with this kind of televised statement?"* And what impact does this have on our children in this high tech world where they have easy access.

He said, *"I think the only difference between me and the other candidates is that I'm more honest and my women are more beautiful."*

I say that he treats beautiful women as if they are his possessions. *"You're disgusting"* is what he said to an opposing lawyer during a court case when she asked for a medical break to pump breast milk for her three-month-old daughter. I ask, *"Who is the one who is most disgusting?*

And, again on the subject of our President's taxes? Should our system of government allow him to withhold his business and personal financial statements from public review and scrutiny? Shouldn't Republicans and Democrats join together to amend the law to make these financial disclosures absolutely, timely and clearly required prior to election without exception?

And I ask him? *"Mr. President, what is it that you are hiding in your tax returns? How long does our system of government allow you to get away with this? Do the American people really have to wait for the stalling process that may even have to go to the Supreme Court for a decision by judges whom you nominated? Is the timing of this issue such that any decision would be made after the next upcoming election? Indeed, if the law allows you do get away with this, the law ought to be urgently changed.*

And on the formerAttorney General of the United States, Don McGhan to fire Robert Mueller, on May 3, 2019 Michael A. Cohen writes:

President Trump. (EVAN VUCCI/AP)

THURSDAY, (May 3, 2019), DONALD Trump told his 60 million followers on Twitter that he had *"never told then-White House Counsel Don McGahn to fire Robert Mueller."* No one truly believes this. Trump was, according to the Mueller Report, obsessed with firing *the special counsel.* He called McGahn at home, telling him "Mueller has to go," and asked him to "call me back when you do it." At the same time, the president told key aides and confidants that he was looking to get rid of Mueller

And consider this. On April 10, 2019, Associated Press - *"Treasury Secretary Steven Mnuchin says his department is unable to provide President Donald Trump's tax returns to Congress by Wednesday's deadline. Mnuchin told House Ways and Means Committee Chairman Richard Neal, who made the request a week ago, that Treasury respects congressional oversight but needs more time to review the "unprecedented request."*

Let's have a bit of fun about Loose Lips Mnuchin initials. *More, Nonsense, Under, Concealed, Hiding In Neverland.*

Finally, on this subject, Secretary Mnuchin says it is *"unprecedented request"* and I say for our President to continue to use *"under audit"* as an excuse is *"unpresidential"*. And to stall the process with such pride and arrogance, until you believe you would be reelected? Watch out Loose Lips Mnuchin. Voters are aware. Voters care. You could be caught in your underwear.

Our President said, *"My Twitter has become so powerful that I can actually make my enemies tell the truth.*

I say, Mr. President, wouldn't it be great for our school children to hear you twitter the following:

"My Twitter has become so powerful, after all of these years, it has stopped the influence of the National Rifle Association in governmental affairs. This includes the banning of any political contributions from the NRA to those who are seeking any political office in any of our 50 United States of America.... and to Republic for which it stands".

Wow! If you had said this in the past, I would stand outside of your White House in my WWII navy suit, and salute you.

Our President said, *My IQ is one of the highest — and you all know it! Please don't feel so stupid or insecure; it's not your fault."*

I say to him. In the view of many citizens throughout the world, your IQ stands for your Idiot Quotes as reflected in this book, *"Loose Lips Sink Ships".*

Our President said, *"I have so many fabulous friends who happen to be gay, but I am a traditionalist."*

And I say to him. Mr. President, Are you are really saying that you have fabulous gay friends but your tradition does not accept gays? If so, isn't this hypocritical? Here's the definition for a traditional person *"one who believes that older ways of doing or thinking about things are better than newer ways: a person who follows a particular and established tradition"*.

And, Mr. President here is a definition for hypocrite – *"a person who puts a false appearance of virtue or religion. Characterized by behavior that contradicts what one claims to believe or feel"*. There's an old saying Mr. President. *"If the shoe fits, wear it"*.

Our President said, *"The other candidates — they went in, they didn't know the air conditioning didn't work. They sweated like dogs…How are they gonna beat ISIS? I don't think it's gonna happen."*

Mr. President, that's like saying, *"Our troops in Iraq. They sweat like dogs. How are they gonna beat ISIS. I don't think it's gonna happen"*.

Our President said, *"Look at those hands, are they small hands? And, [Republican rival Marco Rubio] referred to my hands: 'If they're small, something else must be small.' I guarantee you there's no problem. I guarantee."*

Mr. President. You and Marco Rubio, along with many Republicans, accepted funds from the now beleaguered NRA to support your causes and your wall? Along with the petition to keep you out of the United Kingdom, can we also campaign for you to stop bragging about the size of your hands and/or the size of your ……? As our nation's leader, do you ever stop to think about the example you set for our children with such ongoing vulgarity? Do your loud supporters think about this and/or condone it?

Mr. President, you said, *"Lyin' Ted Cruz just used a picture of Melania from a shoot in his ad. Be careful, Lyin' Ted, or I will spill the beans on your wife!"*

Mr. President. Many of your avid and vocal supporters', who cheer you on, may treat your comments with humor. Sorry, I believe it demeans the office of our US Presidency, not only in the US but in the eyes of the world. (And Ted, again in January of 2019, you stand next to Mr. President in support of the Wall? Really?)

Mr. President, you said, *"The only card [Hillary Clinton] has is the woman's card. She's got nothing else to offer and frankly, if Hillary Clinton were a man, I don't think she'd get 5 percent of the vote. The only thing she's got going is the woman's card, and the beautiful thing is, women don't like her."*

Mr. President. As I write this the jury is still out on Russian Interference in our election. Further, the newspaper headlines read that "Clinton ended up beating Donald Trump by 2.8 million votes."

How about this?

Trump: "My plan (tax plan) is for the working people, and my plan is for jobs."

Reporter: "You wouldn't benefit under your tax plan?"

Trump: "No, I don't benefit. I don't benefit. In fact, very, very strongly, as you see, I think there's very little benefit for people of wealth".

Sorry Mr. President, the rich do benefit far more than their fellow Americans. That is a fact. Consider the digested following news article from a highly respected expert on the new tax law.

"I think it would impact different parts of the base differently," says William Gale, chairman of the Brookings Institute's Economic Studies and who served as an economic adviser to President George H.W. Bush. 'The rich donors who are part of the base would come out quite nicely from this proposal. The proverbial kind of lower-middle-class worker is not going to benefit as much, particularly when the financing of the tax cut is taken into account."

And, further Mr. President, the recent gross national debt surpassed $22 trillion for the first time ever according to data released by the Treasury department on February 12, 2019 under your leadership. And in the past 12 months, the US has added $1 trillion in debt.

And this again leads to your tax returns. And no different than any other past Presidents, are we or are we not entitled to see them from your multiple complex organization structures? How much longer do we have to listen to, *"They are still under audit?"*

Further Mr. President, do you remember this quote. *"Figures don't lie but liars figure".* Your quote that the rich do not benefit is a lie. As the objective news media states, people of wealth do benefit.

By Michael A. Cohen May 3, 2019, 4:33 p.m.

President Trump. (EVAN VUCCI/AP)

LAST THURSDAY, DONALD Trump told his 60 million followers on Twitter that he had "never told then-White House Counsel Don McGahn to fire Robert Mueller." No one truly believes this.

Trump was, according to the Mueller Report, obsessed with firing the special counsel. He called McGahn at home, telling him "Mueller has to go," and asked him to "call me back when you do it."

At the same time, the president told key aides and confidants that he was looking to get rid of Mueller.

In WWII, on board my ship of 2,000 men, any Seaman appearing in front of the Executive Officer for failing to tell the truth about a major offense would be assigned to the brig. I was the Yeoman on board the USS Guam responsible for recording data into the records of the sailors on board. This included any sailor's clearly established lies. Sometimes certain offenses required being sentence to the ship's "Brig".

The Definition of the brig – *"A jail or prison on board a US Navy or Coast Guard vessel"*

On board our ship, Mr. President, you would have been sent to the brig for the following false claims.

You said, *"96 million really want a job and they can't get one"*. Not true. Your quote includes retirees, students and others who are not looking for a job. Only 5.5 million of them want work.

You said, *"You learn very little from a tax return"*.

Mr. President, multiple tax returns in the same year, under different structures, especially related to real estate properties, can reflect an actual or potential conflict of interest or exaggerations of property values which impact the fair and actual taxes due and as I write this, you continue to use the power of your office to do everything possible to prevent the right of the people of our nation, or your avid supporters, to see these complete tax returns.

You said that some states have seen health insurance coverage under the Affordable Care Act increase by 100%. Only Arizona has an average increase that high, and 84 percent with marketplace coverage in 2016 received tax credits to purchase insurance.

You continue to over exaggerate the rise of the Islamic State by blaming President Obama for *'leaving at the wrong time'* from Iraq. President George W. Bush set the withdrawal date. And, just as important, there were numerous other factors in the rise of the terrorist group.

You said that *'nobody even talked about it"*, when hacked emails showed that Hillary Clinton's campaign got debate questions in advance. In fact, there was plenty of press coverage when it was revealed that former CNN contributor Donna Brazile shared questions with Clinton's campaign.

You said that a million of them 'currently want a job. You cited the statistic in the context of a border tax on 'these companies that are leaving the U.S. and getting away with murder.' You said, 'And if our politicians had what it takes, they would have done this year's ago. And you'd have millions more workers right now in the United States that there are 96 million really wanting a job and they can't get one. That's the real number." That's what you said.

Mr. President, according to the latest figures from the Bureau of Labor Statistics, there were 95.8 million people not in the labor force in December. So you are in error to lump them all in as "really wanting a job". According to this government Bureau, only 5.5 million of them "currently want a job." Those not looking for a job include millions of retirees, teenagers and stay-at-home parents. For example, there were "18.3 million people age 75 and older who were not in the workforce in December", the Bureau says.

You said that *'you learn very little'* from a tax return and that *'the only one that cares about my tax returns are the reporters.'*

Mr. President, experts will tell you tax returns give plenty of information. For example - potential conflicts of interest, repeated charitable giving and effective tax rates. Further, polls show that a majority of Americans say that you should release your tax returns.

You were asked if you would release your tax returns to prove that you had no business dealings in Russia. You said, *"I'm not releasing the tax returns because as you know, they're under audit".* You said this during the campaign as well.

Also during the campaign, when you faced questions about releasing your returns, something many 2016 presidential candidates and every major party nominee since the late 1970s have done, you then claimed that *'there's nothing to learn'* from your tax returns. You repeated this in a press conference, stating, *'You learn very little from a tax return.'*

In my sixty years of business experience, I learned that tax returns can show sources of income, deductions taken, potential conflicts, overseas income, and how these affect one's tax situation. They can also show reveal the way someone lives one's life, or conducts business, especially in multiple real estate dealings.

A reporter asked you. *"You don't think the American public is concerned about it?"*

You replied: *'No I don't think so. I won, when I became president. No, I don't think they care at all. I don't think they care at all.'* Mr. President, a previous Pew Research Center poll conducted found that 60 percent of respondents said you have a responsibility to release your tax returns. Other polls have shown similar results.

A CBS News poll conducted Dec. 9-13, 2016, asked whether it was 'necessary' for you to release your tax returns. Sixty percent <u>responded</u> that it was necessary. In addition, a Quinnipiac University poll taken Aug. 18-24, 2016, <u>asked</u> likely voters: *"Do you think Donald Trump should publicly release his tax returns, or not? Seventy-four percent said he should release them, including a majority (62 percent) of Republicans."*

And on this subject of Taxes, Mr. President you publicly said, *"I would <u>not</u> personally benefit from the proposed changes to tax law".* Tax experts say the rich do benefit.

Mr. President, the next time you talk to your base why not just loudly shout with your usual arm waving and finger pointing and say to them: *"You know how that crooked media fuss around with revealing my tax returns. These idiots say that I am the only President in the United States to not release my returns. Yeah, so it's true… but look what I have done for our country in jobs and the stock market. And those who say that seeds for such great results were planted by a previous four year President are idiots".*

This WWII Vet shouts loudly and clearly, is the President of the United States really exempt from the following which all Americans must conform with? The facts say that he is not.

<u>THIS DIGEST IS TAKEN FROM THE TAX INFORMATION CENTER : IRS : AUDITS AND TAX NOTICES.</u>

"How Long Does the IRS Have to Audit Your Tax Return? *There are two answers to this question: the legal answer and the practical answer.*

Legal answer: Three years

First, the legal answer is in the tax law. Technically, except in cases of fraud or a back tax return, the IRS has three years from the date you filed your return (or April 15, whichever is later) to charge you (or, "assess") additional taxes. This three-year timeframe is called the assessment statute of limitations. Additional taxes usually come in the form of an audit or an under reporter notice (called a CP2000). Even though the IRS can legally audit you until the three-year assessment statute ends, in practice, it rarely works this way.

The practical answer: 26 months - The practical answer lies in a procedural policy at the IRS called the "examination cycle." The Internal Revenue Manual (basically, the IRS training guide) says that IRS agents must open and close an audit within 26 months after the return was filed or due (whichever is later). The IRM also says that IRS agents should "strictly adhere to" this guideline, to make sure that the audit and other processing needs are complete within the three-year timeframe. Most audits start a few months after you file your return."

Let this WWII Vet repeat. You are the only president in modern history to not release your tax returns consistent with the law….but nevertheless, on this subject, your base applauds you in your two hour session on March 2, 2019?

Legal Definition of *freedom of the press – Webster's Dictionary:*

: *the right to publish and disseminate information, thoughts, and opinions without restraint or censorship as guaranteed under the First Amendment to the U.S. Constitution*

NOTE: The First Amendment's guarantees of freedom of speech and freedom of the press are closely intertwined, and many cases relating to freedom of the press are couched in terms of the freedom of speech.

Mr. President, you are the first president in the history of the United States, calling the entire Media "crooked". Why not have your current Attorney General to review the First Amendment to the Constitution…..and while at it, ask him to again objectively review all of the pages of the Muller report before he comes to his digested conclusions.

Mr. President, I compare you with impeached President Nixon. Why? In taped phone conversations with the Chairman of the Joint Chiefs of Staff, he said:

The press is your enemy…Enemies. Understand that? … Because they're trying to stick the knife right in our groin.

And by the way, he was eventually impeached.

Mr. President, you said, *"I'm just thinking to myself right now, we should just cancel the election and just give it to Trump, right?"*

Some say, it is impossible for you to change. I say, the US and its neighbors want a change from you. Come on now. I was 20 when you were born. So listen to me. *Turn your arrogant pride and complex leadership into rational humility and common sense and make it work for you and your team.*

Mr. President, you said, *"You know, it really doesn't matter what the media writes as long as you've got a young, and beautiful, piece of ass."*

Mr. President, maybe your supporters do not find this quote seriously offensive. Maybe it's my Christian upbringing and the lovable and respected women in my life. Maybe it's because in my business career, I employed hundreds of women. Maybe it's because, in WWII, on board our ship I also served as the Chaplain's assistant. Then and now, I find your kind of talk offensive to women. And I am disappointed that so many of your men and women followers do not consider your public remarks regarding women shameful. And this WWII Vet says to you and to your followers - "Shame on all of you. Democracy is one thing. Giving bad examples to our children and the world is another". (I wonder how truly Sarah Huckabee feels *about this? I also wonder how truly Reverend Mike Huckabee feels about this? And I repeat, "truly feels".*

Mr. President, you said, *"I thought being President would be easier than my old life."*

Mr. President. It could be a lot easier if you worked on becoming a humble, skillful and effective leader and a respectful listener to qualified, objective and courageous advisors in your remaining term of office, or indeed if you are elected to serve four more years.

Mr. President, you said, *"North Korean leader Kim Jong Un is 27 years old. His father dies, took over a regime. So say what you want but that is not easy, especially at that age."*

There are few in the US, let alone the world, that are not concerned about the devastation of nuclear war. Like many, I pray that we find the road to peace. And when I think of devastation, I especially think of the innocent children who would suffer and die and yes, I mean all children in the world including North Korea. And with that in mind, I pray that you, your team and world leaders develop a change of heart and find the road to peace with children foremost in mind.

And regarding Kim? On April 23, 2019, the news reports that your buddy Kim Jon-un will be meeting with your buddy Putin. Now isn't that interesting?

Mr. President, you said, *"You know, I'm automatically attracted to beautiful — I just start kissing them. It's like a magnet. Just kiss. I don't even wait. And when you're a star, they let you do it. You can do anything….Grab them by the pussy. You can do anything."*

Someone wrote, *"Somehow the gross audio from the Access Hollywood tapes only tanked one career – and it wasn't Donald Trump's".*

No, it did not *"tank your career"* Mr. President….as the results of the election proved. But I wonder what examples are set when your followers do not speak out against such comments, which in our modern world of TV, Newspapers, New Technology, Twitter and Cell Phones, can have a disappointing and negative example and impact on our children and grandchildren.

Mr. President you said, *"You have a bunch of bad hombres down there. (Mexico) You aren't doing enough to stop them. I think your military is scared. Our military isn't, so I might just send them down to take care of it."*

I say, consider this. What harm would it do to say this to the current and future Mexican Presidents,

"You have a bunch of bad hombres down there. I'm sending Jim Mattis, Security of Defense down to see you... to see, if together, in Mexico, we can resolve this issue with a team approach that is fair, reasonable and respectful to all. We don't need a wall. We need to bridge with you in finding and jailing the Mexican bad guys in Mexican prisons and assisting with the Mexican economy. We will spend billions with you on this team effort rather than the wall......and together we will succeed and set an example for the rest of the world". (Note again, in June of 2019, you did work on a plan which we pray will be successful).

(*Note*: President Donald Trump announced on Twitter that Defense Secretary Jim Mattis retired in February 2019. Mattis submitted a letter to Trump saying the president deserves a secretary of defense with views more close to his on things like alliances and building an international order. The move came after Trump abruptly announced that U.S. troops would be withdrawn from Syria, where they'd been fighting ISIS).

Mr. President - Obviously the professional, valued and experienced views of Secretary Mattis were treated with disdain by you. How sad. (*To former Secretary Jim Mattis: This WWII Vet salutes you. You did not cave in but you were caved in by our President).*

Mr. President - Regarding Syria and the suffering parents and children of Syria? You took admiral action with the Syrian airstrike.

Indeed, the fight is not over. I find it difficult to sleep when I look at the photographs and news reels of the Syrian children who have suffered and continue to suffer. I reflect on the fact that my father was born in a part of Lebanon which was once a part of Syria. As fate would have it, I thank God that my father immigrated to the US when he did and where he and my American born mother of Lebanese heritage raised nine children. I also sadly reflect on the historic Hitler persecution of the Jews which indeed makes the current Syrian crises seem minor in comparison.

I can only pray that you, as our President, or your successors, work toward a creative unity with other nations to build bridges of peace throughout the world, whether Jew, Catholic, Protestant or Muslim, rather than the physical or psychological walls of separation that you so loudly and repeatedly proclaim.

And Mr. President – You, as an acknowledged Protestant, should take time to reflect on the Bible - James: 2:14-18: *"What good is it, my brothers, if someone says he has faith but does not have works? Can that faith save him? If a brother or sister is poorly clothed and lacking in daily food, and one of you says to them, 'Go in peace, be warmed and filled,' without giving them the things needed for the body, what good is that? So also faith by itself, if it does not have works, is dead. But someone will say, 'You have faith and I have works.' Show me your faith apart from your works, and I will show you my faith by my works."* And Mr. President, in God's eyes and words, all those *"who are hungry and thirsty should be satisfied"* not only in the US but throughout the world.

Mr. President, you said. *"Yes, Arnold Schwarzenegger did a really bad job as Governor of California and even worse on the Apprentice…but at least he tried hard!"*

Mr. President, Arnold did try hard and there were measures of success. It is not too late for you to try hard…..as well as smart.

Mr. President, you said, *"Why can't we use nuclear weapons?"*

Mr. President. MSNBC stated in a foreign policy meeting, that you asked this question three times. Consider this. Whether it is North Korea, Russia or any part of our world, in addition to many other factors, you and other nations in our world with this capability should carefully reflect on the population of innocent children who would die and/or suffer. (It appears that I repeatedly make statements about caring for children. In all of your decision making, you should to).

Mr. President, you stated: *"The New York Times January 6, 2018 don't write good. They have people over there, like Maggie Haberman and others, they don't – they don't write good. They don't know how to write good."*

Mr. President. There is a feature in Microsoft Word Documents that rates words that you used above and guess what? This quote and your tweets are reflected at the 4th Grade Level. And you are a college graduate from prestigious schools?

Mr. President – A former serviceman gave you his purple heart at a rally. You then said, *"I always wanted to get the Purple Heart. This was much easier"*. And the record shows that you avoided military service on shaky medical grounds. I'll let all of our US Veterans and your vocal supporters at your rallies reflect on this reality.

Mr. President, You said, *"I've had a beautiful…I've had a flawless campaign. You'll be writing books about this campaign."*

Mr. President, indeed, there will many history books, not only about the campaign, but about your Presidency. Keep that closely in mind as you continue your service to the American people and to the world.

Mr. President, you said, *"Russia, if you're listening, I hope you're able to find the 30,000 [Hillary Clinton] emails that are missing. I think you will probably be rewarded mightily by our press."* It appears that Russia indeed was listening to you and yours in their interference with our election.

Mr. President, you said, *"Fake news is at an all-time high. Where is their apology to me for all of the incorrect stories?"*

Mr. President, check these digested quotes taken on January 17, 2018, from "The Two-Way Break News from National Public Radio - Subject: In the Category of "Fake News," the Award Winner is:

"The president saved his last award, not for a specific news organization, but for his claim that there was no collusion with Russia, which he dismissed as a 'hoax.' And last, but not least: Russian collusion is perhaps the greatest hoax perpetrated on the American people. THERE IS NO COLLUSION!'

And Mr. President earlier in that day, in a speech delivered on the Senate floor, Sen. Jeff Flake (R-Ariz.) blasted you for calling the press the —*'enemy of the people'*, a phrase first used by Soviet dictator Josef Stalin. And Sen. Flake added, *'And, of course, the president has it precisely backward — despotism is the enemy of the people. The free press is the despot's enemy, which makes the free press the guardian of democracy. When a figure in power reflexively calls any press that doesn't suit him 'fake news,' it is that person who should be the figure of suspicion, not the press."*

This WWII Veteran stands a long time and salutes Senator Flake. Indeed, *"Free press is the guardian of democracy".*

Definition of despotism — the word used by Sen. Flake — Webster's Dictionary

1a : oppressive absolute (see absolute 2) power and authority exerted by government : rule by a despot an excess of law is despotism, from which free men revolt —S. B. Pettengill

b : oppressive or despotic exercise of power educational despotism

2a : a system of government in which the ruler has unlimited power : absolutism

b : a despotic state enduring the despotism of the czars

Mr. President - Regarding Megyn Kelly just doing her job, you said, *"You could see there was blood coming out of her eyes, blood coming out of her wherever."*

Mr. President. Again, our modern technology enables young and old alike to see and reflect on such unbridled words. Contrary to your supporters who cheer your talks and tweets, how do I and most of world view your words? *Disgusting, immature, insulting, definitely not presidential, and just as important, insulting to all religions.*

Mr. President, you openly state with pride that you are a Christian. And you make constant references to God. Therefore, you should recall these Bible Versus related to Arrogance from the King James Version (KJV) by Relevance. As with all Presidents, you were sworn into office with your hand on a Bible and in this Bible there are these following quotes copied from the Internet.

"*__1 Samuel 2:3__ - Talk no more so exceeding proudly; let [not] arrogancy come out of your mouth: for the LORD [is] a God of knowledge, and by him actions are weighed.*

__Romans 12:3__ - For I say, through the grace given unto me, to every man that is among you, not to think [of himself] more highly than he ought to think; but to think soberly, according as God hath dealt to every man the measure of faith.

__Proverbs 8:13__ - The fear of the LORD [is] to hate evil: pride, and arrogance, and the evil way, and the froward mouth, do I hate. (Definition of froward – adjective (of a person) difficult to deal with, contrary).

__Isaiah 13:11__ - And I will punish the world for [their] evil, and the wicked for their iniquity; and I will cause the arrogancy of the proud to cease, and will lay low the haughtiness of the terrible."

(Definition of arrogant – an attitude of superiority manifested in an overbearing manner or in presumptuous claims or assumptions).

Mr. President, you should take time to humbly reflect on the above biblical "tweet" quotations and so should your supporting base members who claim to be Christians and accept your quotes without any criticism.

Note to the readers: As it pertains to the Islam Religion and the pursuit of world peace the following was digested from the Internet.

Subject: *"Quran quotes that teach Love, Tolerance and Freedom of Religion.*

By the Good News Network – February 9, 2015.

"Islam, according to the Quran, teaches love and compassion for every human being, no matter their religion, says author Adnan Oktar whose television show is watched by millions in Turkey and the Arab world.

He believes the problem for the majority of Muslims is that some groups are following traditions and superstitions invented centuries after the Quran was first sent and the Prophet lived, and these have gotten more radical over time."

Note: To the readers. As a WWII Veteran, I look back on my life in working with others. On Board my ship the USS Guam, I worked side-by-side in the ships office with sailors of Jewish, Protestant and Catholic heritage. In fact, it was Jewish sailor, who created a history of our ship in a beautiful book that I cherish. I recall with sadness that black sailors were limited to serve only in the ship's kitchen. I also recall sailors of the Muslim faith who served with honor.

Our President constantly refers to Muslims in a negative way. Consider that we have troops of the Muslim faith that are currently and faithfully serving in our Armed Forces.

Mr. President, on the subject of "extremism",

*A recent Pew Research Study places the number of Muslims worldwide to be around 1.6 billion (or 23% of the world's population). So doing some basic math, we get that about **.006625% of the Muslim population are "extremist".***

(To the reader - Sadly as I write after Easter Sunday 2019, either these "extremist" or others are responsible for the devastation that occurred in

India. And further, as I dwell on the word "prejudice", this is my simple prayer").

"To the same God of Christians, Jews, Muslims and people of color, I pray that we focus on the pursuit of peace, love and respect for all involved. Amen".

And to Mr. President, this is the Biblical Psalm in the Bible that you swore on when you took office.

Psalms 33 - For David, when he changed his countenance before Achimelech, who dismissed him, and he went his way. I will bless the Lord at all times, his praise shall be always in my mouth. In the Lord shall my soul be praised: let the meek hear and rejoice. O magnify the Lord with me; and let us extol his name together. I sought the Lord, and he heard me; and he delivered me from all my troubles. Come ye to him and be enlightened: and your faces shall not be confounded. This poor man cried, and the Lord heard him: and saved him out of all his troubles. The angel of the Lord shall encamp round about them that fear him: and shall deliver them. Oh taste, and see that the Lord is sweet: blessed is the man that hopeth in him. Fear the Lord, all ye his saints: for there is no want to them that fear him. The rich have wanted, and have suffered hunger: but they that seek the Lord shall not be deprived of any good. Come, children, hearken to me: I will teach you the fear of the Lord. Who is the man that desireth life: who loveth to see good days? Keep thy tongue from evil, and thy lips from speaking guile. Turn away from evil and do good: seek after peace and pursue it. the eyes of the Lord are upon the just: and his ears unto their prayers. But the countenance of the Lord is against them that do evil things: to cut off the remembrance of them from the earth. The just cried, and the Lord heard them: and delivered them out of all their troubles. :1-18 DRC1752

Mr. President, do I simply quote this bible? No, I can almost repeat it from memory.

And as it relates to our Inner City Black Students? Much to my sadness, on board our ship, Black sailors were assigned to the ship's kitchen regardless of their past experiences. In a chapter of my autobiography, "Prisoner of the Truck" I honor every one of these sailors by name).

And, in the past few years, I am impressed and proud of the teachers and the black students with whom I have worked with in my www.YesPa.org not-for-profit foundation. English speaking schools throughout the world have freely downloaded, used the materials and watched my video presentations, thanks to our high tech world. (Hi, Betsy Voss, our Secretary of Education, check it out).

Mr. President, you said, *"I know more about ISIS than the generals do. Believe me."*

Mr. President, consider the above Psalm 33. Example - *"Keep thy tongue from evil and they lips from speaking guile"*. As the military leader of our nation, you should be saying, *"I highly regard and respect the dedication, experience and wisdom of our law makers, our law enforcers and our generals, and believe me, fellow Americans, I will listen to them with dignity and respect."*

Mr. President, you said, *"My use of social media is not presidential? It's MODERN DAY PRESIDENTIAL. Make America Great Again. Believe me. You be the judge."*

Mr. President, when I judge, here's a short summary of a news article which wins this WWII Veteran's admiration.

By *John F. Banzhaf III - a professor of public interest law at the George Washington University Law School.*

"It is said that "loose lips sink ships," but lately loose lips have been sinking President Trump's centerpiece executive orders including Trump's latest on sanctuary cities. In his order, California federal judge **William Orrick III** *cited extensively from the President and from his various spokesmen in staying a new executive order threatening to withhold federal funds from sanctuary cities. Trump called the executive order a "weapon."*

And the opinions that I express, Mr. President, are those of a World War II Veteran who thanks God daily for his many blessings in family, friendships and energy at age 93.

Mr. President, you said, "I heard poorly rated@Morning Joe speaks badly of me (don't watch anymore). Then how come low I.Q. Crazy Mika, along with Psycho Joe came to Mar-a-Lago 3 nights in a row around New Year's Eve, and insisted on joining me. She was bleeding badly from a face-lift. I said no!"

Mr. President. Will it be ever possible to hear you speak in a Presidential tone and manner? Again, have you stopped to think that children either in the news, on their computers, or on their cell phones read or hear your nasty words. Definition of Nasty: *"unpleasant, disagreeable, disgusting, distasteful, awful".*

You said, *"Most politicians would have gone to a meeting like the one Don Jr attended in order to get info on an opponent. That's politics!"*

Mr. President, Donald Junior met with the Russian lawyer to get dirt on Hillary Clinton in the lead-up to the election. The Trump Hotel in Moscow as well – Read the entire Muller report.

You said, *"Eventually we're going to get something done and it's going to be really, really good."*

Mr. President, your sentences remind me of an actual quotation from a kiddy garden child. *"Our President tries to get things done, but my mother said he's not really really good about it".*

You said, *"You know I'm automatically attracted to beautiful – I just start kissing them. It's like a magnet. Just kiss. I don't even wait. And when you're a star, they let you do it. You can do anything. Grab them by the p**sy. You can do anything."*

Mr. President, Sorry, again, current data reflects the significant activity of children on the internet and cell phones. As our national leader, what example do you set for our children with such crude and rude comments?

You said, at the third presidential debate, *"Nobody respects women more than me."* Three minutes later regarding Hillary Clinton you hypocritically said, *"Such a nasty woman."*

Mr. President, the definition of nasty is *"unkind, unpleasant, unfriendly, disagreeable, inconsiderate"* And in my view, you are the one who is *"nasty"*.

You said, *"Why can't we use nuclear weapons?"* – reportedly asking a foreign policy adviser three times during a meeting why the U.S. couldn't use its nuclear weapons stockpile.

Mr. President, in light of the videos of the nuclear devastation witnessed in WWII in Japan and the photos of the thousands of dead and wounded Japanese adults and children, again, do you ever take your remarks seriously? Do you?

On a Gold Star Mother, you said, *"His wife, she was standing there, she had nothing to say. She probably — maybe she wasn't allowed to have anything to say."* —You smeared Ghazala Khan, the mother of a fallen American soldier, by implying that she was not allowed to speak, despite the fact that she has spoken publicly about her son's death (ABC News interview, July 30, 2016)."

How could anyone, including your supporting base, forgive your insensitive, cruel and rude remark to this Gold Star Mother?

Note: "You do know you just attacked a Gold Star family?" one adviser warned Trump Trump didn't know what a Gold Star family was: 'What's that?' he asked." –as reported by New York Magazine."

Mr. President, Possibly, if you have not been a "draft dodger" in your time, you would have understood what a Gold Star Mother is. I clearly remember. I had two first cousins in WWII whose mothers, in honor of their fallen sons, put Gold Stars on their front doors - and their parents were Catholic Syrian-Lebanese born immigrants. And thank God, my mother did not have to endure this sadness.

Mr. President note the date: *"When Iran, when they circle our beautiful destroyers with their little boats, and they make gestures at our people that they shouldn't be allowed to make, they will be shot out of the water."* –Donald

Trump, threatening to go to war with Iran over rude hand gestures, Pensacola, Florida, (Sept. 9, 2016)."

Mr. President, on Iran past and present, instead of your crude ***"shot out of the water"*** threat on Iran, you and your team should carefully consider the following objective and logical review summary dated February 5, 2019.

"Correcting course on Iran: Trump has left us painfully isolated; it's time to reorient our foreign policy – By Suzanne DIMAGGIO AND THOMAS PICKERING – FEBRUARY 5, 2019

"Withdrawing from the deal is seriously damaging the transatlantic alliance. President Trump is strong-arming our European allies to act against their own economic and security interests.

You said, *"that makes me smart."* – you said, responding to Hillary Clinton's suggestion that you pay no federal income tax (Sept. 26, 2016)."

Mr. President, as it pertains to your ongoing and declining supporters who pay their fair of taxes, I wonder why they do not come to the conclusion that you have not only been a smart <u>draft</u> dodger, you have also been a smart <u>tax</u> dodger.

Mr. President, you said, *"Russia, if you're listening, I hope you're able to find the 30,000 emails that are missing. I think you will probably be rewarded mightily by our press."* – calling on Russian espionage services to intervene in the U.S. election and help sabotage Hillary Clinton. The emails in question were deemed "personal," but Trump has previously said he thinks they contain sensitive intelligence, meaning that Trump is hoping Vladimir Putin gains access to classified government information (July 27, 2016)".

Mr. President, Hillary's email behavior, right or wrong, is one thing. Since you were elected our President, your behavior and your family's behavior with Russia is another thing.

Mr. President, you said, *"I've been treated very unfairly by this judge. Now, this judge is of Mexican heritage. I'm building a wall, OK? I'm building a wall."* –Donald Trump, accusing U.S. District Judge Gonzalo Curiel, who is presiding over the fraud case against Trump University, of being biased against him because of his Mexican heritage, despite the fact that he is a U.S. citizen who was born in Indiana (CNN interview, June 5, 2016)"

Mr. President, as President-elect, you agreed to a $25 million settlement to end the fraud cases pending against your now defunct real estate seminar program, Trump University. Schneiderman said, *"Today's $25 million settlement agreement is a stunning reversal by Donald Trump and a major victory for over 6,000 victims of his fraudulent university".*

Mr. President – Whenever I did something naughty as a child, my mother would say to me, *"My, my Fred, how could you do that?"* About the above issue, your supporters should say the same to you. Your above settlement is a clear indication of your guilt. I have learned that integrity in business pays dividends. In my business background, with 6,000 employees under my administration, and in contracts with major US corporations managing their food and vending services, as one example, I learned that a supplier was packing meat products with ice, weighing it and charging us for the ice as well as the meat. When I learned of this, I not only stopped this practice but I also gave a refund to my clients for the cost of the ice. Therefore, when prospective new clients called our existing clients to inquiry about our services, they were told that we were not only excellent in our service but we had unique integrity of operations.

My point is this? With four years of accounting in school, a contractor for food and vending operations and a developer of major resort properties in New York State, including a major ski area and a new village, I know a lot about integrity of operations, Balance Sheets, Income and Cash Flow Statements. And in addition to receiving many outstanding Community Awards for Public Service, I speak with some degree of public experience in my responses to all of your repeated crude comments. And I repeat to you and Attorney General, William Barr, what are you two hiding?

Mr. President, you said about Senator McCain, *"He's not a war hero. He's a war hero because he was captured. I like people that weren't captured."*

Mr. President, as I write this, John McCain died a few months ago. On March 20, 2019, you said that you gave Mr. McCain, "the funeral he wanted, and didn't get a thank you". In fact, you exaggerated the role you played in honoring the Senator's death four days before his 82nd Birthday. And your Lima supporters in hearing this did not boo you? I'll limit my comments to four words. *"How very, very sad".*

Mr. President, you said, *"now this poor guy — you've got to see this guy, 'Ah, I don't know what I said! I don't remember!'"* – You were mocking New York Times investigative reporter Serge Kovaleski, who has a physical disability called arthrogryposis that limits flexibility in his arms, by jerking his arms in front of his body".

And Mr. President you have mocked people with disabilities. More than 60% called the Kovaleski mockery your worst offense and even more people were offended by your attacks on the Khan family, who lost a son in the war in Iraq.

Mr. President, on November 3, 2016, you said, *"I'm also honored to have the greatest temperament that anybody has."*

Mr. President, as reflected on TV, your arrogance is well respected by your supporters but bear in mind there are 325 million US Citizens of which currently 60% do not respect you and this disrespect is growing.

Mr. President, you said, *"I don't think Ivanka would do that, although she does have a very nice figure. I've said if Ivanka weren't my daughter, perhaps I'd be dating her."* –Donald Trump, when asked how he would react if Ivanka posed for Playboy".

Mr. President, Indeed, Ivanka is a beautiful daughter in both looks, speech and mannerism. As it pertains to your past and present behavior regarding such talk, you should listen to her.

Mr. President, you actually said, *"Women: You have to treat them like s--t."*

Loose Lips Sink Ships

Mr. President, here is what you should say about women. *"Women should be treated with respect.* Or maybe you had a problem with your spelling as you did in college and currently in your tweets?

Mr. President, you said, *"I sorta get away with things like that."* —(On bursting into Miss Universe pageant dressing rooms)"

Mr. President – It is time you burst into the hearts of the World's Humanity. It is not too late. Give up the walls that separate us. Build bridges with others that unite us. Give it a try. It is not too late.

Mr. President, you said, *"I could stand in the middle of Fifth Avenue and shoot somebody, and I wouldn't lose any voters, okay? It's, like, incredible."* – Donald Trump, speaking at a rally in Sioux Center, Iowa as the audience laughed, January 23, 2016."

Mr. President how insane. This may be true of your base but they represent a small percentage of our 325 million Americans?

Mr. President, you said, "Hillary Clinton ... started the birther controversy. I finished it." –That's you, falsely claiming that Hillary Clinton started the rumors that President Obama wasn't born in the United States (Sept. 16, 2016)

Mr. President – This is *"childish"* defined as *"immaturity and lack of poise".*

You said, *"40 Wall Street actually was the second-tallest building in downtown Manhattan... And now it's the tallest."* This was you, bragging about your building following the 9/11 attack on the World Trade Center in an interview with a radio station on September 11, 2001.

Mr. President – Speaking of tallest? The more one studies your quotes, the more one is convinced that you constantly tell the tallest lies.

You said, *"Actually, I was only kidding. You can get that baby out of here. Don't worry; I think she really believed me that I love having a baby crying while I'm speaking. That's O.K. People don't understand. That's O.K."* –Donald

Trump, booting a mother and her crying baby from a rally moments after saying *"I love babies"* (August 2, 2016)

Mr. President – When that baby grows up, whoever she is, I hope she writes a book titled *"Trump thru me and my mother out"*. Who knows, she may get even by becoming our President in year 2070.

On November 13, 2015, You said, *"I know more about ISIS than the generals do, believe me… I would bomb the sh**t out of them."*

Mr. President – How about this kind of leadership response instead? *"Any decisions that I make regarding ISIS will involve huddles with my Vice-President, Cabinet Members and our Generals whose experience and input, I will deeply value and respect"*.

You said, *"[Vladimir Putin} is not going into Ukraine, OK, just so you understand. He's not gonna go into Ukraine, all right? You can mark it down. You can put it down."* – apparently unaware that Russia had already annexed Crimea in a 2014 intrusion into Ukraine that left thousands dead (July 31, 2016)

Mr. President – Do members of your staff endorse or respect your quotes? Sarah Huckebee, did you? Really, did you? Also, do you or members of your remaining staff live by and/or endorse or respect the following quotes?

"I always believe that ultimately, if people are paying attention, then we get good government and good leadership. And when we get lazy, as a democracy and civically start taking shortcuts, then it results in bad government and politics. BARACK OBAMA, interview, MSNBC, September 25, 2006"

"All of us are neck deep in politics everyday of our lives. Every organization on earth that involves human beings has its politics. Politics does not have to be a bad thing. Actually politics can be a good thing when we bring people to the table to sit down, work together, compromise and get things done for the common good". BILL GINDLESPERGER, "Politics is about how many friends, not enemies, you can make, *Public Opinion*, May 6, 2016"

"If you have sense enough to realize why flies gather around a restaurant, you should be able to appreciate why men run for office". EDGAR WATSON HOWE, *Country Town Sayings*

"If a political party does not have *its foundation in the determination to advance a cause that is right and that is moral, then it is not a political party; it is merely a conspiracy to seize power"*. DWIGHT D. EISENHOWER, speech, March 6, 1956

"Instead of giving a politician the keys to the city, it might be better to change the locks". DOUG LARSON, attributed, *Phillips' Treasury of Humorous Quotations*

"However [political parties] may now and then answer popular ends, they are likely in the course of time and things, to become potent engines, by which cunning, ambitious, and unprincipled men will be enabled to subvert the power of the people and to usurp for themselves the reins of government, destroying afterwards the very engines which have lifted them to unjust dominion".

GEORGE WASHINGTON, Farewell Address, September 19, 1796

"I used to say that politics was the second-oldest profession. I have come to know that it bears a gross similarity to the first". RONALD REAGAN, speech at a business conference in Los Angeles, California, March 2, 1977

"The majority is never right. Never, I tell you! That's one of these lies in society that no free and intelligent man can help rebelling against. Who are the people that make up the biggest proportion of the population -- the intelligent ones or the fools?" HENRIK IBSEN, *An Enemy of the People*

"The only motive that can keep politics pure is the motive of doing good for one's country and its people". HENRY FORD, "Party Politics", *Ford Ideals*

"The goal in the end is not to win elections. The goal is to change society". PAUL KRUGMAN, *Playboy*, March 2012

"Politics, n. A strife of interests masquerading as a contest of principles. The conduct of public affairs for private advantage". AMBROSE BIERCE, *The Devil's Dictionary*

"In politics, it's what isn't said that matters". K. J. PARKER, *Devices and Desires*

"Politics is not an end, but a means. It is not a product, but a process. It is the art of government. Like other values it has its counterfeits. So much emphasis has been placed upon the false that the significance of the true has been obscured and politics has come to convey the meaning of crafty and cunning selfishness, instead of candid and sincere service". CALVIN COOLIDGE, *Have Faith in Massachusetts*

"You don't have to wait till your party's in power to have an impact on life at home and around the world". BILL CLINTON, speech at Campus Progress National Student Conference, July 13, 2005

"We've come to be consumed by a 24-hour, slash-and-burn, negative ad, bickering, small-minded politics that doesn't move us forward. Sometimes one side is up and the other side is down. But there's no sense that they are coming together in a common-sense, practical, nonideological way to solve the problems that we face". - BARACK OBAMA, *New York Times*, December 11, 2006

"In politics, sunny days and rainy days can change very quickly". GIULIO ANDREOTTI, *"Giulio Andreotti: le frasi celebri e gli aforismi"*, *L'Huffington Post*, June 5, 2013

"I mean, you know, this idea that somebody we disagree with on economic or social policy or something we have to turn into some kind of ogre or demon, I think, is a mistake. I mean, it's like telling the American people or half the American people that don't agree with you they're all fools. That's just not true". – Credit - BILL CLINTON, interview, *Larry King Live*, June 1, 2005

Reading to the Democratic National Convention (July 29, 2016), you said, *"You know what I wanted to. I wanted to hit a couple of those speakers so hard. I would have hit them. No, no. I was going to hit them, I was all set and then I got a call from a highly respected governor... I was gonna hit one guy in particular, a very little guy. I was gonna hit this guy so hard his head would spin and he wouldn't know what the hell happened... I was going to hit a number of those speakers so hard their heads would spin, they'd never recover. And that's what I did with a lot – that's why I still don't have certain people endorsing me: they still haven't recovered." –* 2016)

Mr. President – Just for the fun of it, let me imitate you. *"Yeah, I'm gonna hit him. Yeah, he's our President but I'm gonna hit him so hard he would fall on his face and he wouldn't know what the hell happened. His head would spin and he'd never recover and I would go to jail even though he didn't go to jail for all the issues he got away way with."* (I repeat *"just for the fun of it"*).

"I think I've made a lot of sacrifices. I work very, very hard. I've created thousands and thousands of jobs, tens of thousands of jobs, built great structures. I've had tremendous success. I think I've done a lot." –Donald Trump, rejecting the assertion made at the Democratic convention by Muslim lawyer Khizr Khan, whose son died in Iraq in 2004, that Trump had *"sacrificed nothing and no one."*

Trump was unable to name an actual sacrifice when pressed to elaborate. (ABC News interview, July 30, 2016)

Mr. President - In WWII, we referred to people like you as "Draft Dodgers". Webster's definition of draft dodger - *a person who illegally avoids joining the armed forces".*

Bottom line Mr. President – Draft dodgers should not pick on the father of son who died serving our country. Draft dodgers should not pick on Senator John McCain, whose service as a Veteran, Prisoner of the War, and a Senator were loved and admired by the American people. Your loose lips on this issue are very, very hard for me to forget, and as I believe, with all of objective fellow Americans.

Tweeting a humble brag following the Orlando shooting massacre, June 12, 2016 you said, *"Appreciate the congrats for being right on radical Islamic terrorism, I don't want congrats, I want toughness & vigilance. We must be smart!"*

Mr. President, I'll keep this response very brief. You do not judge a Christian, Muslim, Jew or Atheist by the insane behavior of a few.

On July 29, 2016, you said, *"I've had a beautiful, I've had a flawless campaign. You'll be writing books about this campaign."*

Mr. President – Yes, I am writing this book about this campaign and your current leadership and the facts clearly review that your campaign and your current leadership are far from flawless – as a result of your *"Loose Lips"*.

On February 22, 2016, on how you would handle a protestor in Nevada, sparking a roaring applause from your audience, you said, *"I love the old days, you know? You know what I hate? There's a guy totally disruptive, throwing punches, we're not allowed punch back anymore. ... I'd like to punch him in the face, I'll tell ya."*

Mr. President – This is bonkers. What disturbs me more than your Trump-Punch-in-the-face comment is the *"sparking roaring applause from the audience"*. Indeed, in this great democracy of ours, they are indeed entitled to their point of view but I wonder how other WWII Veterans and the Veterans of all Wars truly feel about all of your quotes.

Synonyms for *"bonkers"* which fits your public quotes:

"balmy, barmy *[chiefly British]*, bats, batty, bedlam, brainsick, bughouse *[slang]*,certifiable, crackbrained, cracked, crackers, crackpot, cranky *[dialect]*, crazed, crazy,cuckoo, daffy, daft, demented, deranged, fruity *[slang]*, gaga, haywire, insane, kooky*(also* kookie*)*, loco *[slang]*, loony *(also* looney*)*, *(or* looney tunes*)*, lunatic,mad, maniacal *(also* maniac*)*, mental, meshuga *(or* meshugge*)*, moonstruck, non compos mentis, nuts, nutty, psycho, psychotic, scatty *[chiefly British]*, screwy,unbalanced, unhinged, unsound, wacko *(also* whacko*)*, wacky *(also* whacky*)*, wud*[chiefly Scottish]*")

Mr. President, you encouraging violence at your rally in Cedar Rapids, Iowa, Feb. 1, 2016.

Ready to throw a tomato, knock the crap out of them, would you? Seriously. Okay? Just knock the hell -- I promise you, I will pay for the legal fees."

Mr. President – Pay for the legal fees? As an eight year old boy who helped his father sell fruits and vegetables off of his truck, the tomato makes me think of other vegetables or fruits like the peach and in 2019, I think about the <u>impeach</u> definition: specifically *: to charge (a public official) before a competent tribunal with misconduct.* Or I could think of a *pear* which rhymes with impair as with your *impaired* mannerism.

You said, *"I don't care. It's a long time ago. And he voted that way and they were also misled. A lot of information was given to people…"* This pertained to your forgiving your running mate, Mike Pence, for voting in favor of the Iraq war, saying he was *"entitled to make a mistake.* (This was in a 60 Minutes interview on July 17, 2016)

Mr. President, on VP Mike Spence, he stands next to you with a good looking firm face. I often wonder. *"What is he really thinking that he dare not say?"* When he goes home, *"What does he truly tell his wife about you, his boss?"*

You said, *"There were people that were cheering on the other side of New Jersey, where you have large Arab populations. They were cheering as the World Trade Center came down."*

Mr. President a November 21, 2015 New York Times article stated the rumors were never substantiated and that thousands and thousands of any group of people could not physically congregate on a rooftop. Mr. President. No different than all of the above. As the media reported, this quotation is an unforgiveable outright lie. It personally offends me and my family of Arabic heritage, Eastern Rite Catholics under the Pope, (which I am), law-abiding US Muslim citizens, and I believe other open-minded US Citizens and I mean "open minded".

Mr. President – My further comment on this subject. With all of my experiences related to WWII, jobs, real estate developments and community services in which I have received major awards, I look you in the eye and I say to you. *"Loose lips Sink Ships"*. And your memory is indeed not only loose, but blatantly and carelessly false.

Mr. President, defending the size of your penis in reference to a joke by Republican rival Marco Rubio, GOP presidential debate, March 3, 2016, you said, *"He referred to my hands, if they're small, something else must be small. I guarantee you there's no problem. I guarantee it."* –

Mr. President – Your base may overlook this, but I wonder how mothers feel about this poor crude-and-rude example for children coming from the then future President of the United States? Consider that in these modern times, current technology spreads all of your comments to children. Imagine a child saying, *"Mom, if our President can say it, why can't I?"*

You said, *"You could see there was blood coming out of her eyes. Blood coming out of her wherever"*. – insulting Fox News anchor Megyn Kelly over questions she asked during the first Republican primary debate.

Mr. President – How your supporting base who have children, can ignore this and your many other *"loose lips"* comments is beyond my comprehension? If a vote were taken, I believe 95% of our US Citizens would clearly call this and other remarks as very un-presidential.

And how about this Mr. President? You said, *"You know, it really doesn't matter what [the media] writes as long as you've got a young and beautiful piece of ass."*

I repeat my response above regarding your utter vulgarity that will go down in history. And don't forget that reality.

You said in a victory press conference in New York on April 26, 2016, *"I think the only card she has is the women's card. She has got nothing else going. Frankly, if Hillary Clinton were a man, I don't think she would get 5% of the vote. And the beautiful thing is women don't like her, ok?"*

Mr. President, as I wrote before, Hillary did receive over two million more votes than you did in the US. Meanwhile, we await the conclusion of the complete Muller findings which may lead to your impeachment.

In a response to remarks by Pope Francis saying that "a person, who thinks only about building walls, wherever they may be, and not building bridges, is not Christian." (February 18, 2016), you said, *"For a religious leader to question a person's faith is disgraceful. I am proud to be a Christian. … If and when the Vatican is attacked by ISIS, which as everyone knows is ISIS' ultimate trophy, I can promise you that the Pope would have only wished and prayed that Donald Trump would have been President because this would not have happened."*

Mr. President – It clearly appears that, in your words as well as your actions, you are not a Christian as you profess to be. Your extensive business experience lacks the building of a single bridge and your political experience, thus far, also reflects your inability to even build just one bridge needed in our United States. And indeed, as I write this in 2019, the people have spoken as reflected in the recent election and control of the House of Representatives by the Democrats.

You said, suggesting that Ted Cruz's father may have been involved in the assassination of President John F. Kennedy, despite the fact that no proof exists of any such link, Fox News interview, May 3, 2016.

"His father was with Lee Harvey Oswald prior to Oswald's being – you know, shot. I mean, the whole thing is ridiculous. What is this, right prior to his being shot, and nobody even brings it up. They don't even talk about that. That was reported, and nobody talks about it."

Mr. President – What shocks me regarding the above is not you. It is Ted Cruz who seems to have ignored this *unbelievable 2016 insult as he stands next to you in a 2019 recent photo near the start of your proposed wall. This WWII Vet has no respect for Ted Cruz. To those who elected Ted, think about* it.

"What do I know about it? All I know is what's on the internet." – You said, on trying to smear a protester who rushed the stage at his campaign rally by tweeting a widely debunked hoax video tying him to ISIS. (Credit - Meet the Press interview, March 13, 2016)

Mr. President, simple stated, *"a widely debunked hoax video"* is a lie - period. Definition of debunk – *"expose the falseness or hollowness of (a myth, idea, or belief)"*. Definition of hoax - *"a humorous or malicious deception"* Note: Possibly my book should have been entitled *"Presidential Hoax's and Debunks"*.

You said, *"When Mexico sends its people, they're not sending their best. They're sending people that have lots of problems...they're bringing drugs, they're bringing crime. They're rapists."*

Mr. President, Mexico or other counties are not sending its people. The people who wish to flee are no different than past immigrants who now live in the US….who were escaping from some form of hardship in the past…in which they could no longer tolerate ….work, famine, religious persecution or otherwise.

You said on Twitter, *"Happy Cinco de Mayo! The best taco bowls are made in Trump Tower Grill. I love Hispanics!"*

Mr. President – Here's what appears to be your past and current byline on Russia. *"I love Russia. One of these days, either myself or family members will have a Trump Tower in Russia serving the "best taco bowls" even after the impeachment of my Presidency or the loss of my reelection"*.

You said at a rally in Portsmouth, New Hampshire: *"We're gonna bring businesses back. We're gonna have businesses that used to be in New Hampshire, that are now in Mexico, come back to New Hampshire, and you can tell them to go f**k themselves. Because they let you down, and they left!"* –You at a rally in Portsmouth, New Hampshire

Mr. President, devoted Christians, Jews and Muslims would all most likely agree that your foul language demeans your office and is harmful to our children. Why could not you just say, *"and you tell them we mean business"*.

Speaking about politicians at a campaign rally in Exeter New Hampshire, you said, *"These people – I'd like to use really foul language. I won't do it. I was going to say they're really full of s**t, but I won't say that".*

Mr. President, how about the word dishonest instead of that vulgar word. Note there is an "s" "h" "i" and a "t" in dishonest so why not spell out "dishonesty" completely?

In a New York Times interview (Maureen Dowd on November 28, 1999), you said, *"My entire life, I've watched politicians bragging about how poor they are, how they came from nothing, how poor their parents and grandparents were. And I said to myself, if they can stay so poor for so many generations, maybe this isn't the kind of person we want to be electing to higher office. How smart can they be? They're morons."*

Mr. President, in responding to this, I feel like a parrot. And it makes me think of this comment and the Webster's dictionary definition of moron: *"a very stupid person; a person affected with mild mental retardation."*

Mr. President, I repeat, you often brag about how rich you are. How Russians have purchased million dollar condos from your family. How, during the Presidential election process, thinking you would not win the Presidential election, you were leading the charge on a Trump Tower in Moscow and how the law allows you to fail to provide your tax returns to the American people. And many of our elected officials and your base allow you to get away with all of this.

And a news review found that at least 63 individuals with Russian passports or addresses bought at least $98.4 million worth of property in seven Trump-branded luxury towers in southern Florida. And a person, who proclaims to be a Christian? And as such, maybe each and every morning, you and your elected officials should consider the following quotation from the bible:

"Now when he saw the crowds, he went up on a mountainside and sat down. His disciples came to Him, and He began to teach them, saying: Blessed are the poor in spirit, for theirs is the kingdom of heaven. Blessed are those who mourn, for they will be comforted. Blessed are the meek, for they will inherit the earth. ⁶Blessed are those who hunger and thirst after righteousness, for they will be filled.⁷Blessed are the merciful, for they shall be shown mercy. Blessed are the pure in heart, for they will see God. Blessed are the peacemakers, for they will be called the children of God. Blessed are those who are persecuted because of righteousness, for theirs is the kingdom of heaven. Blessed are you when people insult you, persecute you and falsely say all kinds of evil against you because of me, rejoice and be glad, because great is your reward in heaven, for in the same way they persecuted the prophets who were before you. The Beatitudes (Matthew 5:1-12)

Mr. President, note the following quoted from the U.S. Poverty September 18 2018

U.S. Poverty Statistics

Here are the current U.S. Poverty Statistics released September 2018 by the U.S. Census Bureau [i]. They represent various categories of the population and the percentage of people within those categories in a poverty status (more on <u>Poverty Threshold page</u>):

> Adults not working - 31%
> Single moms - 26%
> Adults with a disability - 25%
> Adults without a high school diploma - 25%
> Black Americans - 21%
> Foreign born non-citizens - 19%
> Hispanic Americans - 18%
> All children - 18%
> Single dads - 12%
> Seniors - 9%

Married couples - 5%
Adults with college degree or higher - 5%
Full time working adults - 2%

What is the difference between the official and supplemental poverty measures?

It is my understanding that the official poverty measure triples the inflation-adjusted cost of a minimum food diet and creates thresholds. These are based on family size, and ages of householders. Anyone living with an income below their relative <u>poverty threshold</u> is considered to be in poverty.

The U.S. Department of Health and Human Services develops the Federal Poverty Guideline income thresholds. It is based on the official poverty measure estimates which are used to determine eligibility for <u>federal safety net programs</u>, such as Medicaid.

Since the 1960s, new poverty measures provide <u>a more complex understanding of poverty in the United States</u>. The supplemental measure includes basic costs of living that can vary across states. It also includes transfers from safety net programs and in-kind benefits"

You said, in a boast that provoked widespread ridicule from the LGBT community on June 15, 2016:

"The LGBT community, the gay community, the lesbian community — they are so much in favor of what I've been saying over the last three or four days. Ask the gays what they think and what they do, in, not only Saudi Arabia, but many of these countries, and then you tell me — who's your friend, Donald Trump or Hillary Clinton?"

Mr. President – The ridicule you received from the LGBT community was not only justified, it was well deserved.

The news media reported: *"Donald J. Trump is calling for a total and complete shutdown of Muslims entering the United States until our country's representatives can figure out what is going on."*

Mr. President – In the historical rentals of your New York apartments, you and your father allowed discrimination against blacks. You and your family marketed multi-million dollar Condos to Muslims and Russians. As before, I repeat, our US Presidents and Governing Bodies should be more interested in building bridges with the world rather than walls and, in this regard, you have yet to build a single bridge.

In an interview with MSNBC's Joe Scarborough, when pressed to condemn such actions, you said, I think our country does plenty of killing also, Joe", seemingly unconcerned that Russian President Vladimir Putin kills journalists who disagree with him.

Mr. President – Read all the pages *of the recent Muller Report.*

You said, in a tweet quoting fascist Italian dictator Benito Mussolini, "It is better to live one day as a lion than 100 years as a sheep.".

Mr. President – Indeed, you growl as a lion against "fake news" but you have been like a lamb with Russia's Vladimir Putin. Maybe in the future, we should address you as President Benito Muscle Trump?

You said, *"[Hillary Clinton] was gonna beat Obama. I don't know who would be worse, I don't know, how could it be worse? But she was going to beat – she was favored to win – and she got schlonged, she lost, I mean she lost."*

Mr. President – OK. I am a WWII Vet. I was also the Chaplain's assistant on board the USS Guam CB2. I am a Christian. I am the father of five and grandfather of thirteen. I spend my retirement in a not-for-profit mission to help kids and prisoners. Let me tell you that the definition of "schlonged" is disgusting. I did not realize how bad that word is until I just looked it up. And to your avid supporters, both men and women I say take a moment to stop reading and then look it up. Do you find it entertaining or do you find it absolutely disgusting?

You said on Hillary Clinton taking a bathroom break during a Democratic presidential debate.

"I know where she went – it's disgusting, I don't want to talk about it. No, it's too disgusting. Don't say it, it's disgusting." Mr. President – How on earth anyone who is familiar with your repeated and constant disgusting behavior can support you is beyond my comprehension?

You said about the Republican presidential candidate Carly Fiorina. *"Look at that face! Would anyone vote for that? Can you imagine that, the face of our next president I mean, she's a woman, and I'm not supposed to say bad things, but really, folks, come on. Are we serious?"*

Everyone should agree that the President of the United States on this and other Presidential issues should live and honor the definition of "Diplomat". And here is the definition:

"One employed or skilled in <u>diplomacy</u>", *the art and practice of conducting negotiations between nations - skill in handling affairs without arousing <u>hostility</u>"*. Mr. President, this is what you and your yes men should fully practice.

You said, *"All of the women on 'The Apprentice' flirted with me – consciously or unconsciously. That's to be expected."*

Mr. President – With your ongoing arrogance and lack of respect for women you remain a poor example for our children. I parrot, *"how can any of your supporters continue to support or respect you?"*

Mr. President, you praised two audience members who tackled a protester at your rally in South Carolina. *"That was so great. Who was the person who did that? Put up your hand, put up your hand. Bring that person up here. I love that."*

Mr. President – Did you ever attend a church service while you were in College? Just wondering? And if so, do you remember ever reciting the following?

Frederick W. Sarkis

THE EIGHT BEATITUDES OF JESUS

"Blessed are the poor in spirit,
for theirs is the kingdom of heaven.
Blessed are they who mourn,
for they shall be comforted.
Blessed are the meek,
for they shall inherit the earth.
Blessed are they who hunger and thirst for righteousness,
for they shall be satisfied.
Blessed are the merciful,
for they shall obtain mercy.
Blessed are the pure of heart,
for they shall see God.
Blessed are the peacemakers,
for they shall be called children of God.
Blessed are they who are persecuted for the sake of righteousness,
for theirs is the kingdom of heaven."
Gospel of St. Matthew 5:30.10

Mr. President, *"Christ is all loving, all holy and all merciful."* He was a bridge builder not a wall maker. And carefully study each one of the above eight Beatitudes as it relates to those in need within and beyond our borders. And further, as it relates to the Ten Commandments embraced by Christians and Jews, it also relates to the Islam faith as briefly reflected in the following:

"Name of Counselor Ahmad Kutty - Wa `alaykum As-Salamu wa Rahmatullahi wa Barakatuh. In the Name of Allah, Most Gracious, Most Merciful. All praise and thanks are due to Allah, and peace and blessings be upon His Messenger. 'Dear questioner, we would like to thank you for the great confidence you place in us, and we implore Allah Almighty to help us serve His cause and render our work for His sake. The Ten Commandments—with the exception of the fourth one, which deals with observance of the Sabbath—in essence and spirit belong to the perennial religion that allows for no abrogation or alteration, and thus in essence and spirit constitute an integral part of the Qur'anic ethics and laws."

Mr. President, on March 14, 2016, on your campaign rallies, <u>despite documented evidence</u> to the contrary, you said:

"The press is now going, they're saying, 'Oh but there's such violence.' No violence. You know how many people have been hurt at our rallies? I think, like, basically none except maybe somebody got hit once. It's a love fest. These are love fests. And every once in a while ... somebody will stand up and they'll say something.... It's a little disruption, but there's no violence. There's none whatsoever."

Mr. President – Even three years ago in 2016, you treated "documented evidence" with disdain and your supporters applause it?

You said, *"I will build a great wall – and nobody builds walls better than me, believe me —and I'll build them very inexpensively. I will build a great, great wall on our southern border, and I will make Mexico pay for that wall. Mark my words."*

Mr. President, El Paso, Texas transcends the border. Their community chooses to celebrate it. It is a fact that their community has consistently ranked as one of the safest in the United States. (January 18, 2019 - from Robert Farley, the Wire, Fact Check on January 18, 2019). And today, dozens of Fortune 500 companies reside in Juarez, the Mexicana City on the other side of their border fence. And further, the residents eat in restaurants and walk the streets in safety.

Mr. President, vastly overstating the unemployment rate in a claim rated false by Politifact, Sept. 28, 2015, you said:

"I've seen numbers of 24 percent — I actually saw a number of 42 percent unemployment. Forty-two percent. 5.3 percent unemployment -- that is the biggest joke there is in this country. ... The unemployment rate is probably 20 percent, but I will tell you, you have some great economists that will tell you it's a 30, 32. And the highest I've heard so far is 42 percent."

Mr. President – And the world is round – not flat.

You said, *"I think the only difference between me and the other candidates is that I'm more honest and my women are more beautiful."*

Mr. President. The definition of humility is. *"a modest or low view of one's own importance; humbleness"* – Let the reader decide about your humility.

You said, *"The beauty of me is that I'm very rich."*

Mr. President you might have pompously added, *"And I will not openly share my tax returns with the people of the United States, neither with those who elected me and/or those who didn't and my supporting base won't give a damn"*. (Note Mr. President, let's see how your vocal supporters feel when they compare the taxes they paid in 2018 with the taxes they will pay for year 2019 compared to the taxes the rich paid in 2018 compared to 2019).

You said, *"I like kids. I mean, I won't do anything to take care of them. I'll supply funds, and she'll take care of the kids."* –Donald Trump

Mr. President – In 1965, before his death, on a chairlift of a major ski area that I financed, Robert Kennedy actually asked me, *"If I become President of the US, would you be interested in serving our country?"* I replied, *"Yes, I would. I want to be in charge of food and water for the world's disadvantaged. I want to be sure that middle men do not get involve."* Sadly, a few months later he was shot to death. If you have any doubt about my meeting with Robert Kennedy, read a book that I wrote sixteen years ago titled *"Prisoner of the Truck"* and view the photo of my skiing with the then Senator.

And as it relates to your *"liking kids"*, does this include kids South of our Border? Does it include kids of the Muslim faith?

You said, *"I have a great relationship with the blacks."*

Mr. President – Really? You have repeated said that you are *"the least racist person that you've ever known"*. Your record tells a different story. On the campaign trail, you repeatedly made racists and bigoted remarks. You called Mexican immigrants criminals and rapists. You even suggested that a US judge should recuse himself because of his Mexican heritage.

This trend continued in your presidency. You stereotyped a black reporter to pandering white supremacists after they held a violent rally in Charlottesville, to cracking a joke about the Trail of Tears. You have stopped with racist acts only after your 2016 election.

The very first time you appeared in the 1970 pages in the New York Times, the US Department of Justice sued you for racial discrimination. Since then, you have repeatedly appeared in newspaper pages across the world as you inspired more comparable controversies.

Simply misspeaking one or two times is one thing. However, when you take all of your actions and comments together, a clear pattern comes to light – one that suggests that bigotry is not just political opportunism on your part. It is a real element of your personality, character and career.

You said, *"If Hillary Clinton can't satisfy her husband what makes her think she can satisfy America."*

Mr. President – In your book "Art of the Deal", let me quote you.

"After I graduated from the New York Military Academy in 1964, I flirted briefly with the idea of attending film school but in the end, I decided real estate was a much better business. I began by attending Fordham University... but after two years, I decided that as long as I had to be in college, I might as well test myself against the best. I applied to the Wharton School at the University of Pennsylvania and I got in....I was also very glad to get finished. I immediately moved back home and went to work full time with my father."

Just one question Mr. President – Did you ever "flirt" with the idea of taking a course in "mannerism". Here is a quote example taken from the Web. *"Trump has many of the mannerisms and much of the style of a plebiscitary dictator who wields demagogic rhetoric to turn the crowd against liberal institutions"*. Wow!!!

You said, three week before Obama released his long-form birth certificate in 2011,

"I have people that have been studying [Obama's birth certificate] and they cannot believe what they're finding... I would like to have him show his birth certificate, and can I be honest with you, I hope he can. Because if he can't, if he can't, if he wasn't born in this country, which is a real possibility...then he has pulled one of the great cons in the history of politics".

Mr. President – This WWII Vet firmly believe that, unlike President Obama, you will go down as the *"greatest con artist president"* in US History.

In a CNN interview in March 16, 2016, on what will happen if the nomination is taken from you at the Republic Convention, you said, *"I think you'd have riots. I think you'd have riots. I'm representing many, many millions of people. I think you'd have problems like you've never seen before. I wouldn't lead it, but I think bad things will happen."*

Mr. President – You are a graduate of prestigious schools but you are far from being a prestigious graduate. Do you know that prestigious means *"distinguished, respected, esteemed?"*

Also, Mr. President, as far as presidential leadership is concerned, note the following departures from your administration so far and ask yourself if these departures in just the past two years of these highly qualified and respected individuals have anything to do with your failed direction or Presidential leadership?

Sally Yates, US Deputy Attorney General, Preet Bharara, US Attorney for the Southern District of NY, Katie Walsh, Deputy White House Chief of Staff, Michael Flynn, National Security Advisor, K.T. McFarland, Dep. National Security Advisor, Vivek Murthy, Surgeon General, James Comey, FBI Director, Mike Dubke, Communications Director, Walter Schaub, Office of Government Ethics Director, Sean Spicer, WH Press Secretary, Reince Priebus, WH Chief of Staff, Anthony Scaramucci, Communications Director, Steve Bannon, Chief Strategist, Segastian Gorka, Dep. Asst. to the President, Tom Price, HHS Secretary, Richard Cordray, Consumer Financial Protection Bureau Director, Dina Powell, Deb. National Security Advisor, Omarosa ManiGAULT, Communications Director at the WH

Office of Public Liaison, Rick Dearborn, Dep. Chief of Staff, Brenda Fitzgerald, CDC Director, Rob Porter, WH Staff Secretary, Hope Hicks, Communications Director, Gary Cohn, NEC Director, Rex Tillersen, Secretary of State, Andrew McCabe, FBI Dep. Director, H.R. McMaster, National Security Adviser. David Shulkin, Veterans Affairs Secretary as of March 2018.

Announcing your campaign for president, you said, "I will be the greatest jobs president that God ever created."

Mr. President – God ever created? Since you became President, I'll leave that judgement about to God and those who vote in our next election.

You said, "I don't think I've made mistakes. Every time somebody said I made a mistake, they do the polls and my numbers go up, so I guess I haven't made any mistakes." –Donald Trump.

As of 4-24-19 – 51% disapprove. (according to Fox News)

Mr. President, I leave this judgement up to the people.

You said, *"Washington – October 2018. About 44% of the troops had a favorable view of Trump's presidency, the poll showed, compared to 43% who approved".* In your victory speech, you said, "I pledge to every citizen of our land that I will be president for all Americans".

Mr. President, I have not studied favorable views of Past Presidents but can you image troops lined up with the 44% of troops on the left with a favorable view and then a space and the 56% of the troops on the right with an unfavorable view?

Chapter Eight

In Tribute to Past Presidents - 50 Greatest Presidential Quotes of All Time

"Every gun that is made, every warship launched, every rocket fired signifies, in the final sense, a theft from those who hunger and are not fed, those who are cold and are not clothed."
– **Dwight D. Eisenhower (1953-1961)**

"Under the cloud of threatening war, it is humanity hanging from a cross of iron….Is there no other way the world may live?" "So, first of all, let me assert my firm belief that the only thing we have to fear is fear itself." – **Franklin Delano Roosevelt (1933-1945)**

"There is something inherently wrong, something out of accord with the ideals of representative democracy, when one portion of our citizenship turns its activities to private gain amid defensive war while another is fighting, sacrificing, or dying for national preservation."
– **Warren G. Harding (1921-1923)**

"In a storm at sea no one on board can wish the ship to sink, and yet not unfrequently all go down together because too many will direct and no single mind can be allowed to control."
– **Abraham Lincoln (1861-1865)**

"Peace is the best time for improvement and preparation of every kind; it is in peace that our commerce flourishes most, that taxes are most easily paid, and that the revenue is most productive." – **James Monroe (1817-1825)**

Democracy & Government

"But I do have an unyielding belief that all people yearn for certain things: the ability to speak your mind and have a say in how you are governed; confidence in the rule of law and the equal administration of justice; government that is transparent and doesn't steal from the people; the freedom to live as you choose. Those are not just American ideas, they are human rights, and that is why we will support them everywhere." – **Barack Obama (2009-2017)**

"We the people tell the government what to do, it doesn't tell us." – **Ronald Reagan (1981-1989)**

"A president's hardest task is not to do what is right, but to know what is right." – **Lyndon B. Johnson (1963-1969)**

"No government is perfect. One of the chief virtues of a democracy, however, is that its defects are always visible and under democratic processes can be pointed out and corrected." – **Harry S. Truman (1945-1953)**

"You cannot extend the mastery of government over the daily life of a people without somewhere making it master of people's souls and thoughts." – **Herbert Hoover (1929-1933)**

"Being a politician is a poor profession. Being a public servant is a noble one." – **Herbert Hoover (1929-1933)**

"It is not the enactment, but the observance of laws, that creates the character of a nation." – **Calvin Coolidge (1923-1929)**

"I can imagine no greater disservice to the country than to establish a system of censorship that would deny to the people of a free republic like our own their indisputable right to criticize their own public officials." – **Woodrow Wilson (1913-1921)**

*"In the history of mankind many republics have risen, have flourished for a less or greater time, and then have fallen because their citizens lost the power

of governing themselves and thereby of governing their state." – **Theodore Roosevelt (1901-1909)**

"Officeholders are the agents of the people, not their masters." – **Grover Cleveland (1885-1889, 1893-1897)**

"This country, with its institutions, belongs to the people who inhabit it. Whenever they shall grow weary of the existing government, they can exercise their constitutional right of amending it or their revolutionary right to dismember or overthrow it." – **Abraham Lincoln (1861-1865)**

<u>*"A president's hardest task is not to do what is right, but to know what is right.*</u> *The only legitimate right to govern is an express grant of power from the governed."* - **William Henry Harrison (1841)**

"It's time to remember that old wisdom our soldiers will never forget, that whether we are black or brown or white, we all bleed the same red blood of patriots." - **Donald J. Trump (2017-)**

"Change will not come if we wait for some other person, or if we wait for some other time. We are the ones we've been waiting for. We are the change that we seek." - **Barack Obama (2009-2017)**

"It is now our generation's task to carry on what those pioneers began. For our journey is not complete until our wives, our mothers and daughters can earn a living equal to their efforts. Our journey is not complete until our gay brothers and sisters are treated like anyone else under the law – for if we are truly created equal, then surely the love we commit to one another must be equal as well." – **Barack Obama (2009-2017)**

"America has never been united by blood or birth or soil. We are bound by ideals that move us beyond our backgrounds, lift us above our interests and teach us what it means to be citizens." **George W. Bush (2001-2009)**

We must teach our children to resolve their conflicts with words, not weapons." **Bill Clinton (1993-2001)**

"Think about every problem, every challenge, we face. The solution to each starts with education." – **George H.W. Bush (1989-1993)**

"For this is what America is all about. It is the uncrossed desert and the unclimbed ridge. It is the star that is not reached and the harvest that is sleeping in the unplowed ground." – **Lyndon B. Johnson (1963-1969)**

"If national pride is ever justifiable or excusable it is when it springs, not from power or riches, grandeur or glory, but from conviction of national innocence, information, and benevolence." – **John Adams (1797-1801)**

"But should the people of America once become capable of that deep simulation towards one another, and towards foreign nations, which assumes the language of justice and moderation, while it is practicing iniquity and extravagance, and displays in the most captivating manner the charming pictures of candor, frankness, and sincerity, while it is rioting in rapine and insolence, this country will be the most miserable habitation in the world." – – **John Adams (1797-1801)**

"When one side only of a story is heard and often repeated, the human mind becomes impressed with it insensibly." – **George Washington (1789-1797)**

"Liberty without learning is always in peril, and learning without liberty is always in vain." – **John F. Kennedy (1961-1963)**

"Those who want the government to regulate matters of the mind and spirit are like men who are so afraid of being murdered that they commit suicide to avoid assassination." – **Harry S. Truman (1945-1953)**

"I would rather belong to a poor nation that was free than to a rich nation that had ceased to be in love with liberty." – **Woodrow Wilson (1913-1921)**

"The advancement and diffusion of knowledge is the only guardian of true liberty." – **James Madison (1809-1817)**

"We all declare for liberty; but in using the same word we do not all mean the same thing…it follows that each of the things is, by the respective parties, called

by two different and incompatible names — liberty and tyranny." – **Abraham Lincoln (1861-1865)**

"Although in our country the Chief Magistrate must almost of necessity be chosen by a party and stand pledged to its principles and measures, yet in his official action he should not be the President of a part only, but of the whole people of the United States." **James K. Polk (1845-1849)**

"However [political parties] may now and then answer popular ends, they are likely in the course of time and things, to become potent engines, by which cunning, ambitious, and unprincipled men will be enabled to subvert the power of the people and to usurp for themselves the reins of government, destroying afterwards the very engines which have lifted them to unjust dominion." – **George Washington (1789-1797)**

Power

"...Only if you've been in the deepest valley can you ever know how magnificent it is to be on the highest mountain..." – **Richard Nixon (1969-1974)**

"There is nothing more corrupting, nothing more destructive of the noblest and finest feelings of our nature, than the exercise of unlimited power." – **William Henry Harrison (1841)**

Economy - *"We've learned that piling up material goods cannot fill the emptiness of lives which have no confidence or purpose."* – **Jimmy Carter (1977-1981)**

"Economy is idealism in its most practical form." – **Calvin Coolidge (1923-1929)**

Labor - *"I pity the man who wants a coat so cheap that the man or woman who produces the cloth or shapes it into a garment will starve in the process."* - – **Benjamin Harrison (1889-1893)**

"The diffusion of information and arraignment of all abuses at the bar of the public reason; freedom of religion; freedom of the press, and freedom of person under the protection of the habeas corpus, and trial by juries impartially selected. These principles form the bright constellation which has gone before us and guided our steps through an age of revolution and reformation." – **Thomas Jefferson (1801-1809)**

"In a storm at sea no one on board can wish the ship to sink, and yet not unfrequently all go down together because too many will direct and no single mind can be allowed to control." **Abraham Lincoln (1861-1865)**

"Peace is the best time for improvement and preparation of every kind; it is in peace that our commerce flourishes most, that taxes are most easily paid, and that the revenue is most productive." **James Monroe (1817-1825)**

Democracy & Government

"But I do have an unyielding belief that all people yearn for certain things: the ability to speak your mind and have a say in how you are governed; confidence in the rule of law and the equal administration of justice; government that is transparent and doesn't steal from the people; the freedom to live as you choose. Those are not just American ideas, they are human rights, and that is why we will support them everywhere." **Barack Obama (2009-2017)**

"We the people tell the government what to do, it doesn't tell us." **Ronald Reagan (1981-1989)**

"A president's hardest task is not to do what is right, but to know what is right." **Lyndon B. Johnson (1963-1969)**

"Mankind must put an end to war — or war will put an end to mankind". **John F. Kennedy in his 1961 Address to the UN General Assembly.**

"No government is perfect. One of the chief virtues of a democracy, however, is that its defects are always visible and under democratic processes can be pointed out and corrected." **Harry S. Truman (1945-1953)**

"You cannot extend the mastery of government over the daily life of a people without somewhere making it master of people's souls and thoughts." **Herbert Hoover (1929-1933)**

"Being a politician is a poor profession. Being a public servant is a noble one." - **Herbert Hoover (1929-1933)**

"It is not the enactment, but the observance of laws, that creates the character of a nation." **Calvin Coolidge (1923-1929)**

"I can imagine no greater disservice to the country than to establish a system of censorship that would deny to the people of a free republic like our own their indisputable right to criticize their own public officials." **Woodrow Wilson (1913-1921)**

"In the history of mankind many republics have risen, have flourished for a less or greater time, and then have fallen because their citizens lost the power of governing themselves and thereby of governing their state." **Theodore Roosevelt (1901-1909)**

"Officeholders are the agents of the people, not their masters." **Grover Cleveland (1885-1889, 1893-1897)**

"This country, with its institutions, belongs to the people who inhabit it. Whenever they shall grow weary of the existing government, they can exercise their constitutional right of amending it or their revolutionary right to dismember or overthrow it." **Abraham Lincoln (1861-1865)**

<u>A president's hardest task is not to do what is right, but to know what is right.</u>

"The only legitimate right to govern is an express grant of power from the governed." **William Henry Harrison (1841)**

"It's time to remember that old wisdom our soldiers will never forget, that whether we are black or brown or white, we all bleed the same red blood of patriots." **Donald J. Trump (2017)**

"Change will not come if we wait for some other person, or if we wait for some other time. We are the ones we've been waiting for. We are the change that we seek." **Barack Obama (2009-2017)**

"It is now our generation's task to carry on what those pioneers began. For our journey is not complete until our wives, our mothers and daughters can earn a living equal to their efforts. Our journey is not complete until our gay brothers and sisters are treated like anyone else under the law – for if we are truly created equal, then surely the love we commit to one another must be equal as well." **Barack Obama (2009-2017)**

"America has never been united by blood or birth or soil. We are bound by ideals that move us beyond our backgrounds, lift us above our interests and teach us what it means to be citizens." **George W. Bush (2001-2009)**

"We must teach our children to resolve their conflicts with words, not weapons." **Bill Clinton (1993-2001)**

"Think about every problem, every challenge, we face. The solution to each starts with education." **George H.W. Bush (1989-1993)**

"For this is what America is all about. It is the uncrossed desert and the unclimbed ridge. It is the star that is not reached and the harvest that is sleeping in the unplowed ground." **Lyndon B. Johnson (1963-1969)**

"If national pride is ever justifiable or excusable it is when it springs, not from power or riches, grandeur or glory, but from conviction of national innocence, information, and benevolence." **John Adams (1797-1801)**

"<u>We must teach our children to resolve their conflicts with words, not weapons.</u> But should the people of America once become capable of that deep simulation towards one another, and towards foreign nations, which assumes the language of justice and moderation, while it is practicing iniquity and extravagance, and displays in the most captivating manner the charming pictures of candor, frankness, and sincerity, while it is rioting in rapine and insolence, this country will be the most miserable habitation in the world." **John Adams (1797-1801)**

Frederick W. Sarkis

Liberty

"Liberty without learning is always in peril, and learning without liberty is always in vain." **John F. Kennedy (1961-1963)**

"Those who want the government to regulate matters of the mind and spirit are like men who are so afraid of being murdered that they commit suicide to avoid assassination." **Harry S. Truman (1945-1953)**

"I would rather belong to a poor nation that was free than to a rich nation that had ceased to be in love with liberty." **Woodrow Wilson (1913-1921)** *"The advancement and diffusion of knowledge is the only guardian of true liberty."* **James Madison (1809-1817)**

"We all declare for liberty; but in using the same word we do not all mean the same thing...it follows that each of the things is, by the respective parties, called by two different and incompatible names — liberty and tyranny." **Abraham Lincoln (1861-1865)**

"Although in our country the Chief Magistrate must almost of necessity be chosen by a party and stand pledged to its principles and measures, yet in his official action he should not be the President of a part only, but of the whole people of the United States." **James K. Polk (1845-1849)**

"However [political parties] may now and then answer popular ends, they are likely in the course of time and things, to become potent engines, by which cunning, ambitious, and unprincipled men will be enabled to subvert the power of the people and to usurp for themselves the reins of government, destroying afterwards the very engines which have lifted them to unjust dominion." **George Washington (1789-1797)** –

"...Only if you've been in the deepest valley can you ever know how magnificent it is to be on the highest mountain..." **Richard Nixon (1969-1974)**

There is nothing more corrupting, nothing more destructive of the noblest and finest feelings of our nature, than the exercise of unlimited power." **William Henry Harrison (1841)**

Economy - *"We've learned that piling up material goods cannot fill the emptiness of lives which have no confidence or purpose."* **Jimmy Carter (1977-1981)** - *"Economy is idealism in its most practical form."*

"I pity the man who wants a coat so cheap that the man or woman who produces the cloth or shapes it into a garment will starve in the process." **Benjamin Harrison (1889-1893)**

"If we can but prevent the government from wasting the labors of the people, under the pretense of taking care of them, they must become happy." **Unknown**

"The diffusion of information and arraignment of all abuses at the bar of the public reason; freedom of religion; freedom of the press, and freedom of person under the protection of the habeas corpus, and trial by juries impartially selected. These principles form the bright constellation which has gone before us and guided our steps through an age of revolution and reformation." **Thomas Jefferson (1801-1809)**

Chapter Nine

Posted on March 12, 2018

In a campaign speech supporting the Republican candidate in a special House election in Pennsylvania's 18th District, President Donald Trump made several false and misleading statements on a range of topics, from drug smuggling to the stock market.

The president wrongly claimed to have received 52 percent of the women's vote in the 2016 presidential election. He received 41 percent.

Trump said when drug dealers and smugglers are caught *"they don't even put you in jail,"* adding that *"you might get 30 days, 60 days, 90 days. You might get a year."* In fact, with some exceptions, major drug traffickers are subject to mandatory minimum sentences that keep them in prison for years.

Trump falsely claimed that *"everyone"* benefits — *"not rich people"* — from stock market gains. In 2016, only about half of U.S. households owned stocks directly or indirectly, and "the richest 10 percent of households controlled 84 percent of all stock value, according to a paper published last year by the National Bureau of Economic Research.

Trump exaggerated when he said the 313,000 jobs gained in February *"was among the best numbers ever produced in the history of our country."* Over the last 79 years, the monthly jobs gain was higher 133 times, including six times under President Obama. Among the *"best numbers"* were 1.1 million in September 1983 and 942,000 in March 1946.

The president said *"a lot of steel mills are now opening up"* because of his announced tariffs on imported steel. He's right that some companies have announced they would reopen plants. But experts say other industries will lose jobs.

Trump also repeated several claims we've written about before on the trade deficit, the tax cut, wages and the cost of wars in the Middle East.

Several times during his speech, Trump revisited the 2016 campaign and basked in his victory — while not always getting the facts straight.

Trump, March 10: *Women, women, we love you, we love you. Hey, didn't we surprise them with women during the election? Remember, women won't like Donald Trump. I said have I really had that kind of a problem? I don't think so. But women won't like Donald Trump. It will be a rough night for Donald Trump because the women won't come out. We got 52 percent, right, 52, right. And I'm running against a woman. You know, that's not that easy".*

No, it's not right. Trump got 52 percent of the male vote, but only 41 percent of the female vote, according to the exit polls, the first female presidential nominee for either major party, received 54 percent of the women's vote.

The president apparently was referring only to white women. He received 52 percent of the white women vote, while Clinton received 43 percent. But Trump received much lower percentages from minority groups, including black women (4 percent), Latino women (25 percent) and other races (31 percent).

Drug Sentences - Making a pitch for tougher drug penalties, Trump unduly minimized the existing consequences of drug smuggling, saying that when caught, *"they don't even put you in jail. They don't do anything. But you might get 30 days, 60 days, 90 days. You might get a year".*

With some exceptions, those caught smuggling substantial amounts of illegal drugs are subject to mandatory minimum sentences that keep them in prison for years. Even lower-level drug traffickers such as couriers faced an average sentence of 8.4 years in prison in 2016 if they were subject to mandatory minimums and 4.3 years if they were among those who qualified for relief from those minimums.

Nonetheless, here's how Trump put it:

Trump, March 10: *"They catch a drug dealer. They don't even put him in jail. Think of it. You kill one person, you get the death penalty in many states or you get life imprisonment. You think of it. You kill 5,000 people with drugs because you are smuggling them in and you are making a lot of money and people are dying and they don't even put you in jail. They don't do anything. But you might get 30 days, 60 days, 90 days. You might get a year. Actually, drug smugglers face far longer prison sentences".*

The level of drug smuggling described by Trump would fall under 21 U.S.C. § 841, which prohibits manufacturing, distributing or dispensing or possessing with intent to manufacture, distribute or dispense, or 21 U.S.C. § 960, which prohibits import and export of controlled substances. And both carry mandatory minimum sentences of five or 10 years based on the weight of the drugs involved.

For example, 100 grams of heroin or 500 grams of powder cocaine carries a five-year mandatory minimum, while more than 1 kilogram of heroin or 5 kilograms of powder cocaine carries a 10-year mandatory minimum prison sentence.

There are two exceptions to the mandatory minimum sentences, the U.S. Sentencing Commission explained in its October 2017 report *"Mandatory Minimum Penalties for Drug Offenses in the Federal Criminal Justice System."* The first is for those who provide *"substantial assistance"* to authorities, typically meaning that they agree to testify against co-defendants or provide the names of their suppliers. The second is for those who qualify for a *"safety valve"* exception, which is available to some defendants who have a minimal criminal history, did not use or threaten violence or carry a weapon, and who were *"not an organizer, leader, manager or supervisor of others or engaged in a continuing criminal enterprise."*

The U.S. Sentencing Commission breaks down the average sentence by offender function:

- Organization leaders who faced mandatory minimums in 2016 were sentenced to an average of 15.5 years, or just over 10 years if relieved of the mandatory minimum penalty.
- Couriers — defined as those who transport or carry drugs with the assistance of a vehicle or other equipment — were sentenced to an average of 8.4 years in prison if they were subject to mandatory minimums and 4.3 years if they were relieved of the minimums.
- Mules — those who transport or carry drugs *"internally or on their person, often by airplane, or by walking across a border"* — got an average sentence of 6.8 years if they were subject to mandatory minimums or 2.2 years if relieved of the minimum penalty. (See Figure 33 on page 50.)

"These differences may be attributable to the fact that offenders who qualify for safety valve relief are generally less culpable than other offenders and, therefore, would normally receive lower sentences on average," wrote the U.S. Sentencing Commission, a bipartisan, independent agency located in the judicial branch of government.

The Sentencing Commission report notes that the Anti-Drug Abuse Act of 1986 created the two-tier mandatory sentencing structure to target *"major"* and *"serious"* traffickers. But, the commission wrote, the minimums created by the law "often apply to offenders who perform relatively low-level functions."

"Trump's comment doesn't line up with the facts," said Ames Grawert, senior counsel at the Brennan Center for Justice at the New York University School of Law.

Grawert said there are perhaps some defendants in very unusual circumstances who might get a sentence of under a year, but those would be extremely rare. It is much more common, he said, for convicted drug smugglers to receive sentences better measured in years than months, he said.

Not all mules and couriers are subject to laws that carry mandatory minimums because prosecutors have some discretion in what they charge, Grawert said. In 2013, then U.S. Attorney General Eric Holder unveiled the "Smart on Crime" initiative that directed federal prosecutors to steer low-level drug cases away from mandatory minimum sentences to concentrate resources on the most serious offenders. But in May 2017, Attorney General Jeff Sessions reversed that policy with a memo directing federal prosecutors to *"charge and pursue the most serious, readily provable offense."*

"Nobody's getting a so-called slap on the wrist for these kinds of offenses," Marc Mauer, executive director of The Sentencing Project, which advocates criminal justice changes, told us in a phone interview.

Stock Market Gains

As he frequently does, Trump boasted about the stock market gains not only since he took office but going back to Election Day. But this time he added a new wrinkle, falsely claiming that *"everyone"* benefits and *"not rich people."*

Trump, March 10: *"The stock market is up almost 40 percent since Election Day. Think of that, almost 40 percent. Think of that. And, by the way, that's not rich people. That's for everyone."*

The Dow Jones Industrial Average, made up of 30 large corporations, has increased by 28 percent during Trump's first year, (after rising 138 percent under Obama). Trump inflates the stock rise by going back to Nov. 8, 2016, which was Election Day. Since that date, the Dow has increased 38 percent.

More importantly, stock market gains do not benefit everyone.

In a working paper issued by the National Bureau of Economic Research in November, New York University economics professor Edward Nathan Wolff looked at household wealth trends in the United States from 1962 to

2016. In 2016, 49.3 percent of U.S. households owned stock either directly or indirectly (through mutual funds, trust funds or pension plans), Wolff wrote. *"So not everyone benefits when the stock market increases."*

As for *"rich people,"* the term used by Trump, Wolff found that stock ownership was *"highly skewed"* toward the wealthy.

Wolff, November 2017: The concentration of investment type assets generally was very high in 2016. Over 90 percent of the total value of stock shares, bonds, and business equity, and 85 percent of non-home real estate were held by the top 10 percent of households. Stock ownership was also highly skewed by wealth class. The top one percent of households classified by wealth owned 40 percent of all stocks in 2016, the top 10 percent 84 percent, and the top quintile 93 percent.

February Jobs Report - The president boasted about the strong February jobs report, but went too far when he claimed it was among the best in history.

Trump, March 10: We have created more than 300,000 new jobs alone last month. And you saw the numbers yesterday. Yesterday's numbers, job reports was among the best numbers ever produced in the history of our country. The economy added 313,000 jobs in February, according to the Bureau of Labor Statistics. That's a preliminary figure and it could be revised as the bureau receives better information.

To put the February jobs report into some context, we went to the BLS website and downloaded monthly jobs data going back to February 1939. In that 79-year period, the U.S. on average has added 125,000 jobs per month. That includes 730 months when the U.S. added jobs and 219 months when it lost jobs. The median job change during that period was an increase of 157,000. So 313,000 is a strong number. But the U.S. has added more than 313,000 jobs in 133 months Including six times in the six years prior to Trump taking office, ranging from 522,000 in May 2010 to 323,000 in April 2011. Below are the top 10 biggest monthly gains since February 1939.

Largest Payroll Employment Increases		
1983	September	1,115,000
1946	March	942,000
1952	August	779,000
1950	August	734,000
1946	January	720,000
1946	April	716,000
1941	May	713,000
1978	April	702,000
1956	August	676,000
1950	March	654,000

Source: Bureau of Labor Statistics

Many of the months with the strongest job gains were from the 1940s and 1950s, when the U.S. labor market was much smaller, making the large gains even more impressive.

For example, the March 1946 increase of 942,000 jobs represented a 2.4 percent increase in total nonfarm employment in just one month, while the 313,000 jobs in February represented an increase of just 0.2 percent.

Steel Tariffs and Jobs - The president boasted that "a lot of steel mills are now opening up" because of the tariffs he announced on imported steel and aluminum. Some companies have announced they would reopen shuttered plants. But the big picture of the impact on jobs is likely to be mixed, experts say.

While domestic steel companies would benefit from the tariffs, other industries, such as those using imported steel, would be at a disadvantage.

Trump, March 10: They have been talking a little bit about steel over the last little while, haven't they? And we are saving the steel. And a lot of steel mills are now opening up because of what I did. And not all of my friends on Wall Street love it, but we love it because we know what it does. Many plants have just announced, over the last few days, that they are expanding, opening. Steel is back. It's going to be back, too. Steel is back. And aluminum is back.

The Trump administration announced on March 1 that it would impose tariffs of 25 percent on imported steel and 10 percent on imported aluminum to aid domestic producers. A week later, the final White House proclamation included temporary exemptions for Canada and Mexico and the possibility for other countries to also get exemptions. The tariffs go into effect March 23.

As a result of the tariffs, U.S. Steel said it would reopen a Granite City, Illinois, mill that would employ 500 workers. Republic Steel said it could reopen a plant in Lorain, Ohio, and employ 1,000. And Century Aluminum Co. said it would add 300 jobs at a plant in Kentucky.

The *Wall Street Journal* also reported that some companies, including Alcoa, had already announced expansions before the tariffs, but the president's support for such measures played a role. *"Steel and aluminum prices have risen recently on higher domestic demand and piecemeal tariffs against producers in other countries including China, as well as Mr. Trump's support for broader tariffs,"* the *Journal* said in a March 7 article.

However, that article also noted that other companies weren't pleased. California Steel Industries said the tariffs would be harmful. That company, like a Russian-owned plant in Farrell, Pennsylvania, imports steel slabs to roll into sheets. So the costs of that imported steel would go up.

Reuters reported in a March 9 story: *"Bob Miller, Chief Executive Officer of NLMK's U.S. unit, said if his company's customers refuse to accept a 25 percent price hike as a result of the tariffs, nearly 1,200 workers could eventually lose their jobs – and the ones in Farrell would be the first to go when supplies of imported slabs run out."* The Farrell plant employed 780 workers.

And companies that use steel and aluminum in their products — including automakers and home appliance manufacturers — are also concerned about the impact of higher prices for those metals.

In a March 5 report, The Trade Partnership, a consulting firm, estimated that the tariffs could increase jobs in metal industries by 33,464, but decrease jobs in other industries by 179,334. That's a net loss of 146,000. That was before the final White House proclamation, which included exemptions for Canada and Mexico.

On March 12, The Trade Partnership released a new analysis that removed Canada, Mexico and Australia, and factored in retaliation by U.S. trading partners. That analysis estimated a net loss of nearly 470,000 jobs.

Chad P. Bown, a senior fellow at the Peterson Institute for International Economics, wrote in a March 9 op-ed that *"whether Canada and Mexico are eventually hit remains a very important unknown—they are America's first and fourth largest foreign suppliers of the metals, respectively."*

The exemption is an attempt to add some pressure to the negotiations between the countries on the North American Free Trade Agreement, Barry Bosworth, a senior fellow in the Economic Studies Program at the Brookings Institution, told FactCheck.org in an email. "It is a big exception, but just for a short period." he said.

Bosworth expects the net effect of the tariffs on total jobs to be *"near zero."*

"In the past, it has been difficult to give precise measures of the effect because so many other things change," he told us. There's also a competitive gain for car importers that won't pay a higher price for steel compared with domestic automakers. *"I think it will help foreign producers of products with a large steel content (autos, appliances, and construction machinery)."*

Gary Clyde Hufbauer, a nonresident senior fellow at the Peterson Institute for International Economics, expects that *"no more than 10,000 jobs would be created in the steel and aluminum industries,"* but at least triple that number of jobs would be lost, *"sprinkled through the economy."*

He notes that stories about steel companies announcing job creation is *"very visible,"* while job losses throughout the economy *"will be far less visible"* and not as easy to pinpoint.

Repeats on Trade, Wages, War and More

No Trump speech would be complete without a list of false and misleading statements that we have repeatedly debunked.

"We spent $7 trillion in the Middle East over 17-year period."

Trump has repeated versions of this claim numerous times in the past several months without getting it right. This speech was no exception. The U.S. has not spent $7 trillion fighting wars in the Middle East. The Department of Defense says the cost *"for the wars in Afghanistan, Iraq and Syria"* through fiscal year 2018 was an estimated $1.52 trillion.

During the campaign, Trump used a $6 trillion estimate, citing a Reuter's article about a report by Boston University Political Science Professor Neta C. Crawford for the Watson Institute for International Studies at Brown University. Crawford's estimate included amounts spent in the U.S., not just money spent in the Middle East, and it included future costs, not just money already spent. In an update published last year, Crawford said U.S. military spending in the Middle East *"and the additional spending on Homeland Security, and the Departments of Defense and Veterans Affairs since the 9/11 attacks,"* has cost $4.3 trillion in current dollars through fiscal year 2017, and will cost more than $5.6 trillion through the year 2056.

"Wages went up a little bit. You haven't had wages go up in 19 years. Wages are starting to go up."

It's true that wages have risen under Trump. As we've reported before, real, inflation-adjusted wages rose 1.1 percent during the first 11 months of his term for all workers. Average weekly earnings dipped in January 2018, although they remained higher (by 0.62 percent) than January 2017, when Trump took office. The president went too far, though, in claiming that wages haven't gone up in 19 years and are only now *"starting to go up."* As we've written before, wages for all workers increased 4.1 percent during President Obama's eight years.

"You know, we have a big deficit with Canada too."

As we wrote earlier this month, the U.S. had a trade surplus in goods and services of nearly $2.8 billion with Canada in 2017. The U.S. has not had a trade deficit with its neighbors to the north since 2014.

Don't forget Betsy Voss, Secretary of Education - $200,000 given to the Republican Party. Then she becomes Secretary of Education. How insane!!!

I study liars. I've never seen one like President Trump. - *He tells far more lies, and far more cruel ones, than ordinary people do.* By Bella DePaulo - December 8, 2017 - Bella DePaulo, a social scientist, is the author of *"Singled Out: How Singles Are Stereotyped, Stigmatized and Ignored" and "How We Live Now: Redefining Home and Family in the 21st Century."*

"I spent the first two decades of my career as a social scientist studying liars and their lies. I thought I had developed a sense of what to expect from them. Then along came President Trump. His lies are both more frequent and more malicious than ordinary people's."

In research beginning in the mid-1990s, when I was a professor at the University of Virginia, my colleagues and I asked 77 college students and 70 people from the nearby community to keep diaries of all the lies they told every day for a week. They handed them in to us with no names attached. We calculated participants' rates of lying and categorized each lie as either self-serving (told to advantage the liar or protect the liar from embarrassment, blame or other undesired outcomes) or kind (told to advantage, flatter or protect someone else).

At The Washington Post, the Fact Checker feature has been tracking every false and misleading claim and flip-flop made by President Trump this year. The inclusion of misleading statements and flip-flops is consistent with the definition of lying my colleagues and I gave to our participants:

"A lie occurs any time you intentionally try to mislead someone." In the case of Trump's claims, though, it is possible to ascertain only whether they were false or misleading, and not what the president's intentions were. (And while the subjects of my research self-reported how often they lied, Trump's falsehoods were tallied by The Post.)

I categorized the most recent 400 lies that The Post had documented through mid-November in the same way my colleagues and I had categorized the lies of the participants in our study.

The college students in our research told an average of two lies a day, and the community members told one. A more recent study of the lies 1,000 U. S. adults told in the previous 24 hours found that people told an average of 1.65 lies per day; the authors noted that 60 percent of the participants said they told no lies at all, while the top 5 percent of liars told nearly half of all the falsehoods in the study.

In Trump's first 298 days in office, however, he made **1,628** false or misleading claims or flip-flops, by The Post's tally. That's about six per day, far higher than the average rate in our studies. And of course, reporters have access to only a subset of Trump's false statements — the ones he makes publicly — so unless he never stretches the truth in private, his actual rate of lying is almost certainly higher.

That rate has been accelerating. Starting in early October, The Post's tracking showed that Trump told a remarkable **nine lies a day**, outpacing even the biggest liars in our research.

But the flood of deceit isn't the most surprising finding about Trump.

Both the college students and the community members in our study served their own interests with their lies more often than other people's interests. They told lies to try to advantage themselves in the workplace, the marketplace, their personal relationships and just about every other domain of everyday life. For example, a salesperson told a customer that the jeans she was trying on were not too tight, so she could make the sale. The participants also lied to protect themselves psychologically: One college student told a classmate that he wasn't worried about his grades, so the classmate wouldn't think him stupid.

Less often, the participants lied in kind ways, to help other people get what they wanted, look or feel better, or to spare them from embarrassment or blame. For example, a son told his mother he didn't mind taking her shopping, and a woman took sides with a friend who was divorcing, even though she thought her friend was at fault, too.

About half the lies the participants told were self-serving (46 percent for the college students, 57 percent for the community members), compared with about a quarter that were kind (26 percent for the students, 24 percent for the community members). Other lies did not fit either category; they included, for instance, lies told to entertain or to keep conversations running smoothly.

One category of lies was so small that when we reported the results, we just tucked them into a footnote. Those were cruel lies, told to hurt or disparage others. For example, one person told a co-worker that the boss wanted to see him when he really didn't, *"so he'd look like a fool."* Just 0.8 percent of the lies told by the college students and 2.4 percent of the lies told by the community members were mean-spirited.

My colleagues and I found it easy to code each of our participants' lies into just one category. This was not the case for Trump. Close to a quarter of his false statements (24 percent) served several purposes simultaneously.

Nearly two-thirds of Trump's lies (65 percent) were self-serving. Examples included: *"They're big tax cuts — the biggest cuts in the history of our country, actually"* and, about the people who came to see him on a presidential visit to Vietnam last month: *"They were really lined up in the streets by the tens of thousands."*

Slightly less than 10 percent of Trump's lies were kind ones, told to advantage, flatter or protect someone else. An example was his statement on Twitter that "it is a 'miracle' how fast the Las Vegas Metropolitan Police were able to find the demented shooter and stop him from even more killing!" In the broadest sense, it is possible to interpret every lie as ultimately self-serving, but I tried to stick to how statements appeared on the surface.

[*Trump always lashes out when he's cornered. He told me so years ago.*]

Trump told 6.6 times as many self-serving lies as kind ones. That's a much higher ratio than we found for our study participants, who told about double the number of self-centered lies compared with kind ones.

The most stunning way Trump's lies differed from our participants', though, was in their cruelty. An astonishing 50 percent of Trump's lies were hurtful or disparaging. For example, he proclaimed that John Brennan, James Clapper and James Comey, all career intelligence or law enforcement officials, were "*political hacks*." He said that "*the Sloppy Michael Moore Show on Broadway was a TOTAL BOMB and was forced to close.*" Talking about green card applicants, he insisted that other "*countries, they don't put their finest in the lottery system. They put people probably in many cases that they don't want.*" And he claimed that "*Ralph Northam, who is running for Governor of Virginia, is fighting for the violent MS-13 killer gangs & sanctuary cities.*"

The Trump lies that could not be coded into just one category were typically told both to belittle others and enhance himself. For example: "*Senator Bob Corker 'begged' me to endorse him for reelection in Tennessee. I said 'NO' and he dropped out (said he could not win without my endorsement).*"

The sheer frequency of Trump's lies appears to be having an effect, and it may not be the one he is going for. A Politico/Morning Consult poll from late October showed that only 35 percent **of** voters believed that Trump was honest, while 51 percent said he was not honest. (The others said they didn't know or had no opinion.) Results of a Quinnipiac University poll from November were similar: Thirty-seven percent of voters thought Trump was honest, compared with 58 percent who thought he was not.

[*President Trump wants to put on a show. Governing matters less.*]

For fewer than 40 percent of American voters to see the president as honest is truly remarkable. Most humans, most of the time, believe other people. That's our default setting. Usually, we need a reason to disbelieve.

Research on the detection of deception consistently documents this "truth bias." In the typical study, participants observe people making statements and are asked to indicate, each time, whether they think the person is lying or telling the truth. Measuring whether people believe others should be difficult to do accurately, because simply asking the question disrupts the tendency to assume that other people are telling the truth. It gives participants a reason to wonder. And yet, in our statistical summary of more than 200 studies, Charles F. Bond Jr. and I found that participants still believed other people more often than they should have — 58 percent of the time in studies in which only half of the statements were truthful. People are biased toward believing others, even in studies in which they are told explicitly that only half of the statements they will be judging are truths.

By telling so many lies, and so many that are mean-spirited, Trump is violating some of the most fundamental norms of human social interaction and human decency. Many of the rest of us, in turn, have abandoned a norm of our own — we no longer give Trump the benefit of the doubt that we usually give so readily. Trump is likely basing his claim on the fact that the U.S. buys more goods from Canada than it sells to Canada. However, this deficit in goods is more than offset by a surplus in the sales of services (such as travel, transportation and intellectual property). As we've noted before, Trump has a habit of ignoring services when discussing U.S. trade.

"We have a trade deficit of almost $800 billion a year."

Trump makes a similar misstatement here, as he has in the past, referring only to the deficit in goods. When the surplus for services is factored in, the U.S. had a total trade deficit of $568 billion in 2017, according to the U.S. Census Bureau.

"We passed the biggest tax cut in the history of our country."

There have been larger cuts as a percentage of gross domestic product and in inflation-adjusted dollars. The new tax law would cost $1.46 trillion over 10 years, <u>according to the nonpartisan Joint Committee on Taxation</u>. The <u>Committee for a Responsible Federal Budget said</u> that an even more expensive plan previously proposed by Trump would have only been the eighth largest tax cut as a percentage of gross domestic product, and it would have been just the fourth largest cut in inflation-adjusted dollars. CRFB said the tax cut in 1981 under President Ronald Reagan, at 2.9 percent of GDP, is the largest in history. *"If President Trump wanted to pass a tax cut that exceeds the record 2.9 percent of the economy in 1981, it would cost roughly $6.8 trillion over ten years, CRFB wrote"*. — *By Eugene Kiely, Robert Farley and Lori Robertson, with Thomas Nowlan*

Chapter 10

The stunning history of William Barr's crusade to bury evidence to protect Republican presidents - March 25, 2019

By Thom Hartman, Independent Media institute

Commentary

Back in 1992, the last time Bill Barr was U.S. attorney general, iconic New York Times writer William Safire referred to him as "Coverup-General Barr" because of his role in burying evidence of then-President George H.W. Bush's involvement in "Iraqgate" and "Iran-Contra."

General Barr has struck again—this time, in similar fashion, burying Mueller's report and cherry-picking fragments of sentences from it to justify Trump's behavior. In his letter, he notes that Robert Mueller "leaves it to the attorney general to decide whether the conduct described in the report constitutes a crime."

As attorney general, Barr—without showing us even a single complete sentence from the Mueller report—decided there are no crimes here. Just keep moving along.

Barr's history of doing just this sort of thing to help Republican presidents in legal crises explains why Trump brought him back in to head the Justice Department.

Christmas day of 1992, the New York Times featured a screaming all-caps headline across the top of its front page: Attorney General Bill Barr had covered up evidence of crimes by Reagan and Bush in the Iran-Contra scandal.

Earlier that week of Christmas, 1992, George H.W. Bush was on his way out of office. Bill Clinton had won the White House the month before, and in a few weeks would be sworn in as president.

But Bush's biggest concern wasn't that he'd have to leave the White House to retire back to Connecticut, Maine, or Texas (where he had homes) but, rather, that he may end up embroiled even deeper in Iran-Contra and that his colleagues may face time in a federal prison after he left office.

Independent Counsel Lawrence Walsh was closing in fast on him, and Bush's private records, subpoenaed by the independent counsel's office, were the key to it all.

Walsh had been appointed independent counsel in 1986 to investigate the Iran-Contra activities of the Reagan administration and determine if crimes had been committed.

Was the Iran-Contra criminal conspiracy limited, as Reagan and Bush insisted (and Reagan confessed on TV), to later years in the Reagan presidency, in response to a hostage-taking in Lebanon? Or had it started in the 1980 campaign with collusion with the Iranians, as the then-president of Iran asserted? Who knew what, and when? And what was George H.W. Bush's role in it all?

Walsh had zeroed in on documents that were in the possession of Reagan's former defense secretary, Caspar Weinberger, who all the evidence showed was definitely in on the deal, and President Bush's diary that could corroborate it. Elliott Abrams had already been convicted of withholding evidence from Congress, and he may have even more information, too, if it could be pried out of him before he went to prison. But Abrams was keeping mum, apparently anticipating a pardon.

Weinberger, trying to avoid jail himself, was preparing to testify that Bush knew about it and even participated, and Walsh had already, based on information he'd obtained from the investigation into Weinberger, demanded that Bush turn over his diary from the campaign. He was also again hot on the trail of Abrams.

So Bush called in his attorney general, Bill Barr, and asked his advice.

Barr, along with Bush, was already up to his eyeballs in cover-ups of shady behavior by the Reagan administration.

New York Times writer William Safire referred to him not as "Attorney General" but, instead, as "Coverup-General," noting that in another scandal—having to do with Bush selling weapons of mass destruction to Saddam Hussein—Barr was already covering up for Bush, Weinberger, and others from the Reagan administration.

On October 19, 1992, Safire wrote of Barr's unwillingness to appoint an independent counsel to look into Iraqgate:

"Why does the Coverup-General resist independent investigation? Because he knows where it may lead: to Dick Thornburgh, James Baker, Clayton Yeutter, Brent Scowcroft and himself [the people who organized the sale of WMD to Saddam]. He vainly hopes to be able to head it off, or at least be able to use the threat of firing to negotiate a deal."

Now, just short of two months later, Bush was asking Barr for advice on how to avoid another very serious charge in the Iran-Contra crimes. How, he wanted to know, could they shut down Walsh's investigation before Walsh's lawyers got their hands on Bush's diary?

In April of 2001, safely distant from the swirl of D.C. politics, the University of Virginia's Miller Center was compiling oral presidential histories, and interviewed Barr about his time as AG in the Bush White House. They brought up the issue of the Weinberger pardon, which put an end to the Iran-Contra investigation, and Barr's involvement in it.

Turns out, Barr was right in the middle of it.

"There were some people arguing just for [a pardon for] Weinberger, and I said, 'No, in for a penny, in for a pound,'" Barr told the interviewer. "I went over and told the President I thought he should not only pardon Caspar Weinberger, but while he was at it, he should pardon about five others."

Which is exactly what Bush did, on Christmas Eve when most Americans were with family instead of watching the news. The holiday notwithstanding, the result was explosive.

America knew that both Reagan and Bush were up to their necks in Iran-Contra, and Democrats had been talking about impeachment or worse. The independent counsel had already obtained one conviction, three guilty pleas, and two other individuals were lined up for prosecution. And Walsh was closing in fast on Bush himself.

So, when Bush shut the investigation down by pardoning not only Weinberger, but also Abrams and the others involved in the crimes, destroying Walsh's ability to prosecute *anybody*, the New York Times ran the headline all the way across four of the six columns on the front page, screaming in all-caps: BUSH PARDONS 6 IN IRAN AFFAIR, ABORTING A WEINBERGER TRIAL; PROSECUTOR ASSAILS 'COVER-UP.'

Bill Barr had struck.

Chapter Eleven

Who is the real Donald Trump? - Source CNN

**Who is Donald Trump?
An interview with Michael D'Antonio
6786 Words – Digest to 678 words - Final is 666**

**Who is Donald Trump?
An interview with Michael D'Antonio**

CNN) - Heir to a construction fortune, business magnate, New York City tabloid obsession, reality TV star and now, the Republican Party's presumptive presidential nominee. For more than 40 years, Donald Trump has sought, found and sustained a global celebrity. But few understand his personal story -- the source of the drive that has put Trump within touching distance of the White House -- like journalist and writer Michael D'Antonio.

In a wide-ranging conversation, the author of *"The Truth About Trump,"* an unauthorized and comprehensive biography, D'Antonio took CNN.com inside the new GOP standard-bearer's untold journey.

This interview has been edited and condensed.

CNN: Trump's wealth and business credentials have been central to his appeal to voters. Was he born into great wealth, as critics note, or has that been overstated?

Michael D'Antonio: When people ask me about Donald's wealth and whether he's a self-made man, I have to remind them that he was born into one of the wealthiest families in America.

In the 1970s his father was worth $200 million, so Donald will say, *"Oh, I got a loan of a million bucks from my dad,"* and that's true too, but he also could access all that wealth in addition to all of his political connections, so there's some who estimate that if he had parked that money in a mutual fund he'd be just as rich today as he is now with all the machinations of his business life, but hey, he kept us entertained, so let him be a developer, let him be a serial entrepreneur. It's fun to watch.

By the time he was a young teen he was out of the house and enrolled at the New York Military Academy. What was that like for him?

Donald's exile from his family and enrollment in military academy at age 13 must be seen as the formative event of his childhood.

Imagine you're a 13-year-old kid in 1959 and all of a sudden your dad announces on a summer day that you're not going back to school, you're going to a military academy and it's 60 miles away, near West Point. You'll no longer be with your family. You'll no longer be in this comfortable, luxurious home. That's quite a jarring episode in Donald's life.

There was a time in the 1980s when repeated year-end polls ranked Donald Trump among the 10 most admired people in America. You don't do that without trying, so Donald had this strategy of seeking attention from the beginning, doing what it takes to get it, and implementing the strategy, and it's always worked.

So, for a person who has sought the limelight and courted the press, he projects a great disdain for reporters. How does he really view journalists and the news media?

In the current campaign, we've seen, at almost every event, Donald begins by excoriating the press. He'll point them out, and the reporters will have to stand there while the crowd turns and looks at these people he describes as terrible people, the scum of the earth, they're really horrible, and I think that the public, especially people who are true Trump followers, love this. This is red meat to his loyalists.

In fact, Donald doesn't think that. This is a pose. This is a way to set up an enemy and also to discredit the press so that he becomes the reliable source, so if Donald says, *"These reporters are terrible. They're not going to tell the truth. They're lying,"* then who is the faithful Republican voter, or independent voter, to believe? Well, they're to believe Donald Trump.

He doesn't hate the press. He loves the press. The press has been the oxygen for his lungs and the air that pumps up the balloon that is his ego. He started, every day of his life before the campaign, by reviewing

Chapter Twelve

Who Am I?

I am a 93 year old WWII Veteran. In my not-for-profit mission, I spent the past twenty years working with regional and national character education teachers and corrections officials in helping kids and juvenile prisoners to be the best they can be, as reflected on my www.YesPa.org website. I have received regional and national awards for community service, major economic developments and job creations.

On August 19, 2016, I was moved by the following letter to the editor which appeared in the Rochester NY Democrat and Chronicle.

"What are we thinking of Folks?

Let's say your 10-year-old-son is a bully. He pushes people around, calls other kids names, makes fun of the kid with disabilities, and even says bad things about other people's religion or ethnicity. He is forever fabricating tales, and when confronted, refuses to take any responsibility. He is angry, belligerent, impulsive, and is constantly getting into fights. He seems to care only about himself, and he doesn't play well with others. And he will not listen. His behavior is becoming more and more erratic. The school is telling you that he may need professional help.

Now let's say that instead of your 10-year-old-son, we are talking about a candidate for the presidency of the United States. I have to ask: folks, what are we thinking?

Tim McMahon, Geneseo, NY"

I'm one of the folks who read Tim's letter. I sought and obtained his approval to include his letter in my book. How could anyone compare Trump's rhetoric any better? Here is how, as a WWII Vet, I feel about Donald Trump.

Yes, as Secretary of State, in year 2012, Hillary Clinton, did not reflect good judgment in her handling of classified information or in conflicts with the Clinton Foundation. Nevertheless, here's why I supported her.

Whether a parent, child, government official or otherwise, if we have any humility at all, we admit, learn and capitalize on our mistakes. In Hillary's case, she has far more gains in world affairs than she has in losses. She also had the benefit of close counseling with two past presidents who were keenly aware of past mistakes and who had creative ideas to make lemonade out of past lemons.

Now Donald, read my biography, Prisoner of the Truck. Then go ahead and pick on this WWII Navy Veteran of Syrian-Lebanese descent. I'd be glad to debate you under the WWII slogan. "Loose lips sink ships". Name the time and the place.

Chapter Thirteen

<u>*Muslim, Jewish, Christian Prayer for Peace*</u>

Oh God, you are the source of life and peace.

Praised be your name forever.

We know it is you who turn our minds to thoughts of peace.

Hear our prayer in this time of war.

Your power changes hearts.

Muslims, Christians, and Jews remember, and found affirm, that they are followers of the one God, children of Abraham, brothers and sisters; enemies begin to speak to one another; those who are estranged join hands in friendship; nations seek the way of peace together. Strength our resolve to give witness to these truths by the way we live.

Gift to us: Understanding that puts an end to strive; Mercy that quenches hatred, and forgiveness that overcomes vengeance. Empower all people to live in your law of love. Amen

<u>Credits for above - Pax Christi USA, 532 West 8th Street, Eric, Pa 16502-1343 814-453-4955</u>

Chapter Fourteen

<u>Your State of the Union address</u>

Mr. President, here's what you said and here are the facts and what the record shows:

FOOD STAMPS: *Describing progress over the last two years: "Nearly 5 million Americans have been lifted off food stamps."*

THE FACTS: The number of people receiving food stamps actually hasn't declined that much.

<u>BORDER WALL:</u> - *"These (border) agents will tell you where walls go up, illegal crossings go way, way down ... San Diego used to have the most illegal border crossings in our country. In response, a strong security wall was put in place. This powerful barrier almost completely ended illegal crossings ... Simply put, walls work and walls save lives."*

THE FACTS: The Government Accountability Office reported in 2017 that the U.S. has not developed metrics that demonstrate how barriers have contributed to border security.

TARIFFS: *"We recently imposed tariffs on $250 billion of Chinese goods — and now our treasury is receiving billions of dollars."*

THE FACTS: Misleading. Yes, money from tariffs is going into the federal treasury, but it's largely coming from U.S. businesses and consumers. It's not foreign countries that are paying these import taxes by cutting a check to the government.

TRADE-NAFTA - *"Our new U.S.-Mexico-Canada Agreement — will replace NAFTA and deliver for American workers: bringing back our manufacturing jobs, expanding American agriculture, protecting intellectual property, and ensuring that more cars are proudly stamped with the four beautiful words: MADE IN THE USA."*

THE FACTS: It's unlikely to do all those things, since the new agreement largely preserves the structure and substance of NAFTA. In addition, the deal has not been ratified and its chances in Congress are uncertain.

DRUG PRICING: *"Already, as a result of my administration's efforts, in 2018 drug prices experienced their single largest decline in 46 years."*

THE FACTS: You are selectively citing statistics to exaggerate what seems to be a slowdown in prices. A broader look at the data shows that drug prices are still rising, but more moderately. Some independent experts say criticism from Trump and congressional Democrats may be causing pharmaceutical companies to show restraint.

WAGES: TRUMP: *"Wages are rising at the fastest pace in decades, and growing for blue collar workers, who I promised to fight for, they're growing faster than anyone else thought possible."*

THE FACTS: This is an unsupported statement because the data on hourly wages for private workers only go back to 2006, not decades.

MINORITY UNEMPLOYMENT

TRUMP: *"African-American, Hispanic-American and Asian-American unemployment have all reached their lowest levels ever recorded."*

THE FACTS: What you're not saying is that the unemployment rates for all three groups have gone up since reaching record low levels.

HUMAN TRAFFICKING

TRUMP: *"Human traffickers and sex traffickers take advantage of the wide open areas between our ports of entry to smuggle thousands of young girls and women into the United States and to sell them into prostitution and modern-day slavery."*

THE FACTS: Your administration has not supplied evidence that women and girls are smuggled by the "thousands" across remote areas of the border for these purposes. What has been established is nearly 80 percent of international trafficking victims cross through legal ports of entry, a flow that would not be stopped by a border wall.

ECONOMY:

TRUMP: *"In just over two years since the election, we have launched an unprecedented economic boom — a boom that has rarely been seen before. There's been nothing like it. ... An economic miracle is taking place in the United States."*

THE FACTS: You vastly exaggerating what has been a mild improvement in growth and hiring. The economy is healthy but not nearly one of the best in U.S. history.

WOMEN IN WORKFORCE:

TRUMP: *"All Americans can be proud that we have more women in the workforce than ever before."*

THE FACTS: Of course, there are more women working than ever before. But that's due to population growth — and not something that you can credit to any your policies.

ENERGY: TRUMP: *"We have unleashed a revolution in American energy - the United States is now the number one producer of oil and natural gas in the world."*

THE FACT: True, if "we" means you and his recent predecessors. It's not all your credit. The government says the U.S. became the world's top natural gas producer in 2013, under Barack Obama's administration.

February 17, 2019 – You ripped Andrew McCabe's "deranged", hours after the former deputy FBI director said on "60 Minutes" that there had been talk of trying to remove the President from office.

The Fact: McCabe said during the interview that the FBI was justified in launching an investigation into whether Trump was in league with Russia following the firing of then-FBI Director James Comey in 2017. McCabe was fired from the Justice Department last year after being accused of misleading investigators in a probe about leaks to the media.

"I believe I was fired because I opened a case against the president of the United States," McCabe said on *"60 Minutes."*

Mr. President, there is a WWI song called *"Tramp, Tramp, Tramp the boys are marching. Here comes the Kaiser (WWI Germany Dictator) at the door. If I had a submarine I would biff him on the bean and there wouldn't be a Kaiser any more. In closing "Lose Lips Sinks Ships, my song would be, "Trump, Trump, Trump he keeps on tweeting, so much nonsense to deplore, if I had a vote to impeach, he wouldn't be our President any more."*

Chapter Fifteen

As it pertains to Elections - A Salute to Pubic Television and Military Times

Mr. President, I posted this on Nov 21, 2012 during the Election of President Barack O'Bama

Hi, Bill (Moyers) and Mike (Winship),

I'm writing this as a World War II veteran. The election is over. Our U.S. President has been elected. Six billion dollars were spent on the presidential election. Thanks to you and the Canandaigua NY Daily Messenger for the Commentary in the Oct. 30 Daily Messenger, "Plutocrats want to own your vote."

For the past 14 years, in retirement, I have fully supported a free character education program developed with the assistance of regional and national character education teachers as noted on my not-for-profit website **www.YesPa.org**. *Yes Pa is a digest of my authored book "Prisoner of the Truck" — a true story involving being bullied in grammar school and 100 hours a week on my immigrant father's fruit and vegetable truck from age 8 to 14 in the Depression years.*

At age 12, there were three five-minute conversations with my immigrant Pa that led to my turning the truck into a study center. This resulted in outstanding academic and work achievement that enabled me to buy my mother of ten a home before I entered WWII at age 18. Later in life, my business success enabled a major ski area and lake village which includes a golf course and marina.

Since retirement, over 1,700 schools in the US and beyond have freely downloaded and printed the Yes Pa book and Teacher Resource Guidebook. This character education program uniquely involves the parent, teacher and child chapter by chapter. Now in 2012, school smart boards also enable my video talk to students, which follows the reading of the Yes Pa book, which also satisfies state standards for English, Language and Arts.

Your Oct. 30 article makes me want to write another book called "Prisoner of US Politics." The last chapter would speak to an amendment to our Constitution that the U.S. Supreme Court could not question — one which prevents the buying of an elective office; one which prevents favor-seeking after election; one which makes veterans proud of a fair and equitable manner in which their representatives are elected; one which stops political robocalls that frustrate senior citizens. Close to 16 million individuals were members of the United States armed forces during World War II. Close to 291,000 battle deaths and close to 670,000 non-mortal woundings. There are an estimated 1.7 million still living. (Note as of 2012).

The time has come for a change in the manner in which elections can be bought — whether by one party or the other. Veterans Day just passed. I just wonder: How many of all veterans of Wars would agree with this? This veteran wishes to salute both of you for this great article. God bless and help preserve the good and objective work of **www.BillMoyers.com** *and public television.*

Chapter Sixteen

Posted on March 12, 2018

The president wrongly claimed to have received 52 percent of the women's vote in the 2016 presidential election. He received 41 percent.

Trump falsely claimed that *"everyone"* benefits — *"not rich people"* — from stock market gains. In 2016, only about half of U.S. households owned stocks directly or indirectly, and "the richest 10 percent of households controlled 84 percent of all stock value, according to the National Bureau of Economic Research.

Trump exaggerated when he said the 313,000 jobs gained in February *"was among the best numbers ever produced in the history of our country."* Over the last 79 years, the monthly jobs gain was higher 133 times, including six times under President Obama. Among the *"best numbers"* were 1.1 million in September 1983 and 942,000 in March 1946.

Trump got 52 percent of the male vote, but only 41 percent of the female vote, according to the exit polls.

Stock Market Gains

The Dow Jones Industrial Average, made up of 30 large corporations, has increased by 28 percent during Trump's first year, (after rising 138 percent under Obama). Trump inflates the stock rise by going back to Nov. 8,

2016, which was Election Day. Since that date, the Dow has increased 38 percent.

"Wages went up a little bit. You haven't had wages go up in 19 years. Wages are starting to go up."

The president went too far, though, in claiming that wages haven't gone up in 19 years and are only now *"starting to go up."* As we've written before, wages for all workers increased 4.1 percent during President Obama's eight years.

Don't forget Betsy Voss, Secretary of Education - $200,000 given to the Republican Party. Then she becomes Secretary of Education. How insane!!!

In Trump's first 298 days in office, however, he made **1,628** false or misleading claims or flip-flops, by The Post's tally. That's about six per day, far higher than the average rate in our studies. And of course, reporters have access to only a subset of Trump's false statements — the ones he makes publicly — so unless he never stretches the truth in private, his actual rate of lying is almost certainly higher.

Starting in early October, The Post's tracking showed that Trump told a remarkable **nine lies a day**, outpacing even the biggest liars in our research.

The most stunning way Trump's lies differed from our participants', though, was in their cruelty. An astonishing 50 percent of Trump's lies were hurtful or disparaging. For example, he proclaimed that John Brennan, James Clapper and James Comey, all career intelligence or law enforcement officials, were *"political hacks."*

For fewer than 40 percent of American voters to see the president as honest is truly remarkable. Most humans, most of the time, believe other people. That's our default setting. Usually, we need a reason to disbelieve.

— *By Eugene Kiely, Robert Farley and Lori Robertson, with Thomas Nowlan*

Chapter Sixteen

Mr. President, this 93 year old World War II Veteran says to you:

If you can, carefully consider this. Your *"Loose Lips"* not only undermined your team, your *"loose lips"* undermines character education in America. Imagine a classroom teacher modeling that low level of contempt, derision, arrogance, crassness, mean-spirit in the classroom. Imagine the damage this would do to young people in school and at home exposed day after day to that example. The community would not allow it. And yet, you as our national *"teacher"* daily before your *"students"*, in a coast-to-coast *"classroom"*, pollute our best virtues with verbal litter called Tweets.

For just one example, your aggressive endorsement of Alabama's Roy Moore and Pennsylvania's Rick Saccone resulted in two sunken auditorium ships. You are possibly heading for ship-sinking consequences far greater to all Americans, especially when you daily tell all Americans that you will build that wall – no matter what logical input you receive from Democrats, Republicans and World Leaders.

Your *"mouthing off"* is irresponsible and dangerous. You fail in values of compassion, charity and leadership while Vice President Spence stands solidly and silently beside you – not to mention Rudy Giuliani, who once had an *"extraordinary grasp of facts"*.

No matter what urgency's in government exist, you not only shut it down, you fail to learn from it. And you take one of Democracy's greatest gifts, Freedom of the Press and you call it *"Fake News"*.

Your language is a corruptive and dangerous encouragement to throw charity to the wind, to belittle the dignity of others, to spread fear, to promote disrespect and hatred, to accept cynicism and sarcasm as heroic traits?

Your language launches torpedoes at the ship of an enlightened social state, making gaping holes in the social fabric of the country, sinking the hope of *"One nation"*, violating the principles of a republic *"under God"* with liberty and justice for all including those who are disadvantaged and in need of a home or a new way of life in America the Beautiful. You clearly toss overboard the sacred notion of Liberty and Justice for all.

Your supporters should recognize the dangerous, sink-ship consequences of your unprincipled blabbering. With bridging strategies with the Congress, there could be smooth Trump sailing in the interest of both Republicans and Democrats. If you could have won the North Korean issue, for example, this that would be the kind of smooth Trump sailing where credit would be due.

And speaking of China, products that happen to be made in China are still at a surprising low cost. In light of your policies, time will tell how long this will last.

It is a fact that seeds planted in Obama's eight years are a factor in smooth sailing of the stock market and unemployment which under your rule, thus far, have continued.

As noted in your quotes in this book, you appear to be deficient in personality, values, compassion, charity and leadership. I pray that your arrogance and pride become humble regrets, openness and team-work with Congress and leaders throughout the world who peacefully travel under bridges.

Having said all this, on world events such as Russia, China, North Korea, Iran and other Nations, I also pray that you and our elected officials (present and future) find a bridge and not a wall that would hopefully achieve world peace for all mankind.

www.ingramcontent.com/pod-product-compliance
Lightning Source LLC
Chambersburg PA
CBHW020632220526
45464CB00001B/119